The New Conservatism

The New Conservatism

Cultural Criticism and the
Historians' Debate

Jürgen Habermas

edited and translated by
Shierry Weber Nicholsen

introduction by Richard Wolin

The MIT Press, Cambridge, Massachusetts

Second Printing, 1990

This work is composed of essays and interviews previously published in German. With the exception of the two pieces in the section on Culture and Politics and the essay "Work and Weltanschauung: The Heidegger Controversy from a German Perspective," they are taken from the two most recent volumes of Habermas's political writings, *Kleine Politische Schriften V* and *VI*, © 1985, 1987 by Suhrkamp Verlag, Frankfurt am Main, Federal Republic of Germany.

This book was set in Baskerville by DEKR Corporation and printed and bound in the United States of America.

Library of Congress Cataloging-in-Publication Data

Habermas, Jürgen.
  [Selections. English. 1989]
  The new conservatism : cultural criticism and the historians' debate / Jürgen Habermas ; edited and translated by Shierry Weber Nicholsen ; introduction by Richard Wolin.
      p.   cm. — (Studies in contemporary German social thought)
  Essays and interviews previously published in German, many of which were taken from Habermas' Kleine politische Schriften V and VI, c1985, 1987.
  Includes bibliographies and index.
  ISBN 0-262-08188-1
  1. Conservatism. 2. Welfare state. 3. Political culture. 4. Politics and culture. I. Nicholsen, Shierry Weber. II. Title. III. Series.
JC571.H17213 1989   89-12437
320.5—dc20   CIP

Contents

Introduction
Richard Wolin

There are not two Germanys, an evil and a good, but only one, which, through devil's cunning, transformed its best into evil. . . .
Thomas Mann, Germany and the Germans, *1945*

I consider the continued existence of National Socialism *within* democracy potentially more threatening than the continued existence of fascist tendencies *against* democracy.
Theodor Adorno, "What Does Coming to Terms with the Past Mean?"

Until now, Jürgen Habermas has been best known in the English-speaking world as the author of a number of seminal works on the metatheoretical foundations of the human sciences: *Knowledge and Human Interests* (1973), *Communication and the Evolution of Society* (1979), and, what will undoubtedly be viewed historically as his masterwork, the two-volume *Theory of Communicative Action* (1984, 1987).[1] In the Federal Republic of Germany, however, his reputation as a scholar has gone hand in hand with his role as a passionate commentator on a wide range of contemporary political themes—in speeches, interviews, and reviews that have appeared in leading German publications such as *Die Zeit* and *Merkur*.[2] The present volume comprises a variety of occasional political and cultural writings conceived by Habermas in the 1980s–an extremely significant decade in the political life of the Federal Republic—which saw thirteen years of Social Democratic rule (1969–1982) come to an end in favor of a coalition headed by the conservative Christian Democrats. Led by Chancellor Helmut Kohl, the Christian

Democrats were returned to office (along with their junior partners, the Free Democrats) in 1987. The political transformation of the 1980s thus represents in many ways a delayed confirmation of the *Tendenzwende* or ideological shift first visible in Germany in the mid-1970s. The multifarious ramifications of this era of neoconservative stabilization in the Federal Republic—in the political, cultural, and intellectual spheres of life—are explored by Habermas in the essays that make up this volume. And while these texts are integrally related to the peculiarities of the West German historical-political context, many of their insights concerning the decline of the welfare state, the function of scholarship under conditions of democracy, and neoconservatism in general are, *mutatis mutandis*, applicable to conditions of other late capitalist societies.

It has recently become fashionable to deny the existence of a causal relation between an author's theoretical position and his or her political convictions[3]—a standpoint consonant with the poststructuralist interest in exposing the limitations of theory in general, which is always suspected of promoting covert, "foundationalist" tendencies. In this respect, the work of Habermas is refreshingly traditional: the political essays continued in *The New Conservatism* represent a studied, practical complement of his theoretical labors of the past thirty years. Indeed, the relationship between "theory" and "practical life" has always been a paramount concern in Habermas's work. In *Knowledge and Human Interests*, for example, he attempted to demystify the misguided, "objectivistic" self-understanding of the human sciences by demonstrating that the so-called observer is an inextricable element of the network of social relations under study. In a similar vein, in his introduction to *Theory and Practice*,[4] Habermas set forth the program of a revitalized critical theory defined as a "theory of society with a practical intent." That he has remained extremely faithful to this early insistence on the practical implications of all social inquiry is attested to by the political texts in this volume. In essence, they may be read as studies in applied critical theory. For despite his telling criticisms of the shortcomings of the first generation of critical theorists,[5] Habermas has, throughout his work, remained faithful to one of the central insights of Max Hork-

heimer: that what distinguishes "critical" from "traditional"
theory is an active interest in advancing a more rational and
just organization of social life. Or, as he observes in *Theory and
Practice*, "We can, if needs be, distinguish theories according to
whether or not they are structurally related to possible
emancipation."[6]

The central theme that unites the various essays of this volume is the German problem of the *Aufarbeitung der Vergangenheit* or "coming to terms with the past." For years, the "German
question" as perceived by politicians of Western Europe had
been, "How can German aggressiveness be curbed?" But after
1945, this question took on an entirely different, more sinister
meaning. It was rephrased to read, "How could the nation of
Goethe, Kant, and Schiller become the perpetrator of 'crimes
against humanity'?" Or simply, "How was Auschwitz possible?"
One could justifiably say that the very "soul" of the nation is
at stake in the answer to this question. For the development of
a healthy, nonpathological national identity would seem contingent on the forthright acknowledgment of those aspects of
the German tradition that facilitated the catastrophe of 1933–
1945. And that is why recent efforts on the part of certain
German historians—bolstered by an era of conservative stabilization—to circumvent the problem of "coming to terms with
the past" are so disturbing. For what is new about this situation—and here I am referring to what has been called the
"Historians' Debate"—is the attempt not simply to provide dis-
honest and evasive answers to the "German question," as stated
above, but to declare *the very posing of the question itself null and
void.*

Historically, the problem of coming to terms with the past
has not been an easy one; and in the first decade and a half of
the Federal Republic's existence—the "latency period" of the
Adenauer years, which lasted from 1949 until 1963—the nation as a whole did very little of it. Instead, the wrong lesson
seemed to have been learned from twelve years of Nazi rule:
there was not only a rejection of jingoistic-genocidal politics
(which had, after all, brought in its wake unprecedented misery
for the Germans, too, an experience they were far from anx-
ious to repeat) but a total rejection of politics, which, in the

post-Hitler era, seemed irrevocably contaminated. These were years of overwhelming political apathy. German political energies, which had once been so robust, were entirely sublimated into economic reconstruction. The result is well known: the creation of the *Wirtschaftswunder* or economic miracle, which catapulted the Federal Republic, within years of its foundation, to the position of one of the world's leading industrial powers. But democratic societies do not come into being overnight. And many features of the Adenauer regime—the incredible political docility of the general populace, the fact that so many officials from the Nazi years so readily found positions of power and influence in his government—suggested that the essential structure of the traditional *Obrigkeitsstaat* (the authoritarian state of the Bismarck and Wilhelmine periods) remained in place beneath the veneer of democratic respectability.

Such conclusions were generally confirmed by social-psychological studies of German character structure in the 1950s. In his incisive analysis of the results of one such study,[7] Adorno noted that many of the attitudes displayed revealed character traits that were highly "neurotic": "defensive gestures when one isn't attacked; massive affect in situations that do not fully warrant it; lack of affect in the face of the most serious matters; and often simply a repression of what was known or half-known." Instead of "coming to terms with the past," the latter was consistently repressed through a series of familiar, highly inventive rationalizations: only five, not six million Jews were killed; Dresden was as bad as Auschwitz; the politics of the Cold War era confirmed what Hitler had always said about communism anyway—which justified in retrospect the war he launched in the East (and from there it is a short step to the conclusion that Hitler was right about a number of other matters as well); the fate of the "East Germans" (i.e., those driven from the eastern territories at the war's end) was comparable to that of the Jews.

The incapacity of the German nation during these years for any honest expression of grief or remorse was brilliantly satirized in a scene from Günter Grass's *The Tin Drum*, where people require onion-cutting ceremonies to help them shed tears. As one pair of critics astutely observed regarding the German national character of the postwar years: "there is a determining connection between the political and social immobilism and provincialism prevailing in West Germany and the stubbornly maintained rejection of memories, in particular the blocking of any sense of involvement in the events of the Nazi past that are now being so strenuously denied."[8]

Certainly, much has changed in Germany since this initial period, largely through the efforts of the generation of the 1960s, who, refusing to remain satisfied with the strategy of repression pursued by their parents, pressed forcefully for answers to the most troubling questions about the German past.[9] However, just at the point when one is tempted to believe that genuine progress has been made concerning the confrontation with the Nazi years, one runs across studies such as Dieter Bossman's *Was ich über Adolf Hitler gehört habe* (*What I have heard about Adolf Hitler*; Frankfurt, 1977), revealing astonishing ignorance on the part of young Germans concerning their recent past. For example, upon being asked what Hitler had done to the Jews, some of Bossman's young interviewees responded as follows: "Those who were against him, he called Nazis; he put the Nazis into gas chambers" (thirteen year-old); "I think he also killed Jews" (thirteen year-old); "He murdered some 50,000 Jews" (fifteen year-old); "Hitler was himself a Jew" (sixteen year-old).

The work of mourning is essential, not as "penance" but as an indispensable prelude to the formation of autonomous and mature identities for both nations and the individuals who comprise them. As Freud showed in his classic study, "Mourning and Melancholia," unless the labor of mourning has been successfully completed—that is, unless they have sincerely come to terms with the past—individuals exhibit a marked incapacity to live in the present. Instead, they betray a "melancholic" fixation on their "loss," which prevents them from getting on with the business of life. The neurotic symptom-formations that result (as described above by Adorno) can be readily transmitted to the character-structures of future generations, which only compounds the difficulty of confronting the historical trauma that wounded the collective ego. And thus the crimes of the past tend to fade into oblivion, unmourned and thus uncomprehended.

Instances of collective repression are, moreover, far from innocent. They prevent the deformations of national character and social structure that facilitated a pathological course of development from coming to light; instead, these abnormalities remain buried deep within the recesses of the collective psyche, from which they may emerge at some later date in historically altered form. In Germany, these "deformations" are often discussed in terms of the persistence of authoritarian patterns of behavior that are a holdover from traditional, predemocratic forms of social organization.[10]

So long as this incapacity to confront the past exists, there usually follows an inability to live realistically in the present. Thus, historically, one of the salient features of Germany as a nation has been a tendency toward a militant exaggeration of the virtues of "nationalism" as a way of compensating for its relatively late and precarious attainment of nationhood under Bismarck in 1871. Or, as Alexander and Margarete Mitscherlich have expressed it in their landmark study of postwar German character structure, *The Inability to Mourn*: "World-redeeming dreams of ancient greatness arise in peoples in whom the sense of having been left behind by history evokes feelings of impotence and rage."[11]

Such infantile fantasies of collective omnipotence have led, on not a few occasions, to a false estimation of national strength and some correspondingly catastrophic national defeats. The important point is that unless the historical reasons that have led to disaster have been explored—unless the labor of coming to terms with the past is undertaken in earnest—one risks reenacting the same historical cycle yet again as a type of collective "repetition compulsion": one proceeds to invent new, more sophisticated rationalizations and defenses to protect the idealized image of national greatness from the traumatic blows it has most recently endured—and so on, *ad infinitum*.

Thus, in the immediate postwar period, the theory arose that it was the German leaders alone who were to blame for the most heinous of Nazi crimes, thereby absolving rank-and-file Germans from responsibility. In truth, of course, the German populace had given their full and enthusiastic support to Hitler's war aims and policies; and without the alacritous and dedicated cooperation of large segments of German society—from industrialists and the judiciary to public officials and railway personnel—the Third Reich and its atrocities would hardly have been possible.[12]

It is within the context of this longstanding attempt to deny the Nazi past—as well as its possible repercussions for postwar German society—that the arguments of Habermas's adversaries in the Historians' Debate must be understood.[13] Their efforts to trivialize and thus finally have quit with past German sins represent much more than a dubious act of historical reinterpretation: they constitute an insidious rewriting of history by virtue of which "the murdered are to be cheated even out of the one thing that our powerlessness can grant them: remembrance."[14]

It is also important to recognize, however, that the "revisionist" standpoint did not materialize overnight and by chance. Rather, it complemented a carefully orchestrated campaign on the part of the ruling Christian Democratic coalition to remove once and for all the stigma of the Nazi era—perceived as a troublesome blot on the honor of the nation—and to return Germany to the status of a "normal nation."

The centerpiece of this process of "normalization" was to have been the visit of the American President to the German military cemetery at Bitburg on May 8, 1985, the fortieth anniversary of the end of both the Second World War and the Nazi dictatorship. Kohl, who had been shunned at the Allies' commemoration of the landings at Normandy the previous year, had obtained a small degree of consolation in a ceremony with President Mitterand at Verdun, which thus became a sort of "dress rehearsal" for Bitburg.

However, it was the Second, not the First World War that weighed heavily on the German conscience; and Bitburg was to have symbolized the end of Germany's pariah status and return to the fold of political normalcy, a *coup de théâtre* that was to receive international sanction by virtue of the presence of the "leader of the Free World." As is well known, however, the affair backfired spectacularly once it was discovered that forty-seven SS members were also buried in the cemetery at Bitburg.[15] What was intended as a display of German "normalcy" was thereby transformed into a prime example of that country's inclination toward grievous lapses of historical memory.[16]

Unflustered by the Bitburg debacle, the Christian Democratic leadership continued to make "normalization" one of the focal points of the federal election campaign of 1987. Such was the intention of Christian Democratic parliamentary president Alfred Dregger, as he argued vehemently in April 1986 against distinguishing between the "victims" and the "perpetrators" of Nazism in a debate before the Bundestag over a new war memorial. In a similar vein, Franz-Josef Strauss, head of the Christian Socialist Union (the Bavarian allies of the Christian Democrats), repeatedly urged in his campaign addresses that Germany must "emerge from the ruins of the Third Reich and become a normal nation again."

It would not be unfair to say that the major claims of Habermas's antagonists in the Historians' Debate have been perceived by most Western historians as neonationalist provocations.[17] A good example of such "provocation" is the rationale for historical study provided by Michael Stürmer, one of the leading members of the revisionist contingent. Stürmer believes that it falls to historians to provide compensations for the potentially confusing array of value-choices that have arisen with the decline of religion and the rise of modern secularism.[18] According to Stürmer, what is needed is a "higher source of meaning, which, after [the decline of] religion, only the nation and patriotism were able to provide." For Stürmer, it is the task of the historian to assist in the renewal of national self-confidence by providing *positive* images of the past. In his eyes, the historical profession is motivated by the "establishment of inner worldly meaning."[19] For "in a land without history, whoever fills memory, coins the concepts, and interprets the past, wins the future."[20]

In a similar vein, Andreas Hillgruber, in his book, *Two Sorts of Destruction: The Smashing of the German Reich and the End of European Jewry*, suggests that, in scrutinizing Germany's collapse in the East toward the end of World War II, a historian

is faced with the choice of "identifying" with one of three
parties: Hitler, the victorious Red Army, or the German army
trying to defend the civil population from being overrun by
Soviet troops.[21] And in his eyes, the choice is self-evident: the
brave German soldiers, desperately fighting to save the fatherland from the atrocities of the Red Army, win hands down. It
is as if Hillgruber were attempting to apply literally the "positive" approach to historical study recommended by his colleague Stürmer.

But as Habermas points out in "Apologetic Tendencies,"
Hillgruber in effect presents us with a series of false choices.
Why is it the obligation of the responsible historian to "identify"
with *any* of the historical protagonists? In fact, is it not his or
her responsibility (in this case, some forty years after the events
in question have occurred) to arrive at an independent and
morally just verdict regarding the past, rather than to "play
favorites"? Morever, Hillgruber can succeed in his choice of
"protagonists" only by abstracting from some extremely gruesome facts: It was the same "heroic" German army in the East
that established the Jewish ghettos from which concentration
camp victims were chosen, that provided logistical support to
the SS *Einsatzgruppen* charged with exterminating the Jews, that
was responsible for the shooting of thousands of Jews in Serbia
and Poland, and in whose hands some two million Soviet prisoners of war perished during the course of the war, either
from famine or starvation.[22] It was this army that, as an integral
part of Hitler's plans for European domination, served as the
guarantor of all Nazi atrocities in Eastern Europe—from mass
exterminations to the sadistic enslavement of the populations
of the occupied territories. The sad irony of Hillgruber's thesis
is that it was the brutal war of aggression in the East launched
by the German army (a war that resulted in the death of some
twenty million Soviet soldiers and civilians) that was responsible
for unleashing the "revenge" of the Red Army on German soil.

But in addition to the important "material" questions that
have arisen in the debate concerning the manner in which
crucial episodes of the German past should be interpreted,
equally important issues concerning the integrity and function
of scholarship in a democratic society have emerged. Should

the primary role of historical study in a democracy be to facilitate "social integration" through the "establishment of inner-
worldly meaning," as Stürmer claims—an approach that results
in the creation of images of the past with which people can
identify in a positive way, such as Hillgruber's nostalgic portrait
of the German army in the East at the end of the war? Or
should scholarship assume a more skeptical and critical attitude
vis-à-vis the commonplaces of a national past for which Auschwitz has become the unavoidable metaphor, thereby assisting
concretely in the process of "coming to terms with the past"?
Compelling support for the historical importance of a "critical"
approach to scholarship has been provided by the historian
Detlev Peukert, who in a recent essay has argued that what was
historically new about the National Socialist practice of genocide was the fact that it received a theoretical grounding
through a determinate conception of "positive" science,
namely, the idea of basing science on racial categories.[23] Habermas's specific fear is that by subordinating scientific criteria
to an identity-securing function, historical study risks falling
behind conventional standards of liberal scholarship, resulting
in the production of neonationalist "court histories." Indeed,
the very idea championed by Hillgruber that a historian must
in some way "identify" with one or several of the protagonists
of his or her drama represents a throwback to the "empathic"
historiography of German historicism—a school formed in the
German mandarin tradition—for which the writing of history
from a "national" point of view was a common phenomenon.[24]

The most sensational of the theses espoused by Habermas's
opponents in the debate were undoubtedly those set forth by
the Berlin historian and former Heidegger student Ernst
Nolte. In an article that appeared in English,[25] Nolte had revived a choice bit of anti-Semitic propaganda from the early
days of the war: that an alleged declaration by Chaim Weizmann (then president of the Jewish Agency) of September
1939, urging Jews to support the cause of democracy in the
impending world war, "justified" Hitler's treating them as prisoners of war, as well as subsequent deportations.

But it was Nolte's contention, in a June 6, 1986, article in
the *Frankfurter Allgemeine Zeitung*, that the atrocities perpe-

trated by Hitler at Auschwitz were merely an understandable (if exaggerated) "response" to a "more original Asiatic deed" (Stalin's Gulag), of which Hitler considered himself a potential victim, that proved the most offensive and ominous of the revisionist claims. Nolte's argument reads as follows:

A conspicuous shortcoming of the literature on National Socialism is that it doesn't know, or doesn't want to admit, to what extent everything that was later done by the Nazis, with the sole exception of the technical procedure of gassing, had already been described in an extensive literature dating from the early 1920s. . . . Could it be that the Nazis, that Hitler carried out an "Asiatic" deed only because they regarded themselves and those like them as potential or actual victims of an "Asiatic" deed? Was not the Gulag Archipelago more original than Auschwitz? Was not the "class murder" of the Bolsheviks the logical and factual *prius* of the "race murder" of the National Socialists?

And to sum up: the singularity of the Nazi crimes "does not alter the fact that the so-called [*sic*] annihilation of the Jews during the Third Reich was a reaction or a distorted copy and not a first act or an original."[26] Nolte goes on to enumerate an entire series of twentieth-century crimes, in comparison to which the uniqueness of the Holocaust is reduced to "the technical procedure of gassing."

As Habermas is quick to point out, there is a method behind Nolte's madness. With the stroke of a pen, the singularity of the Nazi atrocities is denied: they are reduced to the status of a "copycat" crime; and at that, merely one among many. The gist of Nolte's feeble and transparent efforts to rewrite the saga of Auschwitz may be read as follows: Why continue to blame the Germans? The communists did it first anyway. And after all, during the war we were fighting on the right side—at least in the East.

In face of such claims, Habermas's response was guided by an awareness that it is Germany's willingness to deal forthrightly with the dark side of its national past that will determine the moral fiber of the nation in the future; and that only the "analytical powers of remembrance" can in truth break the nightmarish grip of the past over Germany's present:

The less internal communality a collective context of life has preserved, the more it has maintained itself externally, through the
usurpation and destruction of life that is alien to it, the greater is the
burden of reconciliation imposed on the griefwork and the critical
self-examination of subsequent generations. And does not this very
thesis forbid us to use leveling comparisons to play down the fact
that no one can take our place in the liability required of us? . . .
There is an obligation incumbent upon us in Germany . . . to keep
alive . . . the memory of the sufferings of those who were murdered
by German hands. It is especially these dead who have a claim to the
weak anamnestic power of a solidarity that later generations can
continue to practice only in the medium of a remembrance that is
repeatedly renewed, often desperate, yet continually on one's mind.
If we were to brush aside this Benjaminian legacy, our fellow Jewish
citizens and the sons, daughters, and grandchildren of all those who
were murdered would feel themselves unable to breathe in our country ("On the Public Use of History").

One of the key theoretical arguments Habermas mobilizes in
his refutation of the revisionist position is the distinction between conventional and postconventional identities.[27] Within
the framework of developmental psychology, the formation of
a postconventional identity indicates that an individual has
acquired a capacity to evaluate his or her moral convictions in
terms of general ethical maxims; that beliefs concerning right
and wrong are no longer decided by immediate and particu-
laristic points of reference (e.g., the standpoint of one's peer
group or nation), but instead by appeal to universal principles.
Habermas thus views the revisionists' desire for a return to a
conventional national identity as a potential regression behind
the precarious gains the Federal Republic has made as a democratic nation since its inception forty years ago.

The "conventionalist" perspective comes through most forcefully in the positions of Hillgruber and Stürmer, whose arguments betray no small measure of nostalgia for a highly
mythologized image of the old German Reich: Germany as
master of *Mitteleuropa*, capable of mediating the interests of the
nations to the west and east.[28] Their contributions to the debate
are reminiscent of the traditional nineteenth-century argument
for a German *Sonderbewusstsein*, suggesting a "special" historical
course of development for Germany between east and west.
The same nostalgia is also implicit in Nolte's desire to minimize

the historical significance of Auschwitz, thus paving the way for Germany's return to the status of a "normal nation." But the bankruptcy of the *Sonderbewusstsein* argument was definitively proved at Stalingrad and Auschwitz, that is, by the infamy these two places have come to symbolize for the course of German history. In defiance of this historical lesson, one of the main strategies of Nolte and the others has been to downplay the importance of the years 1933–1945 in relation to the trajectory of German history as a whole. But as the opening citation from Thomas Mann reminds us, the wistful desire to differentiate in cut-and-dried fashion between "good" and "bad" Germanys is based on a dichotomy that fails to hold up under closer historical scrutiny.

It is for this reason that Habermas emphatically insists in "Apologetic Tendencies" that the unqualified opening of the Federal Republic to the political culture of the West "is the great intellectual accomplishment of the postwar period," and that the attempts to revive neonationalist dogmas—whose disastrous outcome is a painful matter of historical record—must be combatted by the "only patriotism that does not alienate us from the West," namely, "a constitutional patriotism."[29] For Habermas, the latter would be a "postconventional patriotism." Indeed, the Western constitutional state may be viewed as a postconventional form of political consciousness, insofar as the inherent distinction between "law" and "right" (which corresponds to a broader distinction between "reality" and "norm") mandates that all concrete legislation be evaluated in light of universal normative precepts embodied in the constitution itself.

Habermas associates the revisionist offensive in the Historians' Debate with a neoconservative backlash against the student and antinuclear movements that seemed to peak in the mid-1980s. Of course, neoconservatism has been a phenomenon common to virtually all Western democracies over the course of the last ten years. But, as Habermas explains in "Neoconservative Cultural Criticism in the United States and West Germany," the pecularities of the German version are especially worthy of note, insofar as its roots are to be found in protofascist ideologies that date from the prewar era.

In a 1984 interview, Habermas recounts his shock as a university student in the immediate postwar years upon learning of the continuities between the leading intellectuals of the pre- and postwar eras, many of whom had been enthusiastic supporters of National Socialism.[30] And although a new generation of thinkers has since come to prominence in the Federal Republic, antidemocratic intellectual habits have been slow to die. In most cases, although the transition to democracy has been grudgingly accepted (which could not have been said for the advocates of a German *Sonderweg* during the days of the Weimar Republic), the dissonances of modernity are perceived as placing such great burdens on the adaptational capacities of social actors that the preservation of "order" (as opposed to "freedom") has become the foremost value in contemporary political life. (One of the concrete and highly controversial political expressions of this mania for order was the *Berufsverbot* or "professional proscription" first decreed in 1972, which aimed at excluding political extremists, sympathizers, and other undesirables from the German civil service.[31]) Hence, those who are perceived as the intellectual and cultural standard bearers of modernity (e.g., artists and critical intellectuals) receive more than their fair share of blame for failures of social integration. But in this way, as Habermas shows, the neoconservatives confuse cause and effect: Responsibility for disturbances of social integration that have their source in functional imperatives of the economic and political-administrative spheres is mistakenly attributed to avant-garde artists and a "new class" of free thinkers.

It is considerations of precisely this nature that dominate the historiographical concerns of Stürmer and Hillgruber, in whose eyes history must take on the affirmative function of reinforcing national consensus. Or, as Habermas remarks in his essay on "Neoconservative Cultural Criticism," "The neoconservatives see their role as, on the one hand, in mobilizing pasts which can be accepted approvingly and, on the other, morally neutralizing other pasts that would provoke only criticism and rejection." The currency of *Ordnungsdenken*—a "philosophy of order"—in West Germany today (evident above all in a preoccupation with questions of "internal security") is at times reminiscent of the typical historical justifications of a paternalistic *Obrigkeitsstaat* during the Bismarck and Wilhelmine periods. Its widespread currency inevitably provokes grave suspicions concerning the prominence of regressive tendencies in the political culture of the Federal Republic. Even Chancellor Helmut Schmidt was compelled to wonder aloud at the time of the "German autumn" (1977) whether the West Germans have "in their souls" a certain "hysteria for order" (*Ordnungshysterie*).[32] This is also a fact that might help to account for the continued prominence of the authoritarian political doctrines of Carl Schmitt in West Germany today.[33]

Since the early 1980s, Habermas has shown considerable interest in exploring the possible links between the politics of neoconservatism and the philosophical implications of what is known as postmodernism. In his view, it is far from coincidental that what were perhaps the two most significant intellectual trends of the 1980s emerged and flourished concomitantly.

His earliest thoughts on the relationship between the two date back to an influential essay of 1980 that appeared in English under the title "Modernity versus Postmodernity."[34] This article was itself a meditation on the conception of modernity advanced in the recently completed *Theory of Communicative Action* as it pertained to the contemporary political spectrum. In concluding the essay, Habermas differentiates between three types of conservatism: "old conservatism," which longs for a return to premodern forms of life; "new conservatism," which accepts the economic and technological features of modernity while attempting to minimize the potentially explosive elements of cultural modernism; and finally, "young conservatism,"[35] which he associates with postmodernism. His description is worth reproducing in full:

The *young conservatives* embrace the fundamental experience of aesthetic modernity—the disclosure of a decentered subjectivity, freed from all constraints of rational cognition and purposiveness, from all imperatives of labor and utility—and in this way break out of the modern world. They thereby ground an intransigent antimodernism through a modernist attitude. They transpose the spontaneous power of the imagination, the experience of self and affectivity, into the remote and the archaic; and in manichean fashion, they counterpose to instrumental reason a principle only accessible via "evocation": be it the will to power or sovereignty, Being or the Dionysian power of the poetic. In France this trend leads from Georges Bataille to Foucault and Derrida. The spirit [*Geist*] of Nietzsche that was reawakened in the 1970s of course hovers over them all.

The theoretical bases of Habermas's critique are complex. They presuppose the theory of modernity developed in *Theory of Communicative Action* and foreshadow the lecture series that was first published in 1985 as *The Philosophical Discourse of Modernity*. Nevertheless, since Habermas's critique of neoconservatism stands in an integral relation to his interpretation of postmodernism (see, for example, the essays "Modern and Postmodern Architecture" and "Taking Aim at the Heart of the Present"), a brief discussion of the conceptual foundations of his position will help facilitate a better understanding of the bases of his political judgments.

Habermas's theory of modernity builds on Max Weber's conception of the "differentiation of the spheres." For Weber, modernity is chiefly characterized by the proliferation of "independent logics" in the value-spheres of science/technology, morality/law, and art.[36] In premodern societies, the development of autonomous cultural spheres was hindered by the predominance of all-encompassing "cosmological world views" (religion, myth), in terms of which all social claims to value and meaning were forced to legitimate themselves. Only since the Enlightenment have these individual value-spheres become *self-legitimating*[37]; that is, for the first time in history, the realms of science, morality, and art have been in a position to develop their own inherent meanings.

On the one hand, the gains of modernity have been indisputable. The institutionalization of professional science, universalistic morality, and autonomous art have led to innumerable cultural benefits; our capacities for technical expertise, political justice/ethical fairness, and aesthetic experience have no doubt been tremendously enhanced. It is this point that separates Habermas most emphatically from the postmodernists: He believes that to fall behind the threshold of possibility represented by the cultural achievements of modernity can only result in "regression"—the species would literally have to "unlearn" valuable cultural skills that were only acquired very late and with great difficulty. And it is precisely such "regressive inclinations" among the postmodernists that he singles out for criticism. By generalizing an *aesthetic* critique of modernity (first elaborated in the late nineteenth century by the artistic avant-garde and Nietzsche), the postmodernists show themselves capable of understanding the modern age solely in terms of *one* of its aspects: *instrumental reason*, which then must be combatted at all costs through the (aesthetic) media of provocation, transgression, and play. In this way, they may be considered heirs to Nietzsche's "total critique" of modern values. For like Nietzsche, they reject the method of "immanent critique," insofar as they proceed from the assumption that the values of modernity are irreparably corrupt.[38]

What is lost above all in the heady whirl of postmodern *jouissance* is a capacity to appreciate the universalistic ethical qualities of modernity. It is facile to dismiss the latter as "instrumental," since their very basis is the (Kantian) notion of treating other persons as "ends in themselves," For this reason, Habermas can justifiably accuse the postmodernists of representing a disguised yet profound *antimodernism*: Because their criticisms of modernity as a "generalized instrumentalism" are so reductive, their "program" is governed by an irrepressible longing to be free of the requirements of modernity at all costs, with the "aesthetic moment" as the sole possible survivor.

On the other hand, Habermas himself has been extremely critical of the developmental trajectory of modernity as an empirical social formation. Hence, he believes that, historically speaking, its normative potentials have been inadequately realized. Above all, the various spheres have not developed in an equitable fashion. Instead, the cognitive-instrumental sphere has attained predominance at the expense of the other two spheres, which in turn find themselves marginalized. Instrumental reason, in alliance with the forces of the economy and state administration, increasingly penetrates the sphere of everyday human life—the "life world"—resulting in the creation of "social pathologies." The basis of the life world is intersubjectivity, not formal reason. In the life world, social action is governed by an orientation toward reaching an *understanding* (i.e., communicative reason), not by a functionalist orientation toward *success* (i.e., the ends-means rationality of instrumental reason). The latter therefore violates the inner logic of the former by attempting to subject it to alien, "functionalist" imperatives that derive from the administrative-economic sphere. The term Habermas has coined to describe this process is felicitous: *the colonization of the life world*.[39]

It is this point that separates Habermas most emphatically from the neoconservatives. They wish to preserve one-sidedly the economic, technical, and managerial achievements of modernity at the expense of its ethical and aesthetic components. From their standpoint, the bureaucratic colonization of the life world is a positive development. For by extending the functionalist logics of economic and administrative rationality to the life world, technocratic imperatives of system-maintenance are furthered. Thus, neoconservative political views incline toward a theory of government by formally trained elites. From this perspective, popular or democratic "inputs" with regard to governmental decision-making having their origin in the life world are perceived as an unnecessary strain on the imperatives of efficient political "management."

It is at this point that aspects of the neoconservative and young conservative (or postmodernist) position intersect, that is, as potential complements to one another under the conditions of late capitalism. If the latter's main contribution to the course of Western cultural development has been "specialists without spirit and sensualists without heart" (Weber)—that is, reified personality types and social relations that correspond to them—the global assault against modernity undertaken by the postmodernists under the banner of *différance* would appear to be a logical historical outgrowth of and response to this trend. That is, the aestheticist pseudoradicalism of postmodernism ("pseudoradical" because thoroughly depoliticized) may be viewed as a type of historical compensation for the overwhelming pressures of "theoretical and practical rationalism" (Weber again) that have been imposed by modernity as a social formation. Or as Adorno once observed: "Total reification objectively hatches its opposite."[40] In Heideggerian parlance, the postmodernist celebrations of *jouissance* serve as a kind of "releasement" from the hyperrationalized life world of late capitalism. Yet, as a type of "compensation," such celebrations ultimately have a system-stabilizing effect, insofar as they provide apparent outlets for frustration while leaving the technical-political infrastructure of the system itself essentially untouched.

The postmodernists have been correctly characterized by Habermas as "young conservatives" insofar as they have abandoned any hopes of conscious social change. Indeed, the word "emancipation" seems to have been stricken from their vocabulary. Instead, their aestheticist perspective is content to fall behind the achievements of modernity, a standpoint Habermas likens to "throwing out the baby with the bathwater":

The farewells sung to cultural modernity and the veneration of capitalist modernization can only confirm those who, with their blanket antimodernism, want to throw out the baby with the bath water. If modernity had nothing to offer but what appears in the commendations of neoconservative apologetics, one could well understand why the intellectual youth of today should not rather return to Nietzsche via Derrida and Heidegger and seek their salvation in the portentous voices of a cultically revived, an authentic Young Conservatism not yet distorted by compromise ("Neoconservative Cultural Criticism in the United States and West Germany").

Habermas's alternative to the extremes of neo- and young conservatism is the rebirth of autonomous political subcultures willing to struggle for the creation of new life forms, that stand in opposition to both the increasing pressures of bureaucratic colonization as well as the postmodernist desire to return to a premodern condition of cultural dedifferentiation. "Success" for these political subcultures would mean the creation of new forms of social solidarity capable of linking "social modernization to other, noncapitalist paths." It is an alternative that can come to fruition only if "the life world can develop out of itself institutions that restrict the systematic inner dynamic of economic and administrative systems of action":

At issue are the integrity and autonomy of life styles, perhaps the protection of traditionally established subcultures or changes in the grammar of traditional forms of life. . . . These forms permit the formation of autonomous public spheres, which also enter into communication with one another as soon as the potential for self-organization and the self-organized employment of communications media is made use of. Forms of self-organization strengthen the collective capacity for action beneath the threshold at which organizational goals become detached from the orientations and attitudes of members of the organization and dependent instead on the interest of autonomous organizations in maintaining themselves. . . . The autonomous public spheres would have to achieve a combination of power and intelligent self-restraint that could make the self-regulating mechanisms of the state and the economy sufficiently sensitive to the goal-oriented results of radical democratic will-formation.[41]

With these words from "The New Obscurity," Habermas articulates a vision of radical democratic practice which, coming amidst a chorus of *fin de siècle* pessimism, one cannot help but admire. As he has demonstrated in his contributions to the *Historians' Debate*, there is still much to be accomplished—contemporary naysayers to the contrary—for the ethico-political program of the Enlightenment, out of which that same radical democratic spirit first emerged. And as a new millennium approaches, inspiration can be found in his program of a "social theory with a practical intent," which is tempered by the genuinely egalitarian sentiment that in "discourses of Enlightenment, there can only be participants."

Notes

1. The aforementioned works all appeared with Beacon Press. Of course, Habermas's considerable influence on Anglo-American intellectual life has by no means been limited to these three books. *Legitimation Crisis* (also published by Beacon), has, since its U.S. publication in 1975, become widely regarded as a standard work on the various political/cultural "crisis-manifestations" in late capitalist societies. And *The Philosophical Discourse of Modernity* (Cambridge, MA, MIT Press), a fascinating critique of post-structuralist thought that appeared late in 1987, has in a very short time achieved a remarkable degree of renown.

For a comprehensive bibliography of Habermas's publications through 1980, as well as of the relevant secondary literature, see Rene Gorzten, *Jürgen Habermas: Eine Bibliographie* (Frankfurt, 1981). For a bibliography of works pertaining to *Theory of Communicative Action*, see Gorzten, "Bibliographie zur *Theorie des kommunikativen Handelns*," in *Kommunikatives Handeln*, eds. A. Honneth and H. Joas (Frankfurt, 1986), pp. 406–416.

Introduction

2. It is perhaps of interest to note the differences between the American and German public spheres. For example, the German Historians' Debate was for the most part carried out in the daily or weekly press rather than in professional journals: most of the contributions by Nolte, Stürmer, Fest, and Hildebrand first appeared in the *Frankfurter Allgemeine Zeitung*; Habermas's main contributions appeared in the liberal news weekly, *Die Zeit*. The debate, consequently, was followed by a wide spectrum of the German public, whereas a parallel scenario (i.e., a major historical controversy concerning national identity being conducted in the daily press) would be difficult to imagine in the context of of the North American publicity. Several other of Habermas's contributions to the present volume ("Political Culture in Germany since 1968," "Taking Aim at the Heart of the Present") also originated as occasional pieces in various German dailies. It seems that in the Federal Republic there is more overlap between the academic sphere and the daily press.

3. Cf. Michel Foucault, "Politics and Ethics: An Interview," *The Foucault Reader*, ed. P. Rabinow (Berkeley, 1984), where Foucault observes: "There is a very tenuous 'analytic' link between a philosophical conception and the concrete political attitude of someone who is appealing to it; the 'best' theories do not constitute a very effective protection against disastrous political choices; certain great themes such as 'humanism' can be used to any end whatever . . ." p. 374. An argument similar to Foucault's has been advanced by Richard Rorty with reference to Heidegger's odious political allegiances in the 1930s (thereby suggesting that they have nothing to do with his prior philosophical outlook) in *The New Republic* (April 11, 1988).

4. (Boston, 1974). The introduction in question was originally written for the fourth German edition of *Theorie und Praxis* (Frankfurt, 1971).

5. Above all, see *Theory of Communicative Action* I, pp. 339–399; as well as "The Entwinement of Myth and Enlightenment," *The Philosophical Discourse of Modernity*, (Cambridge, MA, 1987), pp. 106–130.

6. Habermas, *Theorie und Praxis*, p. 37.

7. "Was bedeutet: Aufarbeitung der Vergangenheit"; reprinted in *Gesammelte Schriften* (Frankfurt, 1977), pp. 555–572. An English translation of the essay has appeared in *Bitburg in Moral and Political Perspective*, ed. G. Hartman (Indianapolis, 1986), pp. 114–129. Many of Adorno's observations are based on an empirical study of German attitudes toward the Hitler years that was undertaken by the Institute for Social Research in the early 1950s, entitled *Gruppenexperiment. Ein Studienbericht*, ed. F. Pollock (Frankfurt, 1955). Adorno's own lengthy "qualitative analysis" of the study's findings has been republished as "Schuld und Abwehr," *Gesammelte Schriften* 9(2) (Frankfurt, 1975), pp. 121–324.

8. Alexander and Margarete Mitscherlich, *The Inability to Mourn*, trans. B. Placzek (New York, 1975), p. xxv. According to the authors, another chief symptom of the German failure to work through its past is a more general "impoverishment of object relations, i.e., of those processes of communication that involve feeling and thought." Ibid., p. 8.

9. At the same time, as Saul Friedländer has pointed out, this generation, by attempting to extend their analysis of fascism to the contemporary West German political scene, ended up by overgeneralizing the concept and thus robbing it of much of its real meaning. Cf. Friedländer, "Some German Struggles with Memory," in *Bitburg in Moral and Political Perspective*, p. 29.

Introduction

10. The standard account of those aspects of traditional German social structure that facilitated the mentality of popular obedience and passivity during the period of Nazi rule is Ralf Dahrendorf's *Society and Democracy in Germany* (New York, 1979).

11. *The Inability to Mourn*, p. 12

12. Or, as Holocaust historian Raul Hilberg has expressed this thought: "The bureaucrats who were involved in the extermination process were not, as far as their moral constitution is concerned, different from the rest of the population. The German wrongdoer was not a special kind of German; what we know about his mind-set pertains to Germany as a whole and not to him alone" (*Merkur* 413, july 1988, p. 541).

13. It would of course be unfair to argue that no attempts have been made to deal honestly with the German past. Chancellor Willy Brandt's moving gesture of contrition before the Auschwitz memorial in Warsaw in 1972 will forever remain a memorable and courageous act on the road to reconciliation with the victims of Nazism.
Ironically, the one event that seems to have triggered the greatest amount of national soul-searching was the showing of the U.S. television miniseries "Holocaust" in West Germany in 1979. Serious doubts, however, have been raised over the extent to which a four-part Hollywood-style dramatization can serve as the vehicle of historical expiation that had been sought for in vain for the previous thirty years. See Siegfried Zielinski, "History as Entertainment and Provocation," *New German Critique* 19 (Winter, 1980) pp. 81–96. (This entire issue is devoted to various appraisals of the West German reception of "Holocaust.")

14. Adorno, "What Does Coming to Terms with the Past Mean?," p. 117.

15. According to official reports, when Bitburg had originally been selected as the site for President Reagan's visit in the winter of 1985, a snow cover prevented German officials from noticing the SS graves. Though most of the Bitburg debate has focused on the presence of the SS graves, Raul Hilberg has correctly pointed out that the German Wehrmacht or regular army was itself hardly an innocent bystander to the politics of genocide. Instead, they often provided logistical support to SS troops charged with exterminating the Jews. Its ranking offices (e.g., Field Marshall Keitel and General Jodl) were hanged as war criminals after the war. In truth, the German army was an integral part of Hitler's Reich and its crimes. See Hilberg, "Bitburg as a Symbol," in *Bitburg in Moral and Political Perspective*, pp. 21–22.

16. The American President only compounded the difficulties of the situation by making a series of embarrassing gaffes: he tried to justify his decision to visit the Bergen-Belsen concentration camp on the morning of his Bitburg trip with the explanation that the men buried in the two grave sites were both "victims"—a macabre equation, to say the least. Then he made the inexplicable claim that "the German people have very few alive that remember even the war, and certainly none that were adults and participating in any way." President Reagan himself was in his thirties during World War II.

17. For a representative sample of views, see Charles Maier, "Immoral Equivalence," *The New Republic* (December, 1986); Saul Friedländer, *Kitsch und Tod: Der Widerschein des Nazismus* (Munich, 1986), especially the "Nachwort," pp. 128ff; and Anson Rabinbach, "German Historians Debate the Nazi Past," *Dissent* (Spring, 1988), pp. 192–200.

18. It is far from coincidental that the historian Stürmer doubles as speechwriter and advisor to Chancellor Kohl.

19. Stürmer, *Dissonanzen des Fortschritts* (Munich, 1982), p. 12.

Introduction

20. Stürmer, "Geschichte in geschichtslosem Land," *Frankfurter Allgemeine Zeitung* (April 25, 1986). Reprinted in *Historikerstreit* (Munich, 1987), pp. 36–38. I will from this point on refer to this volume (which contains most of the important contributions to the debate) as "HS."

21. Hillgruber, *Zweierlei Untergang: Die Zerschlagung des Deutschen Reiches und das Ende des europäischen Judentums* (Berlin, 1986).

22. See Raul Hilberg, "Bitburg as a Symbol," pp. 22–23.

23. Peukert, "Die Genesis der 'Endlosung' aus dem Geiste der Wissenschaft," in *Zerstörung des moralischen Selbstbewusstseins: Chance oder Gefährdung* (Frankfurt, 1988), pp. 24–48.

24. Walter Benjamin criticized German historicism for its de facto writing of history from the standpoint of the "victors" rather than that of the downtrodden. See his "Theses on the Philosophy of History," *Illuminations*, trans. H. Zohn (New York, 1969) pp. 251 ff. For a good account of the nationalistic convictions of German social scientists and historians during the Wilhelmine period, see Fritz Ringer, *The Decline of the German Mandarins* (Cambridge, MA, 1969), pp. 113–127.

25. Nolte, "Between Myth and Revisionism? The Third Reich in the Perspective of the 1980s," in *Aspects of the Third Reich*, ed. H. W. Koch (London, 1985), pp. 17–38. Nolte uses the Weizmann declaration to justify his contention that "it can hardly be denied that Hitler had good reasons to be convinced of his enemies' determination to annihilate him . . ."; a fact which in turn "might justify the thesis that Hitler was allowed to treat the German Jews as prisoners of war and by this means to intern them" (pp. 27–28).
It is far from irrelevant to note in this context that the "Weizmann-declaration" argument has recently been resurrected by the French revisionist historian Robert Faurisson, who espouses the thesis that the Holocaust is a Jewish fabrication. Nor did the gas chambers ever exist, according to Faurisson. The crematoria, moreover, served the "legitimate hygienic function" of protecting SS guards against the threat of infection and disease.

26. Nolte, "Between Myth and Revisionism," p. 36.

27. Habermas develops this concept in the context of a reading of the developmental psychology of Piaget and Kohlberg. See his essay "Historical Materialism and the Development of Normative Structures," *Communication and the Evolution of Society*, trans. T. McCarthy (Boston, 1979), pp. 95–129.

28. Within the context of this introduction, it is difficult to give an adequate account of the significance that "geopolitical thinking"—the idea of Germany as a "nation in the middle"—has had in Germany's historical and political self-understanding over the course of the last two centuries. The explicit revival of the idea of Germany's *Mittellage*, or being situated in the middle, as a prominent feature of the revisionist position, has been critically addressed by Hans-Ulrich Wehler, in *Entsorgung der deutschen Vergangenheit? Ein polemischer Essay zum 'Historikerstreit'* (Munich, 1988); see especially, pp. 174–188. The Historians' Debate has spawned a mass of commentaries in the course of the last two years. Wehler's book, however, is unquestionably one of the more reliable and intelligent works to have appeared on the subject thus far.

29. For a more detailed account of Habermas's distinction between "conventional" and "postconventional" identities with reference to the issues at stake in the *Historikerstreit*, see the essay, "Historical Consciousness and Post-Traditional Identity: Orientation Towards the West in West Germany."

30. "Life Forms, Morality, and the Task of the Philosopher," in *Habermas: Autonomy and Solidarity*, ed. P. Dews (London, 1986), p. 196. "There was no break in terms of persons or courses," observes Habermas; a remark that applied to two of his philosophy teachers, Oskar Becker and Ernst Rothacker.

31. For the historical and political background of the "Berufsverbot," see the essays by W-D Narr and J. Seifert in *New German Critique* 8 (Spring 1976), pp. 21–53.

32. The "German autumn" refers to the whirlwind of terrorist-related events that rocked the Federal Republic in the fall of 1977: the kidnapping of Hans-Martin Schleyer, head of the German employers association, by the Red Army Faction; the hijacking by RAF terrorists of a Lufthansa jet to Mogadishu, Somalia; the rescue of the plane by West German commandoes, at which point Schleyer was executed by his captors; and the mysterious suicides in Stahlheim prison of the RAF leaders Ulrike Meinhof and Andreas Baader.

One of the most sinister aspects of these events was a renewed accusation by leading figures on the German right that critical intellectuals undermined the value-system of the Federal Republic and thus fostered attitudes conducive to terrorism. And thus in the fall of 1977, the CDU's Alfred Dregger, appearing on national television, accused the Frankfurt School of direct responsibility for the recent wave of German terrorism. For Habermas's response to these accusations, see "A Test for Popular Justice: The Accusations Against the Intellectuals," *New German Critique* 12 (Fall 1977), pp. 11–13. The same issue of *New German Critique* also contains observations by Herbert Marcuse and Rudi Dutschke on the German autumn.

Schmidt's remarks were made during a Social Democratic Party congress in Hamburg. He went on to observe, "Trivialization [of terrorism] would be dangerous, but it would be just as dangerous to let panic, exaggeration, and hysteria get the upper hand. What we need is a restful, considered decisiveness." Cited in W. Rohric, *Die Demokratie der Westdeutschen* (Munich, 1988), pp. 134–135.

33. See, for example, the recently published collection, *Complexio Oppositorium: uber Carl Schmitt*, ed. H. Quaritsch (Berlin, 1988); and G. Maschke, *Der Tod Carl Schmitts* (Wien, 1987). For Habermas's critique of Schmitt, see the essay, "The Horrors of Autonomy: Carl Schmitt in English," in this volume. For an explanation of the continuities between Schmitt's authoritarian political philosophy of the 1920s and his partisanship for National Socialism in the 1930s, see my essay "Carl Schmitt, Political Existentialism, and the Total State," in *Theory and Society* (forthcoming).

34. The essay first appeared in *New German Critique* 22 (Winter 1981), pp. 3–14. The German original was entitled "Die Moderne: Ein unvollendetes Projekt," and appeared in *Kleine Politische Schriften*, I–IV (Frankfurt, 1981), pp. 444–464. It was delivered by Habermas on the occasion of his receipt of the Adorno prize, awarded by the city of Frankfurt on September 11, 1980.

35. The specific historical point of reference for Habermas's characterization of "young conservatism" is the "conservative-revolutionary" thinkers who dominated German intellectdual life during the 1920s. Their foremost representatives—Ludwig Klages, the Jünger brothers, Oswald Spengler—were all, like the postmodernists of today, immensely influenced by Nietzsche. Their writings were characterized by an uncompromising critique of the modern age that often relied on the strategy of rehabilitating "archaic" concepts (for example, Klages's concept of the "archaic image" or Ernst Jünger's notion of the "warrior"). As the ensuing citation shows, Habermas perceives significant commonalities between the young conservatives of the 1920s and the postmodernists of today, insofar as both groups seek, by virtue of a shared archaism and aestheticism, to break free of the normative presuppositions of modernity: the autonomous conception of the "self," liberal-democratic forms of government, and a rational theory of knowledge.

36. Weber's clearest articulation of this perspective—implicit in all his work—may be found in "Religious Rejections of the World and Their Directions," in *From Max Weber,* eds. H. Gerth and C. W. Mills (New York, 1946), pp. 323–359.

37. For Habermas's treatment of the problem of the modern need for self-legitimation (*Selbstvergewisserung*), see *The Philosophical Discourse of Modernity* (Cambridge, MA, 1987), pp. 1–22 ("Modernity's Consciousness of Time and its Need for Self-Reassurance").

38. Habermas analyzes the Nietzschean origins of postmodernism in *The Philosophical Discourse of Modernity*, chapter IV, "The Entry into Postmodernism: Nietzsche as a Turning Point."

39. See *Theory of Communicative Action*, vol. 2, pp. 311–396, passim.

40. *Negative Dialectics*, trans. E. B. Ashton (New York, 1973), p. 346.

41. Habermas, "Die Moderne: ein unvollendetes Projekt," p. 462.

Translator's Preface

The essays in this volume (with the exception of those in the section on "Culture and Politics" and the discussion of Heidegger) are taken from the two most recent volumes of Habermas's political writings, *Kleine Politische Schriften* V and VI. In the preface to the earlier of the two volumes, Habermas describes these writings as "positions taken by a political contemporary on themes of the day." They are intended, then, for the public sphere rather than for an expert audience, and range in form from the lecture to the magazine or newspaper article, to the book review or interview. While, as Habermas notes, they follow rules less restrictive than those of scholarly work, the longer essays are highly crafted and intricately argued. All are directly related to Habermas's more systematic and theoretical work, to which they form a valuable complement. The essays employ the conceptualizations developed in the more theoretical work, and with their focus on specific topics and contemporary issues elaborate and exemplify perspectives that emerge from that work. These writings can provide an entry into Habermas's thought and also a way to fuller understanding of his systematic writings.

The nature of these writings has occasioned certain decisions regarding the translation and editing of this volume. Because Habermas uses the terminology of his theoretical work here, I have tried to translate technical terms to be consistent with prior translations of Habermas and to reflect current usage in the social sciences. In translating the longer essays, which were originally delivered as lectures but were also intended for pub-

lication, and are thus examples of a written form suitable for
oral delivery, I have paid special attention to the rhythm of the
sentences, the emphasis within a sentence, and the movement
from one sentence to the next. My aim has been essays that
read well aloud. Because the essays are so intricately crafted, I
have tried to retain the main features of Habermas's style: his
sentence construction, which creates a complex web of cross-
references, his use of unobtrusive metaphors drawn from the
realm of physical phenomena, his punctuation, and his
paragraphing.

Annotations have been kept to a minimum. For the most
part I have annotated only references to contemporary German events and public figures, and then only when necessary
for clarity. Annotations have been kept as unobtrusive as possible by inserting them into Habermas's sentences as bracketed
glosses (all bracketed material in the text is mine).

A number of these essays have previously appeared in English translation, and the earlier translation has been used as
a basis for revision. In all cases the revisions have been substantial, both for stylistic reasons and because the published
German text I have followed is usually more extensive. I would
like to thank the following for permission to use published
translations as a basis for revision in this way: *Philosophy and
Social Criticism*, for Philip Jacobs's translation of "The New
Obscurity"; *New German Critique*, for John Blazek's translation
of "The Idea of the University"; the *Times Literary Supplement*,
for a translation of "The Horrors of Autonomy," which appeared as "Sovereignty and the *Führerdemokratie*"; and *Telos*,
for Russell Berman's translation of "Neoconservative Cultural
Criticism." Also consulted were Helena Tsoskonoglou's translation of "Modern and Postmodern Architecture," which appeared in *9H*, and Sigrid Brauner and Robert Brown's
translation of "Taking Aim at the Heart of the Present," which
appeared in *University Publishing*.

John McCumber's translation of the Heidegger piece, "Work
and Weltanschanung," has been reprinted from *Critical Inquiry*
without change.

Finally, I am indebted to Thomas McCarthy for his gener-
osity in sharing his expertise as a translator of Habermas and
his knowledge of current terminology in the social sciences;
and I would like to thank Arden H. Nicholsen for readings of
draft translations and for illuminating reflections on the conceptual content of Habermas's metaphors. I am also grateful
to Andrei Markovits and Jeremy Shapiro for providing valuable suggestions on specific translation problems. Responsibility for errors and lapses into awkwardness remains my own.

Shierry Weber Nicholsen

1

Neoconservatism

Modern and Postmodern Architecture

The exhibition "The Other Tradition: Architecture in Munich from 1800 to the Present" provides an occasion to reflect on the meaning of a preposition. For the exhibition has unobtrusively taken sides in the debate on *post*modern architecture. Those who use this "post" want to set themselves apart from a past; they cannot yet give a new name to the present, since we do not yet have answers for the identifiable problems of the future. Terms like "post-Enlightenment" or "post-history" serve the same function. Such gestures of hasty dismissal are suited to periods of transition.

At first the "postmodernists" of today seem to be only reiterating the credo of the "postrationalists" of yesterday. Leonardo Benevolo, an important historian of modern architecture, characterizes this postrationalist tendency, which was widespread precisely among young architects between 1930 and 1933, in this way: "Now that the modern movement had been reduced to a system of formal precepts, it was assumed that the origin of its present uneasiness lay in the narrowness and schematic nature of these rules, and it was believed that the remedy still lay in a change of formal direction, in a lessening of the stress on technical features and regularity, in the return to a more human architecture, warmer, freer, and inevitably more closely attached to traditional values. The economic crisis meant that the debate was compressed into a very short space

This essay was initially given as a talk at the opening of the exhibition "The Other Tradition" in November 1981.

of time; the Nazi dictatorship that followed saw to it that it was cut short once and for all and at the same time acted as a touchstone, openly revealing what choices had been concealed beneath the stylistic controversy."[1] I do not want to draw false parallels but rather to note that this is not the first time that modern architecture has been dismissed—and it continues to survive.

The prefix that we encounter in such terms for tendencies and points of view does not always have the same meaning. Common to the -isms formed with the prefix "post" is the sense of *standing back* from something. They express an experience of discontinuity but take different attitudes toward the past that is put at a distance. With the word "postindustrial," for instance, sociologists are only trying to say that industrial capitalism has *developed further*, that the new service sectors have expanded at the expense of the domain of immediate production. With the word "postempiricist," philosophers are indicating that certain normative concepts of science and scientific progress have been *rendered obsolete* by recent research. The "poststructuralists" are trying to carry the familiar theoretical approach of structuralism *to its conclusion* rather than to overcome it. We call "postavant-garde," finally, the contemporary painting that makes expert use of the formal language created by the Modern Movement while renouncing its extravagant hopes for a reconciliation of art and life.

At first the expression "postmodern," as it was applied in America during the 1950s and 1960s to literary trends that wanted to set themselves apart from works of the early modern period, was also used merely to designate new variants within the broad spectrum of late modernism.[2] "Postmodernism" became an emotionally loaded outright political battle cry only in the 1970s, when two opposing camps seized the expression: on the one side the *neoconservatives*, who wanted to get rid of the supposedly subversive contents of a "hostile culture" in favor of revived traditions; and on the other side the radical *critics of growth* for whom the *Neues Bauen*, the New Architecture, had become a symbol for the destruction produced by modernization. Only then did postavant-garde movements, which had formerly shared the orientation of modern architecture—

and were correctly described by Charles Jencks as representative of "late modernism"[3]—become caught up in the conservative mood of the 1970s, paving the way for an intellectually playful but provocative repudiation of the moral principles of modern architecture.[4]

These examples of expressions formed with the prefix "post" do not exhaust the spectrum of attitudes one may take toward a past from which one wants to distance oneself. It is only the presupposition that remains constant: the experience of a discontinuity, a detachment from a form of life or consciousness that one had previously trusted *"naively"* or *"unreflectively."*

These are the expressions with which Schiller and Schlegel, Schelling and Hegel sought at one time to comprehend the experiences of discontinuity of *their* time. The period of the Enlightenment had broken irrevocably the continuum joining their present with the world of immediately experienced traditions, both Christian and Greek. The historical Enlightenment did not determine the historicist thought of the late nineteenth century. Still, the classicists and romanticists born in the eighteenth century did not want to simply accommodate to the break in continuity: rather, they wanted to find *their own* way through a *reflective appropriation* of history. This impulse from the German Idealist philosophy of reconciliation also lies behind the quest for a new, synthetic architectural style that dominated the first half of the nineteenth century.[5] The announcement in which, in 1850, Maximilian II of Bavaria challenged architects to a competition that was to produce the desired new style—and which in fact produced the Maximilianstrasse—reads like an echo of this vividly felt need. It was not until the second half of the nineteenth century that people settled down to living with a pluralism of styles that art history had made contemporary and also objectified.

It was only then that the great accomplishments of historical scholarship, which had distanced the past a second time after the Enlightenment had done so the first time, settled into the form of a Janus-faced *historical consciousness*. On the one hand, historicism signified a continuation and radicalization of the Enlightenment, which, as Nietzsche recognized immediately, defined the conditions for the development of modern identities even more sharply, more mercilessly than before; on the other hand, historicism made historical traditions available in an ideal simultaneity and made it possible for a present that was unstable and trying to escape from itself to dress itself up in borrowed identities. Stylistic pluralism, which had previously been something of an affliction, now became an accomplishment. First the *Jugendstil* and then classical modernity arrived at a response to this situation that remains relevant today. The designation "classical," to be sure, also indicates the distance we have achieved in the meantime on the Modern Movement of our century. This is why we have to be willing to face the question of our own position vis-à-vis the discontinuity that is now opening up again.

Ten years ago Wend Fischer, director of the Neue Sammlung, put together a highly regarded exhibition. His intention was to counteract a veneration with neohistoricist overtones, a nostalgia that at that time had taken possession of the contrast-filled eclecticism of the nineteenth century, the "masked ball of styles." Fischer wanted to reveal tendencies of a "hidden reason" by presenting the nineteenth century as the *prehistory* of modern architecture and functional design. The city's enormous glass palace and its market hall notwithstanding, one has to conduct an incomparably more demanding search to discover similar traces of reason in Munich, a place that tends to turn away from the modern—and to follow them into the present. But the weakness of the impressions that modernity has left here in Munich cannot fully explain the change in the tenor of the exhibition: in comparison with the exhibition of ten years ago, defensive characteristics are more evident today. The debate over postmodernism, which is no longer confined to architectural journals, has reached the points of reference involved in these two attempts at reconstruction. This battle concerns the standpoint from which one looks back into the prehistory of the Modern Movement.

It is not easy to sort out the fronts in this battle. For all agree in their critique of a soulless container architecture, of the absence of relationship to the environment and the solitary arrogance of blocklike office buildings; of monstrous department stores and monumental university buildings and conference centers; of the lack of urbanity and the misanthropy of commuter towns; of housing developments, the brutal posterity of bunker architecture, the mass production of A-frame doghouses; of the destruction of city centers for the sake of the automobile, and so forth[6]—so many catchwords, and no dissent to be found anywhere. From Sigfried Giedion, a passionate advocate of modern architecture for more than a generation, there are critical statements dating from the year 1964 that could have been written today by Oswald Matthias Ungers or Charles Moore.[7] Of course, what one group presents as immanent critique is *opposition to modernity* in the other group; the same grounds on which the one side is encouraged to continue an irreplaceable tradition from a critical perspective are sufficient for the other side to proclaim the postmodern era. And these opposing groups, furthermore, draw opposite conclusions depending on whether they approach the problem as a cosmetic one or in terms of criticism of the system. The *conservatively minded* are content to cover up stylistically what will go on in any case—whether they do so as traditionalists, like Branca, or, like the contemporary Robert Venturi, as a pop artist who turns the spirit of the Modern Movement into a quotation and mixes it ironically with other quotations to form garish texts that glow like neon lights. The radical antimodernists, in contrast, attack the problem at a more fundamental level, wanting to undermine economic and administrative constraints on industrial construction with the aim of dedifferentiating architecture. What one group sees as problems of style the other understands as problems of the decolonization of devastated lifeworlds. Thus those who want to continue the uncompleted project of a modernity that is on the skids see themselves confronted with a variety of opponents who are in accord only in their determination to bid farewell to modernity.

The modern architecture whose origins in Frank Lloyd Wright and Adolf Loos were both organic and rationalist, and which flowered in the most successful works of a Gropius and a Mies van der Rohe, a Le Corbusier and an Alvar Aalto—this architecture remains the first and only binding style, the first and only style to have shaped even everyday life, since the days

of classicism. It is the only architectural movement to have
sprung from the spirit of the avant-garde, the only one equal
in stature to the avant-garde painting, music, and literature of
our century. It continued the line of tradition of Western rationalism and was powerful enough to create models, that is,
to become classical itself and to establish a tradition that from
the beginning transcended national boundaries. How are we
to reconcile these indisputable facts with the fact that those
monstrosities we unanimously condemn arose after World War
II as the successors to, even in the name of, this International
Style? Is the true face of modernity revealed in them—or are
they falsifications of its true spirit? I will move toward a prov-
sional answer by listing the problems that faced architecture in
the nineteenth century, describing the New Architecture's programmatic responses to them, and showing the kinds of problems that could *not* be solved with this program. These
considerations, finally, should permit a judgment on the rec-
ommendation that this exhibition, if I understand its intentions
correctly, is making. How sound is the advice that we steadfastly
appropriate the tradition of modernity and continue it critically, instead of pursuing the escapist movements dominant
today—whether the escape be to a tradition-conscious neohistoricism, to the ultramodern "stageset" architecture presented
at the Venice Biennale in 1980, or into the vitalism of the
simple life in an anonymous, deprofessionalized vernacular
architecture?

   1. In the course of the nineteenth century the industrial
revolution and the accelerated social modernization that followed it confronted architecture and town planning with a new
situation. To note the three best-known challenges: qualitatively new needs for architectural design, new materials and
construction techniques, and the subjection of building to new
functional, primarily economic imperatives.

   With industrial capitalism there arose new *spheres of life* that
evaded both the monumental architecture of court and church
and the old European architecture of the cities and the country.
The diffusion of culture to the middle class and the formation
of a broader educated public interested in the arts called for
new libraries and schools, opera houses and theaters. But those

are conventional tasks. A transport system revolutionized by the railroad presented a different task; not only did it raise the locomotive to a symbol of dynamization and progress, it also gave a new meaning to bridges and tunnels, the familiar structures of transport, and with the construction of railway stations it presented a new task. Railway stations are the characteristic settings for dense and varied but also anonymous and fleeting contacts, the kinds of overstimulating but interpersonally impoverished interactions that were to characterize the sense of life in the big cities. As freeways, airports, and television transmission towers demonstrate, the development of transportation and communication systems has always provided the impetus for innovations.

At that time the same thing was true of commerce, which not only required warehouses and covered markets on a new scale but also brought with it unconventional construction projects: the department store and the exhibition hall. The first large glass palaces, built for industrial exhibitions in London, Munich, and Paris, are fascinating examples. But it was above all industrial production, with its factories, workers' housing developments, and goods produced for mass consumption, that gave rise to areas of life into which principles of form and architectural design did not at first penetrate. The social misery of early industrialism took precedence over its ugliness; its problems called into action the state, bourgeois social reformers, and finally a revolutionary labor movement, not the shaping fantasy of architects—if one disregards utopian designs for the new industrial city (from Robert Owen to Tony Garnier). In the second half of the century, mass-produced articles for daily use that were not subject to the stylistic force of traditional craftsmanship were the first to be perceived as an aesthetic problem. John Ruskin and William Morris tried to bridge the gap between utility and beauty that had arisen in daily life in the industrial world by reforming the applied arts. This reform movement was guided by a broader, forward-looking concept of architecture that was accompanied by the demand that the *whole* physical environment of bourgeois society be given architectural form. Morris in particular recognized the contradiction between democratic demands for what amounted to universal participation in culture and the fact that in industrial capitalism more and more domains of life become alienated from the stamp of cultural forces.

A second challenge for architecture arose from the development of *new materials* (such as glass and iron, steel and cement) and *new methods of production* (especially the use of prefabricated units). In the course of the nineteenth century engineers advanced construction techniques, thereby opening up to architecture construction possibilities that shattered classical limits on the constructive manipulation of surfaces and spaces. Glass palaces made with standardized parts, which had developed out of greenhouse construction, provided fascinated contemporaries with their first impressions of new orders of magnitude and new principles of construction; they revolutionized habits of seeing and altered spectators' spatial sense no less dramatically than the railway altered passengers' exprience of time. In the interior of the London Crystal Palace, repetitive and without a center, it must have seemed to contemporaries that the constraints on all the familiar dimensions of formed space had been removed.

The third challenge is the capitalist *mobilization* of labor power, land, and buildings, of urban *living conditions* in general. This led to the concentration of large masses of people and to the incursion of speculation into the domain of private housing. The processes that led to the recent protests in Kreuzberg [a section of Berlin with an active squatters' movement] and elsewhere originated then: to the extent to which housing construction became an amortizable investment, decisions about the buying and selling of real estate, about construction, demolition, and new construction, about renting and vacating became detached from their ties to family and local tradition; they became, in a word, independent of orientation to use-values. Laws governing the market in construction and housing changed attitudes toward construction and housing. Economic imperatives also determined the uncontrolled growth of the cities, resulting in the need for a kind of town planning that had not been involved in the development of the Baroque cities. The way those two kinds of functional imperatives, those of the market and those of communal and state planning, interacted, intersected, and entangled architecture in a new system of dependencies is demonstrated in grand style in the redevelopment of Paris by Haussmann under Napoleon III. Architects played no appreciable role in this planning.

To understand the impulse from which modern architecture arose, one must bear in mind that the architecture of the second half of the nineteenth century was not only overwhelmed by this third challenge of industrial capitalism; in addition, although it had sensed the other two challenges, it had not met them.

Arbitrary disposition of decontextualized, scientifically objectified styles enabled historicism to veer off into an impotent idealism and to *separate* the sphere of architecture from the banalities of everyday bourgeois life. The plight of the new spheres of life that were alienated from architectonic design was turned into the virtue of releasing utilitarian architecture from artistic demands. Opportunities offered by new possibilities for technical design were seized only to divide the world up between architects and engineers, between style and function, between magnificent facades on the exterior and autonomous arrangements of space in the interior. This is why an architecture that has become historicist cannot oppose the internal dynamic of economic growth, the mobilization of urban living conditions, and the social misery of the masses with much more than a flight into the triumph of spirit and culture over the (disguised) material base. The Berlin "rent barracks" becomes an impressive symbol of this: "The front building, whose historicizing facade was designed to ensure the prestige value of the building, was reserved for the middle bourgeoisie, while the poorer people lived in the back buildings."[8]

2. In historicist architecture, Idealism abandoned its original intentions. To be sure, Schelling and Hegel had also placed architecture lowest in the hierarchy of the arts, for "the material for this first art form is the inherently nonspiritual, i.e., heavy matter, shapeable only according to the laws of gravity."[9] For this reason Hegel thinks that "the spiritual meaning does not reside exclusively in the building . . . but in the fact that this meaning has already attained its existence in freedom outside architecture."[10] But he conceives the purpose that ar-

chitecture is to serve as the totality of the social context of communication and life: "as human individuals assembled as a company or nation."[11] Historicist architecture abandons this idea of reconciliation—the spirit, no longer a force of reconciliation, now feeds the compensatory dynamics of a reality that has been plastered over and hidden behind facades. In the reformist tendencies of the *Jugendstil*, from which modern architecture emerged, protest against this falseness, against an *architecture of repression* and symptom-formation, was already making itself felt. It is no accident that Sigmund Freud developed the bases of his theory of neurosis at the same time.

The Modern Movement took up the challenges to which the architecture of the nineteenth century had not been equal. It overcame stylistic pluralism and the distinctions and divisions to which architecture had accommodated.

To the alienation of the various domains of life from culture in industrial capitalism, the Modern Movement responded with the claim of a style that not only stamped public buildings but also penetrated the practice of everyday life. The spirit of modernity was to spread to the totality of social life-expressions. In this way industrial design could be linked to the reform of the applied arts, the functional design of utilitarian buildings could be linked to the engineering techniques used in buildings for transportation and commerce, and the design of business districts could be linked to the models of the Chicago School. In addition, the new language of form took possession of the exclusive domain of monumental architecture, of churches, theaters, court buildings, ministries, town halls, universities, spas, and so forth; and on the other side it extended into the core domains of industrial production, into housing developments, social housing, and factories.

The new style could not have penetrated all domains of life if modern architecture had not dealt with the second challenge, that of the immensely expanded range of technical design possibilities, with an *inherent aesthetic logic*. The term "functionalism" covers specific key ideas, principles for the construction of spaces and the use of materials, methods of production and organization; functionalism is based on the conviction that forms are supposed to express the use-functions for which a structure is created. But that idea is not so new; even the classicistically inclined Hegel writes, "Need introduces into architecture forms which are wholly and entirely purposeful and belong to the [mathematical] intellect, *viz*. the straight line, the right angle, level surfaces."[12] Furthermore, the expression "functionalism" suggests false ideas. It disguises the fact that the features of modern buildings associated with it are the result of consistently applied autonomous aesthetic laws. What is falsely attributed to functionalism owes its existence instead to an aesthetically motivated constructivism that emerged from new problems posed within art itself. In this constructivism modern architecture was following the experimental path of avant-garde painting.

Initially, modern architecture found itself in a paradoxical situation. On the one hand, architecture had always been a use-oriented art. In contrast to music, painting, and lyric poetry, it is as difficult for architecture to detach itself from practical contexts as it is for literary prose to detach itself from the practice of everyday language—these arts remain caught in the net of everyday practice and everyday communication: Adolf Loos even saw architecture, along with everything that serves a specific purpose, as excluded from the domain of art. On the other hand, architecture is subject to the laws of cultural modernity—like art in general, it succumbs to the compulsion of radical autonomization, the differentiation of a domain of genuine aesthetic experience, a domain that a subjectivity freed from the imperatives of everyday life, from the routines of action and the conventions of perception, can explore in the company of its own spontaneity. Avant-garde art, which has freed itself from perspectivistic perception of the object and from tonality, from imitation and harmony and turned to its own media of representation, was described by Adorno in terms like construction, experiment, and montage. According to him, exemplary works of avant-garde art devote themselves to an esoteric absolutism "at the expense of the reality-oriented purposefulness in which functional structures like bridges or industrial plants seek their formal laws. . . . The autonomous work of art, in contrast, functional only within itself, hopes to achieve what was once known as beauty through its immanent teleology."[13] Adorno, then, opposes the work of art that is functional "in itself" to the structure that is functional for "external purposes." In its most convincing examples, however, modern architecture does not fit within the dichotomy Adorno outlined.

The functionalism of modern architecture coincides instead with the inner logic of a development in art. There were three main groups that concerned themselves with the problems that emerged from Cubist painting: the Purists around Le Corbusier, the circle of Constructivists around Malevich, and especially the De Stijl movement (with van Doesburg, Mondrian, and Oud). Just as de Saussure analyzed the structures of language during that period, so the Dutch Neoplasticists, as they called themselves, investigated the grammar of expressive and formative means, the most universal techniques of the plastic arts, in order to incorporate the latter into the *Gesamtkunstwerk* of a comprehensive architectonic designing of the environment. "In the future," Mondrian wrote, "the realization of pure figurative expression within the encompassable reality of our environment will replace the work of art."[14] In Malevich's and Oud's very early architectural sketches one can see how structures like those of functionalist Bauhaus architecture came out of this experimental relationship to formative means. In 1922, Van Doesburg moved to Weimar and argued for the constructivist bases of functional construction and form in debates with the Bauhaus staff. Despite these controversies, the line of development, which Gropius also followed in his striving for a "new unity of art and technology," is clear; in Bruno Taut's slogan "What functions well, looks good," it is precisely the *inherent aesthetic logic of functionalism,* expressed so clearly in Taut's buildings, that is lost.

While the Modern Movememt recognized and, in principle, responded correctly to the challenges presented by qualitatively new needs and new technical design possibilities, it was essentially helpless in the face of systemic dependencies on the imperatives of the market and administrative planning.

3. The expanded concept of architecture that had inspired the Modern Movement from William Morris on and provided the encouragement to overcome a stylistic pluralism detached

from everyday reality was a mixed blessing. It directed attention to important connections between industrial design, interior decoration, domestic architecture and town planning, but it was also godfather to the attempt on the part of the theoreticians of the New Architecture to see life styles and forms of life as a whole subjected to the dictates of their design tasks. Totalities such as these, however, elude the grasp of planning. When Le Corbusier was finally able to realize his design for an "*unité d'habitation,*" to give concrete form to his idea of a "*cité jardin verticale,*" it was precisely the communal facilities that remained unused—or were gotten rid of. The utopia of a preconceived form of life, on which in an earlier period the sketches of Owens and Fourier had been based, could not be brought to life. And this was due not only to a hopeless underestimation of the complexity and changeability of modern lifeworlds but also to the fact that modernized societies with their systemic interrelationships extend beyond the dimensions of a lifeworld that could be measured by a planner's imagination. The current manifestations of a crisis in modern architecture derive less from a crisis in architecture than from the fact that architecture voluntarily allowed itself to become overburdened.

In addition, with the ambiguities of functionalist ideology, architecture was ill equipped to confront the dangers that the reconstruction period after World War II—the period in which the International Style finally became widespread—brought with it. Gropius, of course, emphasized time and time again that architecture and town planning were intertwined with industry, the economy, transportation, politics, and administration. He was also aware of the process character of planning. But in the framework of the Bauhaus these problems came up in a format tailored to didactic purposes. And the successes of the Modern Movement misled the pioneer to the unfounded expectation that a "unity of culture and production" could be created in *another* sense as well: in this transfiguring light, the economic and political-administrative constraints to which the designing of the environment was subject seemed to be merely questions of organization. When at their meeting in 1949 the Association of American Architects wanted to adopt a regulation that architects were not to operate as building contractors, Gropius protested not against the inadequacy of this means but against the purpose and rationale of the proposal. He reiterated his credo: "Made into an educational discipline, [participation in the arts] would give our environment the unity that is the very basis of culture, embracing everything from a simple chair to the house of worship."[15] In this grand synthesis the contradictions that characterize capitalist modernization precisely in the area of town planning vanish—contradictions between the needs of a formed lifeworld on the one hand and the imperatives transmitted through the media of money and power on the other.

No doubt this false expectation was abetted by a linguistic misunderstanding or rather a categorial error. The means suited to a certain *purpose* are called "functional." A functionalism that tries to construct buildings in accordance with the purposes of their users should be understood in this sense. But we also call decisions that stabilize an anonymous complex of the results of action "functional," without the contents of this *system* necessarily being desired or even recognized by any of those involved in it. What is "system-functional" for the economy and for administration in this sense, as for example an increase in the density of the inner city with rising real estate prices and increasing tax revenues, will prove to be not "functional" at all within the horizon of the lifeworld of the inhabitants and those living nearby. The problems of town planning are not primarily problems of design but rather problems of steering failures, problems of controlling and managing anonymous system imperatives that invade urban lifeworlds and threaten to consume their urban substance.

Today everyone is thinking and talking about the traditional European city; but in 1889 Camillo Sitte, one of the first to compare the medieval with the modern city, was already issuing warnings against *forced naturalness*: "Can one," he asks, "invent and construct, according to a plan, contingencies that history has produced over the course of centuries? Could one have genuine unfeigned pleasure in such *false naiveté*, in such *artificial naturalness?*"[16] Sitte's starting point was the idea of a restoration of urbanity. But after a century of criticism of the metropolis, after a century of innumerable fruitless attempts to keep the cities in equilibrium, to rescue the city centers, to divide urban space into residential and commercial areas, industrial zones and garden suburbs, private and public areas; after efforts to build livable commuter towns, to clean up slum areas, to regulate traffic rationally and so forth, the question arises whether the very *concept* of the city has not been superseded. The traces of the occidental city that Max Weber described, the city of the European bourgeoisie in the High Middle Ages or the urban nobility in Renaissance Upper Italy, the princely *Residenz* city restored by the Baroque master builders—these historical traces have blended in our minds into a diffuse and many-layered concept of the city. It is the kind of concept that Wittgenstein found in the habits and the self-understanding of everyday activity: our concept of the city is connected to a form of life. But in the meantime that form of life has changed so much that the concept that grew out of it can no longer keep pace. As a lifeworld that could be surveyed and grasped, the city could be given architectural form, sensory representation. The social functions of urban life, political and economic, private and public, the functions of cultural and ecclesiastical representation, of work, habitation, recreation, and celebration could be *translated* into purposes, into functions of the time-regulated use of formed spaces. But in the nineteenth century at the latest the city became the point of intersection of functional relationships of a *different* kind. It came to be embedded in abstract systems that as such could no longer be represented aesthetically in concretely existing form. The fact that from the middle of the century up into the late 1880s the great industrial exhibitions were planned as major architectural events betrays an impulse that now seems touching, an impulse of which the Olympiads of today are reminiscent. In arranging an international comparison of the products of their industrial production in vivid and festive form in magnificent halls, governments were literally trying to put the world marketplace on stage and to bring it back within the bounds of the lifeworld. But even the railway stations could no longer give visual form to the functions of the transportation system to which they linked the passengers in the way the city gates had once given visual form to the city's concrete ties to surrounding villages and neighboring cities.

Today, moreover, airports are located far outside the cities, for good reasons. And in the faceless office buildings that dominate the city centers—the banks and government buildings, court buildings and corporate headquarters, the publishing and printing houses, the private and public bureaucracies—one cannot recognize the functional relationships whose nodal points they form. The graphics of company logos and neon advertisements show that differentiations must be made in a medium *other* than that of the architectural language of forms. Venturi, in fact, drew the conclusions from this—when he compared the shopping center signs along the Autobahn to a duck-house in the shape of a duck, thus ridiculing the unity of exterior and interior, of beauty and utility demanded by modern architecture. Another indication that the urban life-world is becoming increasingly mediated by *system relationships that cannot be given form* is the failure of what was probably the most ambitious project of the New Architecture: to this day it has not been possible to integrate social housing projects and factories into the city. The urban agglomerations have outgrown the old concept of the city to which we gave our hearts; that is not the failure of modern architecture, or of any architecture at all.

4. If this diagnosis is not completely wrong, then it merely confirms, first of all, the reigning perplexity and the necessity of seeking new solutions. It also raises doubts about the reactions aroused by the disaster of the simultaneously overburdened and instrumentralized New Architecture. To orient myself at least provisionally in the complex terrain of counter-movements, I have made a typology—oversimplified, of course—and distinguished three tendencies that have one thing in common: in contrast to the self-critical continuation of modernity that this exhibition is implicitly advocating, they rupture the modern style by dissolving the conjunction of avant-garde form-language and uncompromising functionalist principles. Form and function once again diverge programmatically. This is true in the trivial sense of a neohistoricism that transforms department stores into a medieval row of

houses and subway ventilation shafts into pocketbook-size Palladian villas. This return to the eclecticism of the previous century is due, as it was then, to compensatory needs. This traditionalism conforms to the pattern of political neoconservatism in that it redefines problems that lie at a *different* level as questions of style and thus removes them from public consciousness. The escapist reaction is linked to a move toward the affirmative: everything *else* is to remain as it is.

The separation of form and function also characterizes a postmodernism that fits the definition given by Charles Jencks and is completely free of nostalgia—whether it be Eisenmann and Grave, who give artistic autonomy to the formal repertoire of the 1920s, or Hollein and Venturi, who, like surrealistic stage designers, use modern design techniques to entice painterly effects from an aggressive mixture of styles.[17] The language of this stage-set architecture is pledged to a rhetoric that tries to express in code the systemic relationships that can no longer be given architectonic form.

The unity of form and function is ruptured in another way by the alternative architecture that takes as its point of departure questions of ecology and the preservation of historically developed quarters of the city. These efforts, occasionally called "vitalist,"[18] aim primarily at achieving a close connection between architectural design and spatial, cultural, and historical environmental contexts. Something of the impulse of the Modern Movement survives here—now, however, on the defensive. Especially noteworthy are steps toward a community architecture in which those affected are included in the planning process in a way that goes beyond mere rhetoric and plans city districts in dialogue with clients.[19] When the steering mechanisms of the market and administrative bodies function in town planning in such a way as to have dysfunctional consequences for the lifeworld of those concerned—thus cancelling out the "functionalism" that was once intended—then it is only consistent to allow the will-formative communication of participants to enter into competition with the media of money and power.

The longing for dedifferentiated forms of life does, it is true, often give these tendencies a veneer of antimodernism.

Then they ally themselves with the cult of the vernacular and the worship of the banal. This ideology of the uncomplicated renounces the rational potential and the inherent aesthetic logic of cultural modernity. Praising anonymous construction and an architecture without architects indicates the price that this vitalism become critical of the system is ready to pay, even if it has in mind another *Volksgeist* than the one whose glorification in its time supplemented the monumentalism of the Führer's architecture most admirably.

There is a good deal of truth in this opposition to modernity; it takes up the unsolved problems that modern architecture pushed into the background—that is, the colonization of the lifeworld through the imperatives of autonomous economic and administrative systems of action. But we can learn something from all these opposition movements only if we keep one thing in mind: At a fortunate moment in modern architecture, the inherent aesthetic logic of constructivism encountered the use-orientation of a strict functionalism and united spontaneously with it. Traditions live only through such moments, even the one that, from the perspective of Munich, represents "the other tradition."

Notes

1. Leonardo Benevolo, *History of Modern Architecture*, vol. II (Cambridge, MA, 1971), p. 552.

2. M. Köhler, "Postmodernismus," in *Amerikastudien* 22 (1977), p. 8ff.

3. Charles Jencks, *Late Modern Architecture and Other Essays* (New York, 1980).

4. Charles Jencks, *The Language of Postmodern Architecture*, 4th ed. (New York, 1984).

5. M. Brix and M. Steinhauser, "Geschichte im Dienste der Baukunst," in their *Geschichte allein ist zeitgemäss* (Giessen, 1978), p. 255.

6. These descriptions are derived from H. Klotz, "Tendenzen heutiger Architektur in der Bundesrepublik," in *Das Kunstwerk* 32 (1979), p. 6ff.; and J. Paul, "Kulturgeschichtliche Betrachtungen zur deutschen Nachkriegsarchitecktur," in *Das Kunstwerk* 32 (1979), p. 13ff.

7. Sigfried Giedion, *Space, Time and Architecture: The Growth of a New Tradition* (Cam-

bridge, MA, 1965), p. xxvi ff.; Charles Moore, "Eine persönliche Erklärung," in G. R. Blomeyer and B. Tietze, *In Opposition zur Moderne* (Braunschweig, 1977), p. 64ff.

8. M. Brix and M. Steinhauser, *Geschichte allein ist zeitgemäss*, p. 220.

9. G. W. F. Hegel, *Aesthetics*, trans. T. M. Knox (Oxford, 1975), p. 624.

10. Hegel, *Aesthetics*, p. 661.

11. Hegel, *Aesthetics*, p. 655.

12. Hegel, *Aesthetics*, p. 655.

13. Theodor W. Adorno, *Aesthetic Theory* (London, 1984), p. 89 (translation altered).

14. Quoted in Benevolo, *History of Modern Architecture*, vol. II, p. 409.

15. Quoted in Benevolo, *History of Modern Architecture*, vol. II, p. 786.

16. Camillo Sitte, *Der Städtebau* (Leipzig, 1889).

17. V. M. Lampugnani, "Theorie und Architektur in den USA," in *Architekt* 5 (1980), p. 252ff.

18. W. Pohl, "Plädoyer für eine unbefriedete Tradition," in *Bauwelt* 19/20 (1981), p. 768ff.

19. L. Kroll, "Stadtteilplanung mit den Bewohnern," in Blomeyer und Tietze, *In Opposition zur Moderne*, p. 160ff.

Neoconservative Cultural
Criticism in the United States
and West Germany

In the most recent issue of *Monat* (July–September 1982), Norman Podhoretz, the editor of *Commentary* and, next to Irving Kristol, the editor of *Public Interest*, the most influential journalist among neoconservatives in the United States, claims for himself and his friends the credit for a twofold accomplishment. The group of intellectuals designated as "neoconservatives," he claims, shook the position of leftists and liberals in "the world of ideas" and by doing so cleared the way to the presidency for Ronald Reagan. The neoconservatives, of course, are only one of three groups in the ideological clientele of the new president—the others being the primarily Catholic-oriented conservatives who had already grouped themselves around activists like William Buckley during the Cold War phase, and the Protestant fundamentalists, who became the New Right during the 1970s as spokesmen for the "silent majority." In contrast to these two groups, the neoconservatives are not a mass phenomenon. They are to be distinguished especially from the populism of the New Right, and from the attempt to mix religion and politics. Their influence is more easily measured in terms of their intellectual stock than in terms of numbers of votes.

In fact, they have made sure that for the first time in half a century conservatism has become a phenomenon to be taken seriously in the United States. It is an accomplishment of the

This essay was presented at a forum held by the Friedrich Ebert Foundation in Frankfurt shortly before the end of the social-liberal (SPD/FDP) coalition in 1982.

neoconservatives that a conservative government is able to rely on theoretical points of view and not merely on pragmatic considerations and the general climate. That explains the interest of the European conservative parties in this intellectual movement: an example of the interest of the Christian Democratic party in West Germany is the conference sponsored by the Konrad Adenauer Foundation in September of 1981, which brought together German and American neoconservatives.[1]

In the United States as in the Federal Republic, neoconservatism is a matter of loose groupings of intellectuals with common orientations. The neoconservatives in both countries share a collection of critical positions and conceptions that are the result of similar disappointments. From the middle of the 1960s, these social scientists and philosophers found themselves confronted with economic, political, and intellectual developments that did not conform to their primarily affirmative image of Western industrial societies. In this sense, neoconservatism emerges from an attempt to deal with a disappointment. The profiles of neoconservative thought in the United States and the Federal Republic, however, differ as much as do the theories and diagnoses with which these intellectuals, in both countries, began in the 1950s. I will begin by characterizing the American side.

I

The theoretically productive center of American neoconservatism is composed of well-known sociologists with good academic credentials like Daniel Bell, Peter Berger, Nathan Glazer, Seymour Martin Lipset, Robert Nisbet, and Edward Shils. They make no secret of their leftist and liberal pasts. During the 1950s many belonged to the rigidly anticommunist circle around the American Committee for Cultural Freedom, took part in related congresses, and published in the organization's house organ, *Encounter*, the English-language counterpart to *Preuves* and *Monat*. At that time the American government was supporting this well-organized network of enteprises whose aim was to validate the liberal basis of the free world in opposition to the Soviet Union's imperialistic claims to power and against all varieties of theoretical Marxism. Seen against this political background, the intellectual continuity of the American neoconservatives becomes evident. They continue to maintain two important positions that they advocated during the 1950s: on the one hand, anticommunism, understood in terms of the concept of *totalitarianism*, and on the other, antipopulism, based on the *theory of democratic rule by elites*. Both theories were somewhat controversial in the social science of the 1950s, but still widely accepted. The theory of totalitarianism highlighted the negative traits of the enemy's political system by emphasizing the similarities between fascist and communist one-party systems; the other theory explained the advantages of their own political system by claiming that the representative character of the constitutional state with a separation of powers guaranteed both the pluralism of social interests and an optimal selection of leadership personnel. This was the common denominator of liberal social theories that conceptualized modernization processes in such a way that the society that was most advanced industrially, i.e., the United States, was implicitly held up as exemplary.

This normative distinction accorded the status quo could not, of course, withstand the realities of the 1960s and the 1970s. Hence the self-image of Irving Kristol, who sees himself as a liberal cheated by reality. Peter Glotz paraphrased this definition: "Neoconservatism is the net into which the liberal can fall when he begins to fear his own liberalism." What frightened the liberals?

The social and economic changes that brought about the end of the New Deal era and destroyed the old New Deal coalition (in part through upward mobility) cannot be treated here. The changes in foreign policy were more tangible; the neoconservatives reacted to the defeat in Vietnam and Kissinger's détente policies with the feeling that America's resistance to world communism was being crippled by a sort of moral disarmament. Just as the international developments did not fit into the anticommunist project, so the domestic mobilization that gripped society in the wake of the civil rights movement, the student protest, the New Left, the women's movement, and the escapist countercultures did not fit into the wholesome world of a nonideological rule by elites.

In addition, the thematization of poverty in the middle of the 1960s shattered the essentially harmonious picture of the affluent society. The undesired byproducts of the social programs bureaucratically implemented under Johnson soon began to appear. Where these programs nevertheless functioned well, they displeased the neoconservatives even more, since they jeopardized the formal principle of equal opportunity for the sake of improving the collective chances of ethnic minorities and women. McGovern combined all these tendencies in 1972, in a coalition in opposition to the labor unions; that gave the neoconservatives, who had not yet broken with the Democratic Party, the final impetus to do so.

The liberals turned neoconservative did not simply desert; instead, they tried to use their social-scientific talents to explain the facts that were bothering them. I can reproduce only the tenor of those extensive analyses. What is striking is the correspondences between neoconservative doctrines and social-critical approaches in the choice of phenomena to be explained. The crisis phenomena, of course, appear under different descriptions at each point. The neoconservatives look for the causes of crisis not in the mode of functioning of the economy and the state administrative apparatus but in legitimation problems that are culturally determined, and, generally, in the disturbed relationship between democracy and culture. They are concerned with the alleged loss of authority of central institutions, especially the political system. This phenomenon is presented suggestively with key terms like ungovernability, decline in credibility, and loss of legitimacy. The explanation begins with an "inflation" of expectations and claims, heightened by competing political parties, the mass media, and pluralist interests. This pressure of popular expectations "explodes" in a drastic expansion of the volume of state activity. As a result, the steering instruments of state administration are overburdened. This overburdening leads in turn to a loss of legitimacy, especially when the scope of state activity is restricted by pre-parliamentary power blocs and when citizens blame the government for tangible economic losses. This is all the more dangerous the more the loyalty of the population depends on material compensations.

Interestingly, cultural resources stand at both the beginning and the end of this spiral: the so-called *inflation of expectations* and the lack of willingness to assent and obey, a willingness based on tradition and a consensus on values, immune to variations in state services. As Peter Steinfels formulated it in his book *The Neoconservatives*, "The current crisis is primarily a cultural crisis. . . . The problem is that our convictions have gone slack, our morals loose, our manners corrupt."[2]

The neoconservatives' therapeutic proposals arise from this analysis. The state bureaucracies need relief; hence the problems that burden the governmental budget are to be returned from the state to the market. Because investment activity is to be promoted at the same time, the reduction in the volume of state activity has to extend to a restriction of public social services and consumption spending in general. Here support for a monetarist and supply-side economic policy designed to stimulate investment activity through tax reductions is readily accommodated within the neoconservative vision. The more the state withdraws from the economic process, as by privatizing public services, the better it can escape the legitimation demands that arise from its general responsibility for the burdens resulting from a crisis-ridden capitalism.

Other proposals aim directly at the suspected causes. The neoconservatives recommend a stronger decoupling of the executive from broad political will-formation and even a moderating of those democratic principles that raise the level of legitimation too high. "Democracies are always in danger of being overwhelmed by their own normative premises."[3] Behind the utopian exaggeration of the democratic level of justification, behind the luxuriating pressure of expectations passed on to the state through decision-making channels open at the base, certain cultural orientations are operating. This overstimulation of cultural resources must ultimately be blamed on an enemy—the "new class" of intellectuals. By negligence or design, these intellectuals release the explosive contents of cultural modernity; they are the advocates of an "adversary culture"—adversary, that is, from the perspective of the functional exigencies of the state and the economy. Thus the intellectuals become the most visible target of neoconservative criticism: "The new class and its adversary culture must be tamed, under threat of being purged from responsible milieus."[4]

I do not want to go into an extensive critique of the research on ungovernability. The theoretical weakness of those analyses consists in their confusion of cause and effect, as Joachim Heidorn has correctly shown:

At the center of the ungovernability analyses stands not a new order of economic and political relationships among the highly industrialized nations of the West and especially the "Third" world regions of misery and catastrophe, an order which stands high on the agenda of world politics; not the functional weaknesses and accumulating secondary problems of the capitalist economic systems; not the precarious balance between Eastern and Western military blocs; not the dissolution of historically outdated ideologies of growth and the development of a noninstrumental relationship between men and their natural living and environmental conditions—to name only a few of the tasks and challenges to be mastered in the next decade. Instead, the political organizational forms of parliamentary democracy, individual liberties and civil rights, and movements for greater social justice are dragged before the tribunal usurped by investigations of ungovernability.[5]

More interesting than this argumentation from the perspective of political science, however, is the theory of culture that forms its background, especially the interpretation of the cultural crisis presented by Daniel Bell in his book *The Cultural Contradictions of Capitalism.*[6]

II

Bell's starting point is Max Weber's claim that by destroying the Protestant ethic, capitalist development undermines the motivational prerequisites for its own continuity. Bell explains the self-destructive pattern of this development in terms of a split between culture and society. He analyzes the tension between a *modern* society that develops in terms of economic and administrative rationality, and a *modernist* culture that contributes to the destruction of the moral bases of rationalized society. In both cases modernity depends on the process of secularization; but what is good for *secularized* society, i.e., capitalist modernization, is catastrophic for culture, since a culture rendered *profane* brings subversive attitudes to the fore; in any case it contrasts with the religiously anchored willingness to achieve and obey on which an efficient economy and a rational state administration are functionally dependent.

The affirmative stance toward *social* modernity and the devaluation of *cultural* modernity are typical for the evaluative schema implicit in *all* neoconservative diagnoses of the contemporary situation. But Daniel Bell has a complex mind and is a good social theorist—in his analysis of the causes of the cultural crisis he does not proceed in a neoconservative manner at all.

The concept of the new class, which according to neoconservative tenets establishes the predominance of the principle of unlimited self-realization, is rejected by Bell as confused. The so-called new class is composed of individuals who carry the "logic of modernism" to its conclusion in their radical lifestyle but who exercise no significant power. The development of capitalism is determined by very different factors: military needs, technical innovations, and social upheavals. In addition to these structural transformations, a new hedonism, justifying itself through examples from aesthetic modernity, has spread. But, according to Bell, "the engine of modern capitalism has taken over these cultural styles and translated them into marketable commodities. Without the hedonism stimulated by mass consumption, the very structure of the business enterprise would collapse. In the end, this is the cultural contradiction of capitalism: Having lost its original justifications, capitalism has taken over the legitimations of an antibourgeois culture to maintain continuity of its own economic institutions."[7]

In this essay, published in 1979, Bell is not guilty at all of the usual confusion of cause and effect. He does not explain the split between culture and society by claiming that the crisis of authority can simply be ascribed to a culture whose advocates exacerbate the hostility toward the conventions and virtues of an everyday life rationalized by economy and administration. Nevertheless, his analysis of modernism remains biased.

On the one hand, Bell conceives the development of modern art and literature since the middle of the nineteenth century as a consistent development of the inner logic that, in Max Weber's words, is inherent in the sphere of aesthetic value. The avant-garde artist gives authentic expression to the experiences of a decentered subjectivity freed from the constraints of everyday knowledge and activity. The inner logic of the aesthetic is revealed in the abandonment of the temporal and spatial structures of everyday life, in the break with the conventions of perception and goal-oriented activity, and in the dialectic of revelation and shock that gives rise to the breakdown of taboos and the deliberate violation of fundamental moral norms.

On the other hand, Bell is less interested in the new sensibilities and the experiential attainments of aesthetic modernity; instead, he is fascinated by the subversive power of a consciousness that rejects the normalizing achievements of tradition. Bell does not see that the aestheticist neutralization of the good, the useful, and the true—the aesthetic rebellion against all norms—is only the result of a radical differentiation of this sphere of value; the avant-garde purifies aesthetic experience, so to speak, from admixtures of different value spheres. The sociologist's attention is directed solely to the disturbingly anarchistic lifestyles that develop wherever the new mode of experience becomes the center of a subjectivist form of life concentrated on the experience of self and self-realization. Bell makes three central assertions that are in complete accordance with the neoconservative line of argumentation: first, that the avant-garde is finished and modernism has exhausted its creative impulses; second, that this is why Bohemian lifestyles with their hedonistic, unrestrainedly subjective value orientations are spreading and undermining the discipline of bourgeois everyday life; and third, that only the renewal of a religious consciousness, the overcoming of a culture that has become profane, can restore the ethical bases of a secularized society.

Strictly speaking, the complaint about the anomic effects of avant-garde art can refer only to the surrealist program of an *unmediated* transformation of art into life. These attempts at a false superseding of art failed long ago. The mass copying of divergent lifestyles derives from the same misunderstanding— as if one could release the explosive experiential content of modern art in this way and thereby make the reified practice of everyday life more flexible. But these are marginal phenomena. If one examines empirical research into changing values in Western societies, one sees something very different in the new attitudes and the shift of the whole spectrum of values, especially in the younger generation.

"Materialistic" needs for security and subsistence are becoming unimportant in comparison to "postmaterialistic" needs, as the research of Ronald Inglehart shows.[8] The label "postmaterialist" covers a variety of issues: an interest in expanded scope for self-realization and experience of self, an increased sensitivity to the need to protect natural and historical environments, and a more acute sense of vulnerable interpersonal relationships. Certainly Daniel Bell could link these *expressive* attitudes to the dimension of aesthetic experience. Here, however, the identification of culture with art and literature takes its revenge; for value orientations crystallized around expressiveness and self-realization are *also* related to ideals of self-determination and morality. In the postmaterialist scale of values, one also finds orientations characteristic of *moral* sensibility—especially the interest in the protection and extensive exercise of individual liberties and rights to political participation. Expressive self-realization and moral-practical self-determination are two *equal*, mutually complementary components that are equally rooted in cultural modernity. Bell does not see that modern culture is characterized as much by the universalization of law and morality as by the autonomization of art.

The thoroughly profane ideas of justice that are connected with natural law and Kantian ethics emerged from the same process of profanization as the postauratic works of modernism. Bell himself has recourse to these ideas at the end of his book, where he asserts that the economic contradictions of capitalism, evident in governmental budgets, can be solved only with the help of a renewed social contract. He is not satisfied with the neoconservative demand to limit democracy in order to meet the imperatives of an economic growth unchanged in the mechanism of its driving forces. Rather, as a consistent liberal he considers a consensual concept of equality necessary, one "which gives all persons a sense of fairness and inclusion in the society and which promotes a situation where, within the relevant spheres, people *become* more equal so that they can be *treated* equally."[9] On this basis the quasi-naturally established proportions in which the social product is produced, distributed, and used would have to be negotiated anew.

III

The social questions of the 1980s, for which no one has any simple remedies, could be discussed on the basis of such a platform. In the Federal Republic, however, the neoconservatives who could be regarded as the intellectual counterparts of their American colleagues, like Richard Löwenthal or Kurt Sontheimer, do not set the tone. The discussion in Germany is influenced more definitively by rhetoric and the politics of ideas than by social-scientific analysis. The spokespersons are largely philosophers, with the addition of a few historians. Under the impact of neoconservative insights, sociologists are declaring themselves "antisociologists"—a very German phenomenon.

Yet differences in style of thought and presentation depend less on training in specific disciplines than on the lines of tradition in the two political cultures. The philosophical proponents of German neoconservatism—and I will restrict my discussion to this clearly defined central group—did not identify with social modernity through the concepts of an unambiguous liberal theory that subsequently gave way to disappointment. Rather, the theories that formed their point of departure had a Young-Conservative tone and thus a specifically German background. In the *Süddeutsche Zeitung* of August 19, 1982, Hans Heigert, in his Geothe Prize acceptance speech, describes the mentality of the Young Conservatives, those "repressed right-wing intellectuals of the Weimar period," using Ernst Jünger as an example. He emphasizes two components: on the one hand, "rejection of mere progress in civilization, thus anticapitalism, anti-Americanism, the development and glorification of the elite. . . . The heroic deed was to overcome what was common and base, action in itself was to serve liberation"; and on the other hand, "loyalty to what was one's own, safeguarding of roots, accommodation to the flow of history, to the depths of one's people. . . . All of pedagogy was permeated with the propagation of secondary virtues: obedience, duty, service, readiness for sacrifice—faith." After 1945, the survivors and heirs of these right-wing revolutionaries began an operation that separated these two components: they reconciled themselves to the progress of civilization, but they maintained their critique of culture. It is this compromise, this half-hearted acceptance of modernity, that distinguishes the German from the American, the formerly Young-Conservative from the formerly liberal neoconservatives.

Since the time of Hegel, sensitivity to the price that social modernization has exacted of the old European world has been more sharply developed in German intellectuals than in the West. To be sure, since Marx, insight into the dialectic of progress did not prevent the Left from placing its bets on the productive forces of the modern world, while the conservatives persisted in rejection and melancholy. On this side of the front in the European civil war, modernity was not given a differentiated "yes" until this century. With a heroic stance and with many reservations, the Young Conservatives nonetheless did pave the way for this step. The step was then finally taken, in the form of a compromise, by authors like Joachim Ritter, Ernst Forsthoff, and Arnold Gehlen, who spanned the period from before to after World War II.

The compromise consisted in accepting social modernity only under conditions that excluded an affirmation of cultural modernity. As before, industrial capitalism, on its way to a postindustrial society, is shown in such a light that one seems to need an explanation of possible compensations for the demands this society imposes—whether those compensations be through substantive traditions that are immune from attack, through the authoritative substance of a sovereign state power, or through the secondary substantiveness of so-called inherent dynamics. These positions, which were very stimulating theoretically, were worked out in more detail during the 1950s— along the lines of a conservative reconciliation to social modernity that was not necessary for the American liberals of the

time. I will outline three lines of argument (a fourth, the eth-
ological line pursued by Konrad Lorenz, will be omitted, since
it leads to the New Right in France rather than to German
neoconservatism).

1. In his both fasincating and influential interpretation of
Hegel's political writings, Joachim Ritter described the modern
"bourgeois society" that emerged from the French Revolution
as the locus of both emancipation and estrangement. The devaluation of the traditional world, the estrangement from the
historically transmitted life order, is seen positively on the one
hand, as the only form in which citizens of the modern world
achieve and maintain their subjective freedom. On the other
hand, modern economic society reduces human beings to the
status of agents of production and consumption. Because of
its inherent tendency to reduce persons to the mere structure
of their needs, an absolute socialization that negated its own
historical conditions would also destroy the achievements of
subjective freedom. Freedom in the modality of estrangement
can be guaranteed against this danger of a total socialization
only if the devalued powers of tradition "as powers of personal
life, subjectivity and historical roots"[10] nevertheless retain the
strength to compensate for the unavoidable abstractions of
bourgeois society. Social modernity requires for its stabilization,
therefore, a renewal of its own historical substance; in other
words, the desperate—because paradoxical—effort of a traditionalism enlightened by historicism.

2. Conservative constitutional theory attempts to find a different solution with the help of Carl Schmitt's concept of sovereignty. In the early 1950s, a discussion arose about the weight
to be given the welfare-state clause in the West German Basic
Law. Ernst Forsthoff advanced the position that the norms that
established the constitutional-state character of the Federal Republic had to maintain absolute priority over the welfare-state
clause, which should be understood merely as a political rec-
ommendation. The historical-philosophical content of this controversy about legal doctrine[11] becomes intelligible only if one
keeps in mind the premise, reminiscent of Ritter's interpretation of Hegel, that the society that represents the substratum
of welfare-state mass democracy cannot achieve stability im-

manently and requires compensations. For Forsthoff, however, this social dynamic cannot be checked by the counterbalance of a tradition invoked rhetorically; it can be checked only by the sovereign state. Even the constitutional state has, as its substantive center, the supreme power of a sovereign, and this state can develop the power necessary to stabilize social modernity only if, in the extreme case, it is immune to arguments presented in the name of social interests. The guardian of the general welfare must have the political power to decide rather than argue.

This concept derives from Carl Schmitt's theory in that the latter used the capacity to distinguish between friend and enemy as the criterion for a pure concept of the political—purged of all evaluative admixtures of the useful, the true, the beautiful, or the just, and especially the latter. The political was to remain unaffected by issues of moral justification. In this view, social modernity loses its horrors only for a state power whose sovereignty is not threatened by moral disarmament. In later works, Forsthoff was open to technocratic conceptions.[12]

3. Arnold Gehlen follows this third line of argumentation. At the beginning of the 1940s, in his important anthropological work *Man: His Nature and Place in the World*, Gehlen emphasized the extreme plasticity and vulnerability of a human nature which is not fixed in instincts and therefore depends on the regulatory force of archaic quasi-natural institutions.[13] From this perspective, the dismantling of sacred institutions, the loss of authority on the part of the church, the military, and the state, as well as the erosion of the latter's sovereign substance, are signs of a pathological development. This explains the harsh cultural criticism that Gehlen then practiced after the war.[14] According to Gehlen, the psychic energies of an inflated inwardness, the subjectivity of experience and the reflexivity of self-enjoyment rush into the void left by deinstitutionalization. Every step toward emancipation robs the individual of automatic mechanisms for regulating his actions, abandons him without protection to his desultory motivations, strains him with excessive demands for decisions, and renders him increasingly unfree the farther the ideals of self-determination and self-realization are extended. The increasing complexity of so-

ciety causes the scope for responsible action to contract, while at the same time it floods the inner world with irritating stimuli, emotions, and vicarious experience. The tenor of the argument changed in the course of the 1950s, when Gehlen adopted a technocratic thesis that allowed him to see modern society in a new light.

According to this idea, the economy and state administration, technology and science are joined together in the iron cage of modernity to form a system of functional laws that seems to be subject to no outside influences and that takes over leadership from the institutions that have been dismantled. Under these objective constraints, the soothing anthropological tendency to unburden the individual can continue, because time has run out for cultural modernity: the premises of the Enlightenment, Gehlen says, are dead; only its consequences keep on going. A traditionalist revival of the powers of historical roots no longer provides the prescription for the deactivation of modern ideas; instead, the key term is "crystallization." Gehlen calls modern culture "crystallized" because "all the possibilities contained in its basic contents have been developed."[15] In 1960, Gehlen made an attempt to document this thesis, using as an example the development of modern painting. His whole interest is directed toward proving that the avant-garde has played itself out, that it is now only quoting itself, that it has lost the seriousness of its original impulse, that as a harmless oasis of arbitrary subjectivity it was dependent on social processes and has been rendered innocuous by institutionalization. A reflective art has become "incapable of having an enemy."[16]

IV

Against this background it becomes clear that the changed scene of the 1960s—with the revival of a militant social criticism and an Enlightenment tradition mobilized in its full breadth, with an antiauthoritarian movement, with a new avant-garde movement in the visual arts and an aesthetically inspired counterculture—revived everything the neoconservative theoreticians had thought dead. Theoreticians like Ritter, Forsthoff, and Gehlen had become reconciled to social modernity only on the assumption that cultural modernity had been put to rest. While American liberals were forced to search for new arguments for an unforeseen situation, the philosophers among the German neoconservatives were faced with a relatively easy task. The argumentative arsenals of their teachers supplied the necessary ammunition to combat on the practical level, as the machinations of a domestic enemy, whatever contradicted their theory. They had only to name the agents responsible for the disagreeable phenomena that seemed to shake the foundations of the compromise, those who had unleashed a cultural revolution. This turn to the practical and the polemical explains why the German neoconservatives could tread a beaten path and were not compelled to offer much that was new. New indeed, however, is the professor who courageously takes his stand on the semantic front of the civil war.

The neoconservative doctrine that filtered down through the press into the everyday politics of the Federal Republic during the 1970s follows a simple pattern. The modern world is focused on technical progress and capitalist growth; any social dynamic ultimately based on private investment is modern and desirable; the motivational resources that nourish this dynamic are also in need of protection. Danger, in contrast, lies in cultural transformations, motivational and attitudinal changes, and shifts in patterns of values and identities, which are attributed, through a kind of intellectual short circuit, to the entry of cultural innovations into the lifeworld. For this reason the legacy of tradition should be preserved in static form as far as possible.

The therapeutic suggestions that have penetrated into everyday politics in the Federal Republic in recent years can be reduced to three elements: (1) All phenomena that do not correspond to the picture outlined by Ritter, Forsthoff, or Gehlen of a compensatorily pacified modernity are personalized and moralized, i.e., blamed on left-wing intellectuals, who are carrying on a cultural revolution in order to ensure their own authority, the "priestly rule of a new class." (2) The explosive contents of cultural modernity, which nourish this cultural revolution, must be deactivated—where possible, by declaring them passé: We have in actuality reached the safe shores of posthistory, the postenlightenment, or postmodernity—but the slowpokes still caught up in the dogmatic slumber of "humanitarianism" haven't noticed it yet. (3) The socially undesirable byproducts of an economic growth that lacks political direction are transposed to the level of a "spiritual-moral crisis,"[17] and they require compensation through straightforward common sense, historical consciousness, and religion. These three recommendations will be commented upon separately.

1. The *critique of intellectuals*, to which Arnold Gehlen devoted the work of his last decade[18] and which Helmut Schelsky expanded into a theory of the "new class," draws on three sources. First, it mobilizes the clichés that have accumulated in the "history of an insult" since the days of the anti-Semitic campaign against Captain Alfred Dreyfus (1894). Dietz Bering has traced this history,[19] and he included in his book a lexicon of "cuts" and epithets that goes from "abstract," "abstruse," "agitator," and "arrogant," to "critical," "cynical," "decadent," "formalist," "free-floating," "lacking in substance," "mechanistic," "opportunistic," "racially foreign," "radical," and "revolutionary," to "rootless," "soulless," and "unworldly." To one who has looked through this register of nearly one thousand terms, the most recent critique of intellectuals does not have much new to say.

Further, the allegation of an intellectual theocracy is based on certain trends; for example, in postindustrial societies the proportion of academic occupations grows, and the significance of the systems of science, scholarship, and education generally increases. Of the intellectual professions, Schelsky of course selects only teachers and publicists, ministers and social workers, scholars in the humanities, and philosophers, and characterizes them as an exploitative class of mediators of meaning— while others do the real work. This fantastic construction fits no one, with the possible exception of the neoconservative intellectuals themselves. But not even they believe in it. Richard Löwenthal provides a convincing critique of the logical fallacies implicit in the concept of the "new class": "The first false equation is between a social sector and a class. The second false equation is between influence and power. The third false equation is between eschatological hopes, necessarily implying a short-term outbreak of chiliastic faith, and a long-term religion capable of giving cultural form to everyday life."[20]

The last element is the linking of the intellectuals to the crisis in the educational system. The educational reforms necessitated by sociostructural changes but long postponed in the Federal Republic did indeed take place during a period in which educational policy was influenced by liberal and moderately leftist goals. And it was in fact the making of reforms that led to the full recognition of the dangers of legal regulation and bureaucratization as well as the dangers of a scientization of pedagogy, of an inadequately professionalized realm of activity. But the neoconservatives misrepresent those unintended consequences as cultural revolutionary intentions, and they were able to use these consequences, which met with general disapproval, as a pretext for mobilizing middle-class resentment because antiintellectual agitation provided the missing link needed to suggest a fatal nexus of social criticism, educational reform, and left-wing terrorism.[21] Subsequent biographical analyses of terrorist careers have dissolved this fantasy into thin air.[22] Today, moreover, those rash authors are asking themselves what would happen if one tried to explain right-wing terrorism in terms of the same model of objective accountability, a model that today finds an echo only in the domain of Stalinist rule.

2. The thesis of the *exhaustion of cultural modernity* refers to all three components: to science and scholarship with their technical successes, to avant-garde art, and to the universalist morality conceptualized by Rousseau and Kant.

As far as science and scholarship is concerned, the message is simple. If scientific and scholarly progress has become "uninteresting in terms of the politics of ideas," if the solution of scientific and scholarly problems no longer touches our life problems,[23] then the encapsulated expert cultures have little to offer everyday life but technical innovations and sociotechnical recommendations. Since the Enlightenment, according to this thesis, scientific and scholarly knowledge has been useful only for technical progress and for economic and administrative planning. The capacity to orient practice is ascribed only to historical scholarship, where narrative is used to give contemporary form to traditions and to guarantee continuities. Hence the revaluation of narrative procedures in the *Geisteswissenschaften* as well as the distrust of history as a social science and the devaluation of sociology and of social sciences in general, disciplines that can be used to diagnose the contemporary period. This would never have occurred to the American neoconservatives, since their spokespersons are almost exclusively sociologists. From this perspective one can understand the opposition to school reforms that result in social science materials being incorporated into the curriculum. One might regard this social-scientific curricular thrust, which occurred several decades earlier in the United States, with greater calm if one were to recall the debate carried on between the champions of the Humaniora and the champions of the natural-scientific Realia at the end of the nineteenth century.

The thesis of a post-Enlightenment, furthermore, is anything but convincing. Certainly, metaphysical and religious worldviews have disintegrated. The empirical sciences do not provide a substitute for them. Yet the wide distribution of popular scientific literature indicates that cosmological findings regarding the origin and development of the universe, biochemical discoveries about the mechanisms of heredity, and especially anthropological and ethnological insights into the natural history of human behavior and the evolution of our species; that psychological findings on the development of intelligence in children, the development of the moral consciousness, affects, and motivations of the child, the psychology of mental illness, and social-scientific insights into the origin and development of modern societies—that all this still touches the self-understanding of contemporary subjects. These findings also alter the standards for the discussion of life problems for which the empirical sciences themselves have no ready answers. Ultimately, one would have to ask the neoconservatives, who want to put science and scholarship at such a distance, how they plan to justify their glib answers to the much lamented crisis of orientation—if not with arguments that can stand up to scientific examination. It is certainly important to exercise caution by treating hypothetical, i.e., provisional knowledge carefully; a healthy dose of skepticism is also called for with regard to the scope and efficacy of disciplines that depend on hermeneutic access to their object domain; and the concern is certainly legitimate that the autonomy of everyday practice within the lifeworld needs to be protected from the unmediated and largely professionally unsupervised interventions of experts—in the family and at school as much as in the gray areas of social services, which are questionable often enough.

With regard to the plastic and graphic arts, Gehlen claimed as late as 1960 that the avant-garde had lost its powers of contagion—we, so he thought, have learned to live side by side with contemporary art. Looking back over the past two decades, Hans Sedlmayer comes to different conclusions. He is convinced that "aesthetic anarchism [is] much more dangerous than political [anarchism]."[24] Sedlmayer sees a "black line" linking the early Romanticism of Jena with contemporary avant-garde art via Baudelaire and surrealism. He conjures up the dangers of an artistic practice that begins by abstracting from all nonaesthetic orders, banishes justice and truth as well as beauty from art, and then destroys the boundaries of the aesthetic work to exercise a subversive influence in the everyday bourgeois world. The uniformity of modern architecture appears as merely the reverse side of anarchism in painting, music, and literature: "The rejection of art, logic, ethics, modesty; the church, the state, the family; the classical European tradition and all religion—has penetrated newspapers and journals, film and television, theater and Happenings, and the practice of life."[25] Of course it is not the complaint that is neoconservative but the reaction to it—the programmatic dismissal of modernity and the proclamation of the "postmodern." This expression carries with it the implicit assertion that avant-garde art has reached its end, has exhausted its creativity, and is going around in unproductive circles.

"Postmodern" is also the key term in a recent debate in the field of architecture. (See, for example, *Der Architekt* 1982, and my essay "Modern and Postmodern Architecture" in the present volume.) This is not an accident, for with its functionalist ideology modern architecture was poorly armed against the economic imperatives that accompanied the reconstruction period after World War II, thus the same period in which the International Style first achieved success on a broad scale. But the disaster of an architecture that was both instrumentalized and overburdened has as yet called forth no alternative that does not either lead back to an uncreative historicism or itself draw on the creativity of a modernity that has ostensibly been defeated. It is true that contemporary postavant-garde art, which has given up surrealist dreams, does not emit any clear signals. But the works that might fill the negative slogan of "postmodernity" with positive content are nowhere to be found.

From a neoconservative standpoint it is not only the sensitization potential of contemporary art and the enlightenment potential of the sciences that must be interpreted away or played down; it is above all the explosive force of universalist principles of morality that must be deactivated. A morality is universalist if it accords validity only to norms that *all* those concerned could approve on the basis of full consideration and without duress. No one will object to that—basic rights and the very principles of our constitutions are norms which we assume fulfill the condition that they are capable of finding such universal approval. I do not want to go into the problems that result when such abstract principles are applied to concrete life situations. Only one aspect of the relationship between morality and ethical life is of interest here, for it in particular arouses the suspicion of the conservatives. A universalist morality, by its very nature, recognizes no limits; it subjects even political action to moral scrutiny, although not so directly as our personal relationships. In an extreme case this kind of moralization can even encourage terrorist actions—so runs an old anti-Enlightenment theme. Even the terrorist, who sees himself as a last, lonely advocate of justice, could try to realize the freedom he is struggling for through direct violent action in the name of universal principles.[26] It should not be difficult to demonstrate the inconsistency or the error in the imaginary moral reflections of the individual terrorist. But the neoconservatives present this extreme case only in order to put the more general problem of restricting moral motives in politics in the proper light. They want to minimize the burdens of moral justification on the political system.

In this effort they either follow Hobbes and Carl Schmitt and proceed from the claim that the state has first and foremost to legitimize itself by accomplishing its central task of guaranteeing the peace, i.e., defending against foreign and domestic enemies. Hence the priority of the problem of internal security and especially the formulation of a purported competition between the constitutional state and democracy. Or they follow the technocracy thesis and proceed on the premise that the state must act primarily as an arbiter guaranteeing the appropriate distribution of jurisdictions so that the inherent dynamics of functionally specified subsectors can operate "independently of the general political will-formation."[27] Hence the preference for depoliticized steering institutions in the formulation of a purported competition between the principle of a separation of powers on the one hand and democracy on the other. In both cases the arguments boil down to the claim that the state order should be relieved of the burden of democratic clashes of opinion about social-political goals. The moral-practical element from which politics is to acquire detachment is a democratization of decision-making processes that would necessarily place political action under the controversial perspective of social justice and desirable forms of life in general.

The relevance of these considerations is obvious in a situation in which the central issue is the degree of social injustice we are prepared to accept, given the fiscal crisis of the state, in order to set back in motion an economic growth whose dynamic mechanism remains unchanged. This capitalist mechanism requires, for example, that the distribution of jobs be regulated solely by the job market, even if the reserve army of the unemployed continues to grow.

3. The programmatic dismissal of cultural modernity is to make room for a healthy sense of tradition. When cultural modernity has closed all the avenues leading to everyday practice and the expert cultures have also been adequately seques-

tered, the staying powers of common sense, historical consciousness, and religion come into their own. The birth of the post-Enlightenment, however, calls for the midwifery of neoconservatism, which is focused on a "courage to educate," that is, on an educational policy that tailors elementary education to basic skills and secondary virtues (industriousness, discipline, and neatness). At the same time it emphasizes a "courage for the past" in schools, the family, and the state. The neoconservatives see their role as, on the one hand, mobilizing pasts that can be accepted approvingly and, on the other hand, morally neutralizing other pasts that would provoke only criticism and rejection. Walter Benjamin called "empathy with the victor" one of the signs of historicism. That is what the neoconservatives are recommending to us today. When, in the spirit of Benjamin, Gustav Heinemann called for the adoption of the perspective of the *defeated*, the unsuccessful rebels and revolutionaries, he had to put up with the rejoinder that this orientation toward the ideals of his own past was a "fixation of immaturity."[28] In the same vein, one finds artful attempts to interpret the National Socialist period in such a way that any reference to fascism can be denounced as a sign of the "universal domination of sophistry."[29]

With this question, of course, we are still in the realm of modernity—and of modern theology. This way of posing the question leads away from a traditional revival of religious consciousness and obligates us to understand the whole spectrum of movements and impulses that, for example, are filling contemporary church conclaves in West Germany. On the one hand, religious fundamentalism draws on very heterogeneous sources; on the other hand, the nonfundamentalist currents release the very forces of problematicization, including forces with a political impact, that the neoconservatives would like to hold in check. It is precisely here that Schelsky's mediators of meaning or Lübbe's ideological guides, horizon-openers, experts on reflection on goals, and pathfinders are congregating. Whereas Daniel Bell analyzes without bias the different orientations of new congregational and communitarian religiosity inside and outside the churches,[30] the German neoconservatives are often concerned with only one issue: the powers of social cohesion implicit in a religious tradition that they understand solely as a substantive tradition unburdened by any requirements for proof. Lübbe considers this functionalist interpretation of religion as a "practice of mastering contingencies" to be advantageous precisely because it ignores the aspect of the validity of religious belief: "The functional definition permits us to pass over . . . the difficulties of a hermeneutic representation of the lasting meaning of old doctrines. In a practical life-context, function is not something we would characterize as 'true' or 'false.' Rather, we call ways of fulfilling functions of a practical nature 'practical' or 'impractical.'"[31] But traditions cannot be revived simply by demonstrating their beneficial effects. The retreat into functionalism does not solve the dilemma in which every mere traditionalism has been entangled since the historicist enlightenment. Horkheimer pointed this out in 1946: "Precisely the fact that today tradition must be invoked shows that it has lost its power."[32]

I do not want to be misunderstood: the nonrenewable resources of our natural environment and the symbolic structures of our lifeworld—both the historically developed and the specifically modern forms of life—need protection. But they can be protected only if we know what is threatening the lifeworld. The neoconservatives confuse cause and effect. In place of the economic and administrative imperatives, the so-called objective constraints that are monetarizing and bureaucratizing more and more domains of life and increasingly transforming relationships into commodities and objects of administration—in place of these true sources of social crisis the neoconservatives put the specter of a subversively degenerate culture. This false analysis explains why neoconservatives, when they are forced to choose, do not regard the lifeworld, including the domain of the family, as so sacred as they claim. Whereas the Christian Democrats have no reservations about the proliferation of private television networks in the Federal Republic, in questions of media policy the Social Democrats are the guardians of tradition. We must proceed gently with the substance of established forms of life, to the extent to which those forms have not already been destroyed by the dynamics of the growth of social modernization. The only question is, *who* protects them when the situation becomes serious.

V

The political culture of the Federal Republic would be in worse condition today if it had not adopted and assimilated ideas from American political culture during the first decades after the war. For the first time, the Federal Republic opened itself without reservation to the West; at that time we adopted the political theory of the Enlightenment, we came to understood the power of a pluralism borne initially by religious sects to shape attitudes, and we came to know the radical democratic spirit of American pragmatism, from Peirce to Mead and Dewey. The German neoconservatives are turning away from these traditions and drawing on other sources. They are reaching back to a German constitutionalism that retained of democracy little more than the constitutional state, to themes from a Lutheran state ecclesiasticism rooted in a pessimistic anthropology, and to the motifs of a Young Conservatism whose heirs could achieve only a half-hearted compromise with modernity. Bismarck broke the back of political liberalism in Germany. It is no historical accident that the domestic political shift to neoconservatism was brought about by the national-liberal wing of the Free Democratic Party; these days it is becoming clear that the social liberals were not strong enough to pay off the questionable debts of German liberalism. For the political culture of West Germany, this shift threatens to complete an unfortunate vicious circle. The farewells sung to cultural modernity and the veneration of capitalist modernization can only confirm those who, with their blanket antimodernism, want to throw out the baby with the bath water. If modernity had nothing to offer but what appears in the commendations of neoconservative apologetics, one could well understand why the intellectual youth of today should not rather return to Nietzsche via Derrida and Heidegger and seek their salvation in the portentous voices of a cultically revived, an authentic Young Conservatism not yet distorted by compromise.

Notes

1. H.Rühle et al., eds., *Der Neokonservatismus in den Vereinigten Staaten* (St. Augustin, 1982). I am indebted to Helmut Dubiel for numerous suggestions. See his recently published study *Was ist Neokonservatismus?* (Frankfurt, 1985).

2. Peter Steinfels, *The Neoconservatives* (New York, 1979), p. 55.

3. P. Graf Kielmannsegg, *Demokratieprinzip und Regierbarkeit* (Stuttgart, 1977), p. 122.

4. Steinfels, p. 65.

5. Joachim Heidorn, *Legitimität und Regierbarkeit* (Berlin, 1982), p. 249.

6. Daniel Bell, *The Cultural Contradictions in Capitalism* (New York, 1976).

7. Daniel Bell, "The New Class: A Muddled Concept," in his *The Winding Passage* (Cambridge, MA, 1980), p. 163f.

8. H. KIages and P. Kmiecak, eds., *Wertwandel und gesellschaftlicher Wandel* (Frankfurt, 1979), pp. 179–365.

9. Bell, *Cultural Contradictions*, p. 282.

10. Joachim Ritter, "Hegel und die französische Revolution," in his *Metaphysik und Politik* (Frankfurt, 1969), p. 183ff.

11. Ernst Forsthoff, ed., *Rechtsstaatlichkeit und Sozialstaatlichkeit* (Darmstadt, 1968).

12. Ernst Forsthoff, *Der Staat in der Industriegesellschaft* (Munich, 1971).

13. Arnold Gehlen, *Der Mensch* (Berlin, 1940). In English as *Man: His Nature and Place in the World* (New York, 1987).

14. Arnold Gehlen, *Urmensch und Spätkultur* (Frankfurt & Bonn, 1956); Gehlen, *Die Seele im technischen Zeitalter* (Hamburg, 1957).

15. Arnold Gehlen, "Uber kulturelle Kristallisationen," in his *Studien zur Anthropologie und Soziologie* (Neuwied, 1963), p. 321.

16. Arnold Gehlen, *Zeitbilder* (Frankfurt, 1965), pp. 202–233.

17. See Helmut Kohl's speech in the West German Bundestag on September 9, 1982.

18. Arnold Gehlen, *Moral und Hypermoral* (Frankfurt, 1969); also the essays in his *Einblicke* (Frankfurt, 1978), pp. 253–530.

19. Dietz Bering, *Die Intellektuellen* (Stuttgart, 1978).

20. Richard Löwenthal, *Gesellschaftswandel und Kulturkritik* (Frankfurt, 1979), p. 38.

21. Günther Rohrmoser, *Ideologische Ursachen des Terrorismus 1, Ideologien und Strategien* (Cologne, 1981), p. 273ff.

22. H. Jäger, G. Schmidtchen, L. Süllwold, *Analysen zum Terrorismus 2, Lebenslaufanalysen* (Cologne, 1981).

23. Hermann Lübbe, "Wissenschaft nach der Aufklärung," in his *Philosophie nach der Aufklärung* (Dusseldorf, 1980), p. 45ff.

24. Hans Sedlmayer, "Aesthetischer Anarchismus in Romantik und Moderne," in *Scheidewege* 8 (1978), p. 174ff.; the quotation in the text is from p. 195.

25. Sedlmayer, p. 195.

26. Hermann Lübbe, "Freiheit und Terror," in his *Philosophie nach der Aufklärung*, p. 239ff.

27. Helmut Schelsky, *Systemüberwindung, Demokratisierung, Gewaltenteilung* (Munich, 1973), p. 58.

28. Hermann Lübbe, *Zwischen Trend und Tradition* (Zurich, 1981), p. 17.

29. G. Rohrmoser, *Zäsur* (Stuttgart, 1980), p. 27.

30. Daniel Bell, "The Return of the Sacred," in *The Winding Passage*, p. 324ff.

31. Hermann Lübbe, "Religion nach der Aufklärung," in his *Philosophie nach der Aufklärung*, p. 69.

32. Max Horkheimer, *Kritik der instrumentellen Vernunft* (Frankfurt, 1974), p. 41.

2

The New Obscurity: The Crisis of the Welfare State and the Exhaustion of Utopian Energies

I

Since the late eighteenth century a new time consciousness has been developing in Western culture.[1] Whereas in the Christian West the "New Age" [*neue Zeit*] had designated the future age that would dawn only on Judgment Day, from the late eighteenth century on the "modern age" [*Neuzeit*] means one's own period, the present. The present is understood at each point as a transition to something new; it lives with an awareness that historical events are accelerating and an expectation that the future will be different. The epochal new beginning that marked the modern world's break with the world of the Christian Middle Ages and antiquity is repeated, as it were, in every present moment that brings forth something new. The present perpetuates the break with the past in the form of a continual renewal. The horizon of anticipations opening onto the future and referring to the present also governs the way the past is grasped. Since the end of the eighteenth century, history has been conceived as a process that is world-encompassing and problem-generating. Time in that process is thought of as a scarce resource for the future-oriented mastery of problems left us by the past. Exemplary periods in the past that the present might have been able to use without hestitation for orientation have faded into insignificance. Modernity can no

This text is based on a talk given to the *Cortes* on November 26, 1984, at the invitation of the President of the Spanish Parliament.

longer derive the standards it uses for orientation from models offered by other epochs. Modernity sees itself as dependent exclusively upon itself—it has to draw on itself for its normativity. From now on the authentic present is the locus in which innovation and the continuation of tradition are intertwined.

This devaluation of an exemplary past and the necessity to extract substantive normative principles from one's own, modern experiences and forms of life accounts for the altered structure of the "Zeitgeist." The Zeitgeist becomes the medium in which political thought and political discussion will henceforth move. The Zeitgeist receives impulses from two contrary but interdependent and mutually interpenetrating currents of thought: it is ignited by the clash of historical and utopian thought.[2] At first these two modes of thought seem mutually exclusive. Historical thought, saturated with actual experience, seems destined to criticize utopian schemes; utopian thought with its exuberance seems to have the function of opening up alternatives for action and margins of possibility that push beyond historical continuities. But in fact modern time consciousness has opened up a horizon in which utopian thought fuses with historical thought. Certainly the movement of utopian energies into historical consciousness characterizes the Zeitgeist that has stamped the political public sphere of modern peoples since the days of the French Revolution. Infected by the Zeitgeist's focus on the significance of the current moment and attempting to hold firm under the pressure of current problems, political thought becomes charged with utopian energies—but at the same time this excess of expectations is to be controlled by the conservative counterweight of historical experience.

Since the early nineteenth century, "utopia" has become a polemical political concept that everyone uses against everyone else. The accusation was first advanced against the abstract thought of the Enlightenment and its liberal heirs, then, naturally, against socialists and communists, but also against the conservative Ultras—against the former because they evoked an abstract future, against the latter because they evoked an abstract past. Because all are infected with utopian thought, no one wants to be a utopian.[3] Thomas More's Utopia, Campanella's City of the Sun, Bacon's New Atlantis—these spatial utopias conceived during the Renaissance could appropriately be called "*novels* of the state," because their authors never left any doubt about the fictitious character of the narratives. They had translated notions of paradise back into historical spaces and earthly antiworlds; they had transformed eschatological expectations back into profane life possibilities. As Fourier noted, the classical utopias of a better life, a less threatened life, were presented as a "dream of the good—without the means to realize the dream, without a method." Despite their critical relationship to their times, they had as yet no contact with history. That situation did not change until Mercier, a follower of Rousseau, in a novel of the future about Paris in the year 2440, shifted the Fortunate Isles from spatially distant regions into a distant future—thus depicting eschatological expectations for a future restoration of paradise in terms of a secular axis of historical progress.[4] But as soon as utopia and history came into contact in this way, the classical form of utopia changed; the state novel lost its novelistic features. From now on those who were the most sensitive to the utopian energies of the *Zeitgeist* would be the ones who most energetically pursued the fusion of utopian with historical thought. Robert Owen and Saint-Simon, Fourier and Proudhon emphatically rejected utopianism; and they in turn were accused by Marx and Engels of being "utopian socialists." Not until this century did Ernst Bloch and Karl Mannheim purge the expression "utopia" of the association of "utopianism" and rehabilitate it as a legitimate medium for depicting alternative life possibilities that are seen as inherent in the historical process itself. A utopian perspective is inscribed within politically active historical consciousness itself.

This, in any case, is how things seemed to stand—until yesterday. Today it seems as though utopian energies have been used up, as if they have retreated from historical thought. The horizon of the future has contracted and has changed both the *Zeitgeist* and politics in fundamental ways. The future is negatively cathected; we see outlined on the threshold of the twenty-first century the horrifying panorama of a worldwide threat to universal life interests: the spiral of the arms race, the uncontrolled spread of nuclear weapons, the structural impoverishment of developing countries, problems of environmental overload, and the nearly catastrophic operations of high technology are the catchwords that have penetrated public consciousness by way of the mass media. The reponses of the intellectuals reflect as much bewilderment as those of the politicians. It is by no means only realism when a forthrightly accepted bewilderment increasingly takes the place of attempts at orientation directed toward the future. The situation may be objectively obscure. Obscurity is nonetheless also a function of a society's assessment of its own readiness to take action. What is at stake is Western culture's confidence in itself.

II

Granted, there are good reasons for this exhaustion of utopian energies. The classical utopias depicted the conditions for a life of dignity, for socially organized happiness; the social utopias fused with historical thought, the utopias that have influenced political discussion since the nineteenth century, awaken more realistic expectations. They present science, technology, and planning as promising and unerring instruments for the rational control of nature and society. Since then, this very expectation has been shaken by massive evidence. Nuclear energy, weapons technology, the penetration of space, genetic research and biotechnical intervention in human behavior, information processing, data management and new communications media are technologies which by their very nature have conflicting consequences. The more complex the systems requiring steering become, the greater the probability of dysfunctional secondary effects. We experience on a daily basis the transformation of productive forces into destructive forces, of planning capacities into potentials for disruption. It is no wonder, then, that the theories gaining in influence today are primarily those that try to show how the very forces that make for increasing power, the forces from which modernity once derived its self-consciousness and its utopian expectations, are in actuality turning autonomy into dependence, emancipation into oppression, and reason into irrationality. Derrida concludes from Heidegger's critique of modern subjectivity that we can escape from the treadmill of Western logocentrism only through aimless provocation. Instead of trying to master foreground contingencies *in* the world, he says, we should surrender to the mysteriously encoded contingencies through which the world discloses itself. Foucault radicalizes Horkheimer and Adorno's critique of instrumental reason to make it a theory of the Eternal Return of power. His proclamation of a cycle of power that is always the same returning in discourse formations that are always new cannot help but extinguish the last spark of utopia and destroy the last traces of Western culture's self-confidence.

On the intellectual scene the suspicion is spreading that the exhaustion of utopian energies is not just an indication of a transitory mood of cultural pessimism but rather goes deeper. It could indicate a change in modern time consciousness as such. Perhaps the amalgam of historical and utopian thought is disintegrating; perhaps the structure of the *Zeitgeist* and the overall situation of politics are changing. Perhaps historical consciousness is being *relieved* of its utopian energies: just as at the end of the eighteenth century, with the temporalization of utopias, hopes for paradise moved into the mundane sphere, so today, two hundred years later, utopian expectations are losing their secular character and once again assuming religious form.

I consider this thesis of the onset of the postmodern period to be unfounded. Neither the structure of the *Zeitgeist* nor the mode of debating future life possibilities has changed; utopian energies as such are not withdrawing from historical consciousness. Rather, what has come to an end is a particular utopia that in the past crystallized around the potential of a society based on social labor.

The classical social theorists from Marx to Max Weber agreed that the structure of bourgeois society was stamped by abstract labor, by the type of labor for payment that is regulated by market forces, valorized in capitalistic form, and organized in the form of business enterprise. Because the form of this abstract labor displayed such power to penetrate all spheres and put its stamp on them, utopian expectations too could be directed toward the sphere of production, in short, to the emancipation of labor from alien control. The utopias of the early socialists took concrete form in the image of the phalanstery, a labor-based social organization of free and equal producers. The communal form of life of workers in free association was supposed to arise from the proper organization of production itself. This idea of worker self-management continued to inspire the protest movement of the late 1960s.[5] For all his critique of early socialism, Marx too, in the first part of the *German Ideology*, was pursuing the same utopian idea of a society based on social labor: "Thus things have now come to such a pass that . . . individuals must appropriate the existing totality of productive forces . . . to achieve self-activity. . . . The appropriation of these forces is itself nothing more than the development of the individual capacities corresponding to the material instruments production. . . . Only at this stage does self-activity coincide with material life, which corresponds to the development of individuals into complete individuals and the casting-off of natural limitations." (Marx and Engels, *The German Ideology*, ed. C. J. Arthur, New York, 1970, pp. 92–93.)

The utopian idea of a society based on social labor has lost its persuasive power—and not simply because the forces of production have lost their innocence or because the abolition of private ownership of the means of production clearly has not led in and of itself to workers' self-management. Rather, it is above all because that utopia has lost its point of reference in reality: the power of abstract labor to create structure and give form to society. Claus Offe has compiled convincing "indications of the objectively decreasing power of matters of labor, production, and earnings to determine the constitution and development of society as a whole."[6]

Anyone who looks at one of the rare pieces of writing that dares to announce a utopian reference in its title today—I am thinking of Andre Gorz's *Paths to Paradise*—will find this diagnosis confirmed. Gorz bases his proposal to disengage labor and income through a guaranteed minimum income on the ending of the Marxian expectation that self-directed activity and material life could still become one and the same.

But why should the diminishing persuasive power of a utopia of social labor be of significance to the broader public, and why

should it help to explain a *general* exhaustion of utopian impulses? We should remember that it was not only intellectuals
whom this utopia attracted. It inspired the European labor
movement, and in our century it left its traces in three very
different but historically influential programs. The political
movements corresponding to these programs established themselves in reaction to the consequences of World War I and the
economic crisis: Soviet Communism in Russia, authoritarian
corporatism in Fascist Italy, in Nazi Germany, and in Falangist
Spain; and social-democratic reformism in the mass democracies of the West. Only this latter project of a social welfare state
has adopted as its own the legacy of the bourgeois emancipation movements, the democratic constitutional state.. Although
this project emerged from the social-democratic tradition, it
has by no means been pursued only by social-democratic governments. Since World War II, all the governing parties in the
Western countries have won their majorities more or less explicitly under the banner of welfare-state objectives. Since the
middle of the 1970s, however, awareness of the limitations
of the welfare state project has been growing—without as yet a
clear alternative in view. Thus I will formulate my thesis as
follows: the New Obscurity is part of a situation in which a
welfare state program that continues to be nourished by a
utopia of social labor is losing its power to project future possibilities for a collectively better and less endangered way of
life.

III

In the welfare state project, of course, the utopian core, liberation from alienated labor, took a different form. Emancipated living conditions worthy of human beings are no longer
to emerge directly from the revolutionizing of labor conditions,
that is, from the transformation of alienated labor into self-
directed activity. Nevertheless, reformed conditions of employment retain a position of central importance in this project as
well.[7] They remain the reference point not only for measures
designed to humanize labor that continues to be largely heteronomous but also and especially for compensatory measures

designed to assume the burden of the fundamental risks of wage labor (accident, illness, loss of employment, lack of provision for old age). As a result, all those able to work must be incorporated into this streamlined and cushioned system of employment; hence the goal of full employment. The compensatory process functions only if the role of the full-time wage earner becomes the norm. For the burdens that continue to be connected with the cushioned status of dependent wage labor, the citizen is compensated in his role as client of the welfare state bureaucracies with legal claims, and in his role as consumer of mass-produced goods, with buying power. The lever for the pacification of class antagonisms thus continues to be the neutralization of the conflict potential inherent in the status of the wage laborer.

This goal is to be reached through social welfare legislation and collective bargaining on wage scales by independent parties. Welfare state policies derive their legitimation from general elections and find their social base in autonomous labor unions and in labor parties. It is of course the power and the capacity for action of an interventionist state apparatus that ultimately determine the success of the project. This apparatus is supposed to intervene in the economic system with the aim of protecting capitalist growth, smoothing out crises, and safeguarding simultaneously both jobs and the competitiveness of business in the international marketplace, so that increases are generated from which redistributions can be made without discouraging private investors. This throws some light on the *methodological* side of the project: the welfare state compromise and the pacification of class antagonisms are to be achieved by using democratically legitimated state power to protect and restrain the quasi-natural process of capitalist growth. The *substantive* side of the project is nourished by the residues of a utopia of social labor: as the status of the employee is normalized through rights to political participation and social ownership, the general population gains the opportunity to live in freedom, social justice, and increasing prosperity. The presupposition here is that peaceful coexistence between democracy and capitalism can be ensured through state intervention.

In the developed industrial societies of the West this precarious condition could, by and large, be fulfilled, at least under the favorable constellation of factors in the postwar and reconstruction periods. But what I want to deal with here is not the changed constellation that has existed since the 1970s, not external circumstances, but the internal difficulties that arise for the welfare state as a result of its own successes.[8] In this regard two questions repeatedly arise. First, does the interventionist state have sufficient power at its disposal, and can it operate efficiently enough to keep the capitalist system under control as intended in its program? Second, is the use of political power the correct method for reaching the substantive goal of promoting and safeguarding emancipated forms of life worthy of human beings? Thus we are concerned first with the question of the degree to which capitalism and democracy can be reconciled, and second with the question whether new forms of life can be created through legal-bureaucratic means.

From the beginning, the national state has proved too narrow a framework to adequately guarantee Keynesian economic policies against external factors—against the imperatives of the world market and the investment policies of business enterprises operating on a worldwide scale. But the limits of the state's power and capacity to intervene internally are still more evident. Here, the more successfully the welfare state puts through its programs, the more clearly it runs into the opposition of private investors. There are many causes, of course, of a decreasing profitability of business, declining willingness to invest, and falling rates of growth. But conditions for the valorization of capital do not remain unaffected by the results of social welfare policies, either in actual fact or—and especially not—in the subjective perception of business enterprises. In addition, rising costs for wages and benefits strengthen the tendency to invest in rationalizing production, investments which—under the banner of a second industrial revolution—so substantially increase the productivity of labor and so substantially decrease the labor time necessary to society as a whole that despite the secular trend toward shortening the work week more and more labor power is unused. Be that as it may, in a situation in which insufficient willingness to invest, economic stagnation, increasing unemployment, and the crisis in public budgets can be suggestively connected in the perception of the public with the costs of the welfare state, the structural limitations under which the welfare state compromise was worked out and maintained become quite evident. Because the welfare state may not interfere with the economic system's mode of functioning, it has no possibility of influencing private investment activity other than through interventions that conform to the economic system. Nor would it have the power to do so, because the redistribution of income is essentially limited to a horizontal reshuffling within the group of the dependently employed and does not touch the class-specific structure of wealth, in particular the distribution of ownership of the means of production. Thus it is precisely the successful welfare state that skids into a situation in which it becomes apparent, as Claus Offe has shown, that the welfare state itself it not an autonomous "source of prosperity" and cannot guarantee employment security as a civil right.

In such a situation the welfare state is immediately in danger of its social base slipping away. In times of crisis the upwardly mobile groups of voters who received the greatest direct benefits from the welfare state development can develop a mentality concerned with maintaining their standard of living and may ally themselves with the old middle class, and in general with the strata concerned with "productivity," to form a defensive coalition opposing underprivileged or marginalized groups. Such a regrouping of the electoral base threatens primarily parties like the Democrats in the United States, the English Labour Party, or the German Social-Democratic Party, which for decades have been able to count on a firm welfare state clientele. At the same time, labor unions come under pressure through the changed situation in the labor market; their power to make effective threats is diminished, they lose members and contributions and see themselves forced into a politics of alliances tailored to the short-term interests of those who are still employed.

Even if under more favorable conditions the welfare state could retard or completely avoid the side effects of its own success that are jeopardizing the very conditions of its functioning, a further problem would remain unresolved. Advocates of the welfare state project had always looked in only one direction. In the foreground stood the task of controlling quasi-natural economic power and diverting the destructive consequences of crisis-prone economic growth from the lifeworld of dependent workers. Government power achieved by parliamentary means seemed both an innocent and an indispensable resource; faced with the systemic inner logic of the economy, the interventionist state had to draw on that power for its strength and its capacity for action. The reformers had seen active state intervention, not only in the economic cycle but also in the life cycle of its citizens, as completely unproblematic—reforming the conditions of life of the employed was, after all, the goal of the welfare state program. And in fact a relatively high degree of social justice has been achieved in this way.

But the very people who acknowledge this historical achievement on the part of the welfare state and who refrain from cheap criticism of its weaknesses have come to recognize the failure that derives not from any particular obstacle or from a halfhearted realization of the project but from a specific narrowness of vision on the part of the project itself. All skepticism about the medium of power, which may be indispensable but is only seemingly innocent, has been removed from awareness. Social welfare programs need a great deal of power to achieve the force of law financed by public budgets—and thus to be implemented within the lifeworld of their beneficiaries. Thus an ever denser net of legal norms, of governmental and paragovernmental bureaucracies is spread over the daily life of its potential and actual clients.

Extensive discussions of excessive legal regulation and bureaucratization in general and the counterproductive effects of government social welfare policy in particular, and of the professionalization and scientization of social services, have made one thing clear: the legal and administrative means through which welfare state programs are implemented are not a passive medium with no properties of its own. On the contrary, they are linked with a practice that isolates individual facts, a practice of normalization and surveillance. Foucault has traced the reifying and subjectivizing power of this practice down to its very finest capillary ramifications in everyday communication. Certainly, the deformations of a lifeworld that is regimented, dissected, controlled, and watched over are more subtle than the obvious forms of material exploitation and impoverishment; but social conflicts that have been shifted over into the psychological and physical domains and internalized are no less destructive for all that. In short, a contradiction between its goal and its method is inherent in the welfare state project as such. Its goal is the establishment of forms of life that are structured in an egalitarian way and that at the same time open up arenas for individual self-realization and spontaneity. But evidently this goal cannot be reached via the direct route of putting political programs into legal and administrative form. Generating forms of life exceeds the capacities of the medium of power.

IV

I have discussed the obstacles that the successful welfare state puts in its own path in the context of two problems. I do not mean to say thereby that the development of the welfare state has been a misguided specialization. On the contrary, the institutions of the welfare state represent as much of an advance in the political system as those of the democratic constitutional state, an advance to which there is no identifiable alternative in societies of our type—either with regard to the functions that the welfare state fulfills or with regard to the normatively justified demands that it satisfies. In particular, nations that have lagged behind in the development of the social welfare state have no plausible reason for deviating from this path. It is precisely this lack of alternatives, and perhaps even the irreversibility of these still controversial compromise structures, that now confront us with the dilemma that the developed forms of capitalism can no more live without the welfare state than they can live with its further expansion. The more or less bewildered reactions to this dilemma indicate that the potential of the utopian idea of a laboring society to stimulate new developments in the political sphere has been exhausted.

Following Claus Offe, one can distinguish three patterns of

response to this dilemma in countries such as the Federal Republic of Germany and the United States.[9] The more conservative wing of the social-democratic parties, which defends the legitimacy of industrial society and the welfare state, finds itself on the defensive. I intend this characterization in a broad sense, so that it can be applied, for example, both to the Mondale wing of the Democratic Party in the United States and to the second government under Miterrand in France. The legitimists delete from the welfare state project precisely the components it had derived from the utopian idea of a laboring society. They renounce the goal of overcoming heteronomous labor so that the status of a free citizen with equal rights extends into the sphere of production and can become the nucleus around which autonomous forms of life crystallize. Today the legitimists are the true conservatives, who want to stabilize what has been achieved. They hope to find a point of equilibrium between the development of a welfare state and modernization based on a market economy. The disturbed balance between orientations to democratic use-values and a toned-down version of the intrinsic capitalist dynamic is to be restored. This program focuses on preserving the existing achievements of the welfare state. It fails to recognize, however, the potentials for resistance accumulating in the wake of progressive bureaucratic erosion of communicatively structured lifeworlds that have been emancipated from quasi-natural contexts. Nor does it take seriously the shifts in the social and labor-union base on which welfare state policies have hitherto been able to rely. With shifts in the structure of the electorate and a weakening of the position of the labor unions, these policies are threatened with a desperate race against time.

On the rise is neoconservatism, which is also oriented to industrial society but decidedly critical of the social welfare state. The Reagan administration and the government of Margaret Thatcher made their entrance under its banner; the conservative government in the Federal Republic of Germany has moved into the same position. Basically, neoconservatism is characterized by three components.

First, a supply-side economic policy is supposed to improve conditions for the valorization of capital and set the process of capital accumulation back in motion. It is willing to accept a relatively high unemployment rate, which is intended to be only temporary. As the statistics in the United States show, the shifts in income are to the disadvantage of the poorer groups in the population, while only those who possess large amounts of capital realize definite increases in income. Hand in hand with this come definite reductions in social welfare services. Second, the costs of legitimating the political system are to be reduced. "Inflation of rising expectations" and "ungovernability" are the slogans of a policy that aims at a greater detachment of administration from public will-formation. In this context, neocorporatist developments are promoted, and there is thus an activation of the nongovernmental steering potential of large-scale organizations, primarily business organizations and labor unions. The transfer of normatively regulated parliamentary powers to systems that merely function, without normative regulation, turns the state into one partner among others in the negotiation. The displacement of jurisdiction onto the neocorporate gray areas withdraws more and more social matters from a decision-making process that is obligated by constitutional norms to give equal consideration to all who are concerned in any specific matter.[10] Third, cultural policy is assigned the task of operating on two fronts. On the one hand, it is to discredit intellectuals as the social bearers of modernism, at once obsessed with power and unproductive; for postmaterial values, especially expressive needs for self-realization and the critical judgments of a universalist Enlightenment morality, are seen as a threat to the motivational bases of a functioning society of social labor and a depoliticized public sphere. On the other hand, traditional culture and the stabilizing forces of conventional morality, patriotism, bourgeois religion, and folk culture are to be cultivated. Their function is to compensate the private lifeworld for personal burdens and to cushion it against the pressures of a competitive society and accelerated modernization.

The neoconservative policy has a certain chance to gain ascendancy if it finds a base in the bipartite segmented society it is promoting. The groups that have been excluded or marginalized have no veto power, since they represent a segregated minority that has been isolated from the production process. The pattern of relations between the metropolises and the underdeveloped peripheral areas that has increasingly become established in the international arena seems to be repeating itself within the developed capitalist societies: the established powers are less and less dependent for their own reproduction on the labor and willingness to cooperate of those who are impoverished and disenfranchised. But a policy has to be able to function as well as to simply gain acceptance. A definite termination of the welfare state compromise, however, would necessarily leave gaps in functioning that could be closed only through repression or demoralization.

A third and contrasting pattern of reaction is shown in the dissidence of the critics of growth, who have an ambivalent attitude toward the welfare state. Thus in the new social movements of the Federal Republic, for instance, minorities of the most diverse origins have joined in an "antiproductivist alliance"—the old and the young, women and the unemployed, gays and the handicapped, believers and nonbelievers. What units them is their rejection of the productivist vision of progress that the legitimists share with the neoconservatives. For those two parties, the key to a modernization of society as free as possible from crisis lies in correctly distributing the burden of problems between the two subsystems, the state and the economy. The one group sees the cause of crises in the unfettered inner dynamic of the economy; the other sees it in the bureaucratic restraints imposed on that dynamic. The corresponding therapies are the social restraint of capitalism on the one hand, or the transfer of problems from the planning body back to the market on the other hand. The one group sees the source of the disturbances in a monetarized labor force; the other, in the bureaucratic crippling of private enterprise. But both sides agree that the interactive domains of the lifeworld that are in need of protection can adopt only a passive role vis-à-vis the actual motors of social modernization, the state and the economy. Both sides are convinced that the lifeworld can be sufficiently decoupled from those two subsystems and protected from encroachments by the system if the state and the

economy can be brought into the proper complementary relationship and can provide each other with mutual stabilization.

Only the dissident critics of industrial society start from the
premise that the lifeworld is equally threatened by commodi-
fication *and* bureaucratization—neither of the two media,
money and power, and is by nature "more innocent" than the
other. Only the dissidents also consider it necessary to
strengthen the autonomy of a lifeworld that is threatened in
its vital foundations and its communicative infrastructure.
They are the only ones to demand that the inner dynamic of
subsystems regulated by money and power be broken, or at
least checked, by forms of organization that are closer to the
base and self-administered. In this context, concepts of a dual
economy and proposals for the decoupling of social security
and employment come into play.[11] This dedifferentiation is to
apply not only to the role of the wage earner but also to that
of the consumer, the citizen, and the client of the welfare state
bureaucracies. The dissident critics of industrial society thus
inherit the welfare state program in the radical-democratic
components abandoned by the legitimists. But insofar as they
do not go beyond mere dissidence, insofar as they remain
caught in the fundamentalism of the Great Refusal and offer
no more than the negative program of dedifferentiation and
a halt to growth, they fall back behind *one* insight of the welfare
state project.

The formula of the social containment of capitalism held
more than mere resignation in the face of the fact that the
framework of a complex market economy could no longer be
broken up from within and restructured democratically by
means of the simple recipes of workers' self-management. That
formula also contained the insight that an external and indirect
attempt to gain influence on mechanisms of self-regulation
requires something new, namely a highly innovative combination of power and intelligent self-restraint. At first this insight
was based on the notion that society could act upon itself
without risk, using the neutral means of political and administrative power. If not only capitalism but the interventionist
state itself is now to be "socially contained," the task becomes
considerably more complicated. For then that combination of

power and intelligent self-restraint can no longer be entrusted to the state's planning capacity.

If curbs and indirect regulation are now to be directed against the internal dynamics of public administration as well, the necessary potentials for reflection and steering must be sought elsewhere, namely, in a completely altered relationship between autonomous, self-organized public spheres on the one hand and domains of action regulated by money and administrative power on the other. This leads to the difficult task of making possible a democratic generalization of interest positions and a universalist justification of norms *below* the threshold of party apparatuses that have become independent complex organizations and have, so to speak, migrated into the political system. Any naturally generated pluralism of defensive subcultures arising only on the basis of spontaneous refusal would have to develop separately from norms of civil equality. It would then constitute only a sphere that was a mirror image of the neocorporatist gray areas.

V

The development of the welfare state has arrived at an impasse. With it, the energies of the utopian idea of a laboring society have exhausted themselves. The responses of the legitimists and the neoconservatives move within the medium of a *Zeitgeist* which at this point can only be defensive; they are the expression of a historical consciousness that has been robbed of its utopian dimension. The dissident critics of a growth-oriented society also remain on the defensive. Their response could be turned to the offensive only if the welfare state project were neither simply maintained nor simply terminated but rather continued on a higher level of reflection. A welfare state project that has become reflective, that is directed not only to restraining the capitalist economy but to controlling the state itself would, of course, lose labor as its central point of reference. For it is no longer a question of protecting full employment, which has been raised to the status of a norm. A reflective welfare state project could not even limit itself to introducing a guaranteed minimum income in order to break the spell that the labor market casts on the life history of all those capable of working—including the growing and increasingly marginalized potential of those who only stand in reserve. This step would be revolutionary, but not revolutionary enough—not even if the lifeworld could be protected not only against all the inhuman imperatives of the employment system but also against the counterproductive side effects of an administrative system designed to provide for the whole of existence.

Such barriers to the interchange between system and lifeworld would prove functional only if a new distribution of power arose at the same time. Modern societies have at their disposal three resources with which to satisfy the need for steering: money, power, and solidarity. The respective spheres of influence of these three resources would have to be brought into a new balance. By this I mean that the integrative social force of solidarity would have to be able to maintain itself in the face of the "forces" of the other two regulatory resources, money and administrative power. The domains of life that specialize in the transmission of traditional values and cultural knowledge, in the integration of groups and the socialization of new generations, have always been dependent on solidarity. But a political will-formation that was to have an influence on the boundaries and the interchange between these communicatively structured spheres of life on the one hand and the state and the economy on the other would have to draw from the same source. That, by the way, is not so different from the normative ideas of our social studies textbooks, according to which society influences itself and its development through democratically legitimated authority.

According to this official version, political power springs from public will-formation and flows, as it were, through the state apparatus via legislation and administration, returning to a Janus-faced public that takes the form of a public of citizens at the entrance to the state and a public of clients at its exit. This is approximately how the citizens and the clients of public administration see the cycle of political power from their perspective. From the perspective of the political system, the same cycle, purged of all normative admixtures, presents itself differently. In this unofficial version, of which systems theory

keeps reminding us, citizens and clients are members of the
political system. In this description it is above all the meaning
of the legitimation process that has changed. Interest groups
and parties use their organizational power to create assent and
loyalty to their organizational goals. The state administration
not only structures but also largely controls the legislative process; it in turn has to make compromises with powerful clients.
Parties, legislative bodies, and bureaucracies must take account
of the undeclared pressure of functional imperatives and bring
them into accord with public opinion—the result is "symbolic
politics." The government too must be concerned with supporting the masses and supporting the private investors at the
same time.

In trying to fit these two contrary descriptions together into
a realistic image, one can use the model, current in political
science, of different arenas superimposed on one another.
Claus Offe, for instance, distinguishes three such arenas. In
the first, easily identifiable political elites within the state apparatus make their decisions. Beneath this lies a second arena
in which a multitude of anonymous groups and collective
agents influence one another, form coalitions, control access to
the means of production and communication, and, already less
visibly, preestablish through their social power the margins
within which political questions can be thematized and decided.
Beneath them, finally, lies a third arena in which subtle communication flows determine the form of political culture and,
with the help of definitions of reality, compete for what Gram-
sci called cultural hegemony—this is where shifts in the trend
of the *Zeitgeist* take place. The interaction among these arenas
is not easily grasped. Up to now processes in the middle arena
seem to have had priority. Whatever the empirical answer turns
out to be, our practical problem can in any case be seen more
readily now: any project that wants to shift the balance in favor
of regulation through solidarity has to mobilize the lower arena
against the two upper ones.

In the lower arena conflicts are not directly for money or
power but rather for definitions. At issue are the integrity and
autonomy of life styles, perhaps the protection of traditionally
established subcultures or changes in the grammar of tradi-

tional forms of life. Regionalist movements are examples of the former, feminist or ecological movements examples of the latter. For the most part these battles remain latent; they take place within the microsphere of everyday communication, and only now and then do they consolidate into public discourses and higher-level forms of intersubjectivity. These forms permit the formation of autonomous public spheres, which also enter into communication with one another as soon as the potential for self-organization and the self-organized employment of communications media is made use of. Forms of self-organization strengthen the collective capacity for action beneath the threshold at which organizational goals become detached from the orientations and attitudes of members of the organization and dependent instead on the interest of autonomous organizations in maintaining themselves. In organizations that remain close to the base, the capacity for action will always fall short of the capacity for reflection. That need not be an obstacle to accomplishing the task that occupies the foreground in continuing the welfare state project. The autonomous public spheres would have to achieve a combination of power and intelligent self-restraint that could make the self-regulating mechanisms of the state and the economy sufficiently sensitive to the goal-oriented results of radical democratic will-formation. Presumably, that can happen only if political parties relinquish *one* of their functions without replacing it, that is, without simply making room for a functional equivalent—the function of *generating* mass loyalty.

These reflections become more provisional, indeed vaguer, the more they approach the no-man's-land of the normative. There it is already easier to mark off negative boundaries. When the welfare state project becomes reflective, it takes leave of the utopian idea of a laboring society. The latter had used the contrast between living and dead labor, the idea of self-determined activity, to orient itself. In doing so, it had to presuppose that the subcultural forms of life of industrial workers were a source of solidarity. It had to presuppose that cooperative relationships within the factory would even intensify the naturally operative solidarity of the workers' subculture. But since then these subcultures have largely disintegrated. And it is somewhat doubtful whether their power to create solidarity can be regenerated in the workplace. Be that as it may, what was previously a presupposition or a condition of the utopian idea of a laboring society has now become a theme for discussion. And with this theme the utopian accents have moved from the concept of labor to the concept of communication. I speak only of "accents," because with the shift of paradigm from a society based on social labor to a society based on communication the form of linkage to the utopian tradition has also changed.

Of course, the utopian dimension of historical consciousness and political debate has by no means been completely closed off with the departure of the utopian contents of a laboring society. As utopian oases dry up, a desert of banality and bewilderment spreads. I hold to my thesis that the self-reassurance of modernity is spurred on, as before, by a consciousness of the significance of the present moment in which historical and utopian thought are fused with one another. But with the disappearance of the utopian contents of the laboring society, two illusions that have cast a spell over the self-understanding of modernity disappear as well. The first illusion stems from an inadequate differentiation.

In utopian conceptions of a well-ordered society, the dimensions of happiness and emancipation coincided with the dimensions of increasing power and the production of social wealth. Sketches of rational forms of life entered into a deceptive symbiosis with the rational domination of nature and the mobilization of societal energies. The instrumental reason released in the forces of production, and the functionalist reason developed in capacities for organization and planning were to pave the way for a life that was at once humane, egalitarian, and libertarian. Ultimately, the potential for consensual relationships was to issue directly from the productivity of work relationships. The persistence of this confusion is reflected even in its critical reversal, as for example when the normalizing achievements of complex centralized organizations are lumped together with the generalizing achievements of moral universalism.[12]

Still more fundamental is the abandonment of the methodological illusion that was connected with projections of a concrete totality of future life possibilities. The utopian content of a society based on communication is limited to the formal aspects of an undamaged intersubjectivity. To the extent to which it suggests a concrete form of life, even the expression "the ideal speech situation" is misleading. What can be outlined normatively are the necessary but general conditions for the communicative practice of everyday life and for a procedure of discursive will-formation that would put participants *themselves* in a position to realize concrete possibilities for a better and less threatened life, on *their own* initiative and in accordance with *their own* needs and insights.[13] From Hegel through Carl Schmitt down to our day, a critique of utopia that has issued dire warnings against Jacobinism has been wrong in denouncing the supposedly unavoidable marriage of utopia and terror. Nevertheless, it is utopian in the negative sense to confuse a highly developed communicative infrastructure of *possible* forms of life with a specific totality, in the singular, representing the successful life.

Notes

1. I am following the outstanding work of Reinhart Koselleck, *Vergangene Zukunft* (Frankfurt, 1979); English translation *Futures Past: On the Semantics of Historical Time* (Cambridge, MA, 1985).

2. On this theme see J. Rüsen, "Utopie und Geschichte," in W. Vosskamp, ed., *Utopieforschung* (Stuttgart, 1982), vol. I, p. 356ff.

3. L. Holscher, "Der Begriff der Utopie als historische Kategorie," in Vosskamp, *Utopieforschung*, vol. I, p. 402ff.

4. Reinhart Kosselleck, "Die Verzeitlichung der Utopie," in Vosskamp, vol. III, p. 1ff.; R. Trousson, "Utopie, Geschichte, Fortschritt," in Vosskamp, vol. III, p. 15ff.

5. Oskar Negt has recently published another noteworthy study from this perspective: *Lebendige Arbeit, enteignete Zeit* (Frankfurt, 1984).

6. Claus Offe, "Arbeit als soziologische Schlüsselkategorie," in his *Arbeitsgesellschaft— Strukturprobleme und Zukunftsperspektiven* (Frankfurt, 1984), p. 20.

7. From this perspective see also the recent work of H. Kern and M. Schumann, *Das Ende der Arbeitsteilung?* (Munich, 1984).

8. On this theme see Claus Offe, "Zu einigen Widersprüchen des modernen Sozial-staaates," in his *Arbeitsgesellschaft*, p. 323ff.; and John Keane, *Public Life and Late Capitalism* (Cambridge, 1984), chapter 1, p. 10ff.

9. Claus Offe, "Perspektiven auf die Zukunft des Arbeitsmarktes," in his *Arbeitsgesellschaft*, p. 340ff.

10. Claus Offe, "Korporatismus als System nichtstaatlicher Machtsteurerung," in *Geschichte und Gesellschaft* (10 (1984), p. 234ff.; on the systems-theoretical justification of neocorporatism see H. Wilke, *Entzauberung des Staates* (*Königstein, 1983*).

11. Th. Schmid, *Befreiung von falscher Arbeit. Thesen zum garantierten Mindesteinkommen* (Berlin, 1984).

12. See Jean-Francois Lyotard, *The Postmodern Condition: A Report on Knowledge* (Minneapolis, 1984). For a critical perspective, see Axel Honneth, "Der Affekt gegen das Allgemeine," in *Merkur* 430, December 1984, p. 893ff.

13. Karl-Otto Apel, "Ist die Ethik der idealen Kommunikationsgemeinschaft einer Utopie?" in Vosskamp, vol. I, p. 325ff.

3
Heinrich Heine and the Role
of the Intellectual in Germany

I

In 1916, Kurt Hiller published a manifesto with the expressionistic title "The Goal. An Appeal to the Active Spirit," in which eighteen intellectuals spoke in favor of progressive demands. Theodor Heuss [later first president of the Federal Republic], then thirty-two years old, took this publication as the occasion for a critique of the politicization of writers, a process he considered questionable. Heuss pointed to precursors like Ulrich von Hutten and the pamphlet-writing Humanists, Voltaire and the Encyclopedists, Arndt and Görres, spokesmen for the opposition to Napoleon, and finally Börne, Heine, and the Young Germany group. Heuss pointed out that these writers had emerged in periods *prior to* the development of a parliament and a party system. In those days political will-formation did not stand under the wholesome discipline of tactics and organization. Even the intellectuals of the *Vormärz*, the period prior to the revolution of March 1848, could afford a certain idealism, as they were not involved in the considerations of expediency that accompany everyday political activity. Such idealism, however, Heuss continued, could no longer serve as a model for his contemporaries, lest they run the risk "of losing their footing in realities that are shifting." "When

This text is based on Habermas's opening address to the February 1986 conference on "Young Germany in 1835: Literature and Censorship in the Pre-1848 Period," organized by the Heinrich Heine Institute in Düsseldorf.

[the theater critic Alfred] Kerr, for instance," Heuss went on to say, "began giving his journalism a political coloration, one felt that he was thinking of Heinrich Heine. But not much will come of it. Our everyday political activity, which is broader, more complex, and down-to-earth, would show only a weak response to Heine's political journalism and his pointed formulations; besides, this kind of politics of the literati seems significant only when one reads it in literary history. In political and social history it is present only as a nuance, not as a shaping force."[1] The influence of Friedrich Naumann is unmistakable here, as is that of Max Weber, who, three years later, in a famous lecture on "Politics as a Vocation," was to make a similar distinction between the "sterile excitation" of the intellectual and the objectivity and rationality of the professional politician. To the professional politician Weber ascribed realistic detachment, a sense of proportion, competence, and a willingness to accept responsibility—to the writer and philosopher engaged in politics as a dilettante, in contrast, a "romanticism of the intellectually interesting . . . devoid of all feeling of objective responsibility."[2] Weber is using a formula of attack here that might have come out of the armory of Heine's numerous adversaries. I will return to this critique of the role of the intellectual, which was taken up again by Schumpeter and Gehlen. First, however, we must deal with the question whether the intellectuals with whom Max Weber and the young Heuss were confronted at the time of World War I did in fact orient themselves to Heine. Was it even possible for them to be led astray by the model of Heine, as Heuss presumes?

Certainly the observation that the intellectual takes on a different role with the development of a parliamentary system is correct. In fact, the intellectual acquires a *specific* role only when he is able to address a public opinion formed by the press and the struggle between political parties. Only in the constitutional state does the political public sphere become the medium of, and serve to reinforce, the process of democratic will-formation. Here the intellectual finds his place. Even the word "intellectual" was first coined in the France of the Dreyfus Affair. In January of 1898, Émile Zola published an open letter to the President of the Republic that contained grave accusations against the military and the legal system; the following day, a manifesto appeared in the same newspaper, likewise protesting against infringements of rights in the trial of Captain Dreyfus, who had been convicted of espionage. It bore over a hundred signatures, including those of prominent writers and scholars. Soon thereafter it was publicly referred to as the "manifesto of the intellectuals." Anatole France spoke at the time of the "intellectual" as an educated person acting "without a political mandate" when, in the interest of public matters, he makes use of the means of his profession outside the sphere of his profession—that is, in the political public sphere. What will reappear in Max Weber as the irresponsibility of the political dilettante is here still considered responsibility for the whole without official jurisdiction.

With the appeal and acquittal of the unjustly accused Jewish captain, the Dreyfusards had achieved a tangible success. Their indirect success—preventing the Third Republic from slipping into a new Bonapartism—did still more to establish the role of the "universal intellectual" (Foucault), which, from Zola to Sartre, has been a recurrent and impressive feature of the Parisian scene. The definition is clear: when intellectuals, using arguments sharpened by rhetoric, intervene on behalf of rights that have been violated and truths that have been suppressed, reforms that are overdue and progress that has been delayed, they address themselves to a public sphere that is capable of response, alert and informed. They count on a recognition of universalist values; they rely on a halfway functional constitutional state and on a democracy that for its part survives only by virtue of the involvement of citizens who are as suspicious as they are combative. In terms of its normative self-understanding, this type belongs to a world in which politics has not shrunk to state activity; in the world of the intellectual, a political culture of opposition complements the institutions of the state. Heinrich Heine is both close to this world and distant from it.

His distance from it can be measured by the relationship of the Parisian emigrés to the Restoration Germany of the period prior to 1848. Heine cannot yet be an intellectual in the sense of the Dreyfus supporters, because he is kept at a distance

from the formation of political opinion in the states of the
German Confederation in two ways: physically, through his
exile, and intellectually, by censorship. In *Germany, A Winter's
Tale,* Heine compares the censorship with the customs union
that unites his splintered fatherland economically:

It will give us unity
that's, so to speak, external.
The spirit we'll get from Censorship
that's truly ideal and eternal.
A spiritual unity comes from there,
a one-ness in all our thinking.[3]

Anyone who is familiar with Heine's lifelong struggle with
censorship and who knows that anticipated interventions by
the censor exercised a direct formative influence on the style
of his texts will not underestimate the weight of these sarcastic
verses or the ironic truth hidden in them.

The unifying definitions provided by censorship, with which
the Frankfurt Assembly tried in 1832 to ward off conditions
like those in France, transformed the "splintered fatherland"
in fact into a negative version of the arena of public opinion,
which was both reserved for and denied to future intellectuals.
For the intellectual already existed—but only in the anticipa-
tory perception of the censorship officials. As potential midwife
of a political public sphere that would emerge from the literary
one, the intellectual cast his shadow ahead of him. He would,
of course, be able to exercise his functions there only when the
spirit of public opinion had been incorporated into the power
of the state—through a parliamentary system. Until that time,
power had to present itself to the potential intellectual, to
Heine and his contemporaries, as something that merely stood
in opposition to them, an authority that fended off through
censorship the spirit that undermined all morals and religion.
Only after 1848 did the principle of the free expression of
opinion gain at least gradual acceptance in Germany. Parallel-
ing changes in the educational system, there took place a structural transformation from a bourgeois public sphere still
centered in literary activity to a politically functioning public
sphere in which new possibilities for manipulation arose with

a mass press and a mass public, possibilities of which Bismarck immediately availed himself. Peter Uwe Hohendahl has described this transformation of the "institution of literature."[4] But even under these new conditions Heine, the protointellectual, was not repatriated into an empire unified under Prussia—neither as an outstanding writer nor as a prototypical intellectual. The indications that the history of Heine's influence was a negative one became more marked; Heine did not establish a tradition.[5]

In France it was different. Here Heine's texts were granted a different effective history. From the figure of the forerunner that Heine incorporated in a very German variant, the intellectual developed into an acknowledged part of the political culture: "One does not arrest Voltaire."[6] The Dreyfus Affair makes this clear: Heine would have been able to recognize himself in the role of the intellectual, which received its name and its specific function only a half-century later. After all, he had fought on similar fronts and exposed himself to the same denunciations. His mockery, lightfooted but heavy in spirit, of the authoritarian conditions in an officialdom already negated by even a defeated Napoleon; his merciless taunting of opportunism and Restoration middle-class morality; his sensitivity to the (by no means fine) distinctions between republican and Old German nationalism; his fear of the dark energies of a populism that was breaking out in revolt against reason itself—this lifelong battle, fought with the weapons of the poet, was nourished by the same inspirations, the same partisan support of the universalism and individualism of the Enlightenment as the *j'accuse* of Émile Zola and the manifesto of his friends.

These affinities are reflected in the reactions of the opponents in each case. In 1898, the authoritarian, nationalistic, and anti-Semitic opponents had within a few weeks crowned the figure and name of the intellectual with a wreath of pejorative connotations. Maurice Barrès, spokesman for the Action Française, distinguished himself in this. Dietz Bering has studied the image of the intellectual as enemy that came into being during that period: In the intellectual, who thinks abstractly and in general terms, lack of instincts and roots is linked to a lack of patriotic sentiment and loyalty, to unbounded decadence and instability of character, to the destructive addiction to criticism characteristic of the "person of foreign descent," the Jew, to whom nothing is sacred.[7] Anyone who compares these interpretations with the commonplaces of the contemporary criticism of Heine will be surprised by the convergences; in polemical characterizations of the Dreyfus party, the attributes used by outraged critics of Heine's time to describe his person seem simply to have congealed into the stereotype of a role.

But in Germany, where the Dreyfus Affair was followed attentively, no stratum of intellectuals with affinities to Heine had developed by the time of World War I. In Germany it was not the role of the intellectual but only the negatively charged role stereotype of his opponents that was received. Bering has shown that even the handful of influential literary figures and scholars who until 1933 had futilely attempted to create public influence for a radical-democratic humanism like Heine's, even intellectuals like Heinrich Mann, Ernst Troeltsch, and Alfred Döblin did not dare to use the word "intellectual" in a simple positive sense. Karl Mannheim, of course, had developed a sociology of the free-floating intellectual. In the German milieu, however, anyone whose attitude toward intellectuals was positive used in preference a derivative of the word *Geist,* whose meanings have been so splendidly codified in Grimm's dictionary*; he spoke rather of *"geistige Menschen"* ["mental or spiritual men"] or, succinctly, of the *"Geistigen"* ["the mental or spiritual ones"]—for then one could easily make the association to the *"Geistesmenschen"* ["men of the spirit"], the *"geistig Schaffenden"* ["those working in the medium of mind or spirit"], even the *"Geistesadel"* ["aristocracy of mind or spirit"].[8] The corresponding term on the Left was the *"geistigen Arbeiter"* ["mental or spiritual workers"]. One of the few exceptions was Siegfried Kracauer's exchange with Döblin, still worth reading, which

---

*The German word *Geist* has a range of meaning centered in "mind" and "spirit" but extending from "ghost" to "wit." I have not attempted genuine translations of the various formations built on the word *Geist* given as examples here because doing so would require the use of the word "intellectual." Instead I have indicated, by using derivatives of the words "mind" and "spirit," the approximate relationship of the formation to the word *Geist.* (translator's note)

he titled *"Minimalforderungen an die Intellektuellen"* ["Minimal Demands on Intellectuals"].[9]

Adorno, who urged us to "resist anti-intellectual agitation, whatever guise it may take," and who heard in the expression *"geistiger Mensch"* the echo of the German academics' "elitist desires for authority"—even Adorno spoke of *"geistige Menschen"* rather than of intellectuals, and then explained with a bad conscience: "The term *'geistiger Mensch'* may be abominable, but one only realizes that there is such a thing when one becomes aware of the still more abominable fact that such and such a person is not a *'geistiger Mensch.'"*[10] The objective spirit prevails even in Adorno's hesitant opposition to it. Before World War I a critique of intellectuals had arisen in Germany, where there were no self-avowed intellectuals. Between the wars this critique developed a power that was little short of normative. In 1918, in his *Reflections of a Nonpolitical Man,* which he later retracted, Thomas Mann captured the result of the processes of marginalization that had associated the intellectual with an external enemy, with "a foreign race's heroism on the barricades,"[11] hence with the civilization of the West, and had assigned him his place in the zone of tension between culture and civilization, blood and intellect, between the systematic-creative orientation of the spirit and the methodologically restricted orientation of the intellect, with metaphysics and poetry on the one side and "the literature of the streets" on the other. In an explicit analogy to the Dreyfus trial, Mann wrote, "Anyone who is engaged in a spiritual struggle on the side of the civilization *entente* against the forces of the 'saber,' against Germany, is an intellectual."[12]

This interpretation, in which the Other is always made the intellectual, was more or less acceptable to all camps, by no means only the exponents of the youth movement like Hans Blüher or the folk-nationalists like Ernst von Salomon, who needed only to join one of the fronts already developed in France. Each of the four most important factions in the intellectual life of the Weimar Republic had a reason to devalue the others as dubious intellectuals. Let me mention the most important groups, which will occupy us for some time.

First there are the unpolitical among the writers, and the

mandarins among the scholars. For Hermann Hesse or the early Thomas Mann, for Ernst Robert Curtius or Karl Jaspers,[13] the sphere of the mind and the sphere of power are so separate from one another that a "politicization of the mind" would have to seem like a betrayal of the vocation of the creative and cultured personality. On the other side stand theoreticians oriented to *Realpolitik*, like Max Weber or the young Heuss. They harbor the suspicion that in the course of the politicization of writers and philosophers a frivolous, incompetent, unstable element would invade the domain that ought to be reserved for the specialized rationality of the professional politician. Both sides fear from the intellectual a mixing of categories that would do better to remain separate—whether because otherwise the division of labor in political activity would pull the esoteric spirit down into everyday opportunism and contaminate it, or because conversely the normal functioning of political activity would be ruined by rapturous enthusiasms stemming from an ethics of conviction. The activists around Kurt Hiller, and expressionist spirits in general, like René Schickele, Carl Einstein, and Ernst Bloch, form the third group, the group mentioned at the beginning of this essay. By entering the political arena, at least in terms of their rhetoric, these intellectuals seem to confirm the fears and the definitions of the other two factions. Typically, they confuse intellectual influence within a democratic public sphere with possession of political power, and they dream of an International, a convention, an Areopagus of united intellectuals. Accordingly, this emphasis on "spirit and deed" also fails to lead to a balanced assessment of the role of the intellectual. These activists share with the apolitical poet-princes and mandarin scholars the cultural-elitist claim to something higher, while with the *Real*politicians they share the false assumption that for the intellectual political commitment must mean struggling for a position *of his own* within political activity itself. Fourth, this attitude naturally provokes the intellectuals who, like Georg Lukács or Johannes R. Becher, have actually crossed the line to become professional politicians or professional revolutionaries and subordinated themselves to a party apparatus, and who thus do in fact have political power at their disposal. These left-wing party intellectuals have internalized Bebel's working-class distrust of "class traitors" and turncoats and tried to kill off the bourgeois in themselves: "The intellectual . . . has to burn the greater part of what he owes to his bourgeois descent before he can march in rank and file with the proletarian army."[14] These "head-workers" are extremely critical of the vacillation and opportunism, unreliability, and ideological claims to power of the "petit-bourgeois intelligentsia." Of course no ritual of self-purification, no matter how masochistic, shakes the party intellectuals in their conviction, founded on the philosophy of history, that the intellectual who has overcome his individualism and achieved a proletarian orientation has an avant-garde function of world-historical significance to fulfill.

In the spectrum of writers and professors who took any kind of stand on the conflicts of World War I and the Weimar situation, then, we can distinguish four groups of intellectuals who did not want to be intellectuals. All of them were caught in the dilemma of self-disavowal that in other countries is posed only for the right-wing intellectual. Of course there were right-wing intellectuals, who formed a fifth group, in Weimar as well: Wilhelm Stapel, for example, who took arms against the "slogans" of artistic and intellectual freedom by opposing to the "ruined brains in the cafes of the literati" who "blow on Heinrich Heine's freedom trumpet" "the naive feeling of an honest people." The national, self-disavowing intellectual should "not cultivate a spirituality lying beyond the people; he should represent the spirituality of his *own* people."[15] In Germany that privilege was not reserved for those on the Right; almost all the intellectuals disavowed themselves as intellectuals by assuming the pseudonym of *"Geistigen." As* intellectuals, they engaged only in mutual accusations. Many of these accusations were not even unjustified. But in opposition to Theodor Heuss, who derives the wretchedness of the German intellectuals from the false model of Heine and the false identification with the intellectuals of the pre–1848 period, I will defend the thesis that, on the contrary, orientation to the model of Heine could only have furthered the institutionalization of the role of the intellectual—something that, unfortunately, miscarried in Weimar.

Counterfactual assertions about historical developments that did not take place are difficult to support. Let me, then, try to demonstrate that the things that made Heine a politically committed writer ran counter to the self-understanding of most Weimar intellectuals as I have just sketched it. Kindred spirits like Tucholsky remain the exception. Heine's evaluation of his own literary-political journalism would have saved him from two misunderstandings that arose in Germany. The first misunderstanding concerns the autonomy of art, science, and scholarship vis-à-vis politics: it was believed that public political involvement on the part of writers and scholars would necessarily mean a dedifferentiation of cultural spheres that had developed their own inherent logics, and that it would necessarily result in the fusion of those spheres with politics. The other misunderstanding concerns the kind of political commitment with which the intellectual is involved: influence on the political public sphere was confused with incorporation into the operations of the political power struggle. In addition, the two misunderstandings appeared in conjunction with an enthusiastic-elitist self-understanding on the part of those with an academic education. For Heine, in contrast, the opposition between mind and power, which was constituted in practical form by censorship, lacked the connotations that accompany the typically German opposition of enthusiasm and cynicism. Heine did not share the prejudices of the Weimar intellectuals about their own role. But before I go into these structural incompatibilities I need to point out something more trivial. From 1848 to 1945, the very *content* of his writings kept Heine an outsider.

II

1. Adorno traces the fact that despite all attempts at conciliation Heine evokes discomfort and a sharp climate of rejection to the nonaffirmative and undiluted quality of the concept of enlightenment he maintained.[16] Heine was and did in fact remain the representative of a radical Enlightenment—the question, however, is to what kind of radicalness he owed the unacceptability of his thought, the actual formulation of which

tended to be cunning and ingratiating. "With polite irony, he refuses to immediately smuggle back in through the back door—or the basement door to the depths—what he has just demolished."[17] Is that an adequate explanation? To be sure, genuine enlightenment produces goods that are bulky and difficult to handle, especially for a voyage on the streams of German tradition. But Heine's ideas were very much the ideas of his time: "The people of Alsace and Lorraine will rejoin Germany if we complete what the French have begun; if we surpass them in deeds as we have already done in the realm of thought; if we rise to the heights required by the farthest consequences of that thought; if we destroy servitude down to its last hideaway, heaven; if we save the god that dwells within people from his degradation; if we become the redeemers of God; if we restore to their proper dignity the poor people disinherited of happiness, genius scorned and beauty ravished. . . ."[18] The French Revolution as a point of departure; Saint-Simonism, the Young Hegelian philosophy of the deed and the Feuerbachian critique of religion as a background; the radicalization of the bourgeois revolution, thus the social intensification of the political revolution as the driving force behind Heine's prose and a good part of his lyrical production[19]—on this fabric woven of radical Enlightenment, materialist and rational-utopian thought, Heine collaborated vigorously, but still only as one among many. His love for his native land was the wound that Heine tried to conceal from the public—but where is the thorn on which the public, at any rate the German public, rubbed itself sore? Is it located *only* in the intransigence of his Enlightenment stance?

It sounds blasphemous to say that men will redeem God, but that is only an old motif that Baader, Schelling, and Hegel had borrowed long before from Protestant (and Jewish) mysticism and reworked into the productivity of determinate negation. Even as a student, Heine was already, if we may trust his later report,[20] a young Hegelian in relation to his famous professor: he wanted to understand Hegel as a discreet atheist and a secret revolutionary. It is again the left-wing Hegel through whose eyes Heine deciphers the history of religion and philosophy. In that history there appear, one after the other: a

Luther who installs reason as the supreme judge in religious disputes, who paves the way for freedom of thought and creates the language for future revolutions in which even the poorest people will be able to express their needs in Biblical language; a Lessing who continues on from Luther, who now liberates Christianity, which has already been freed from tradition, from the empty shell of the letter, from "rigid service of the Word"; a Kant who carries on from Lessing, and as the great destroyer in the realm of thought far surpasses the petit-bourgeois Robespierre in terrorism, who destroys all lines of argument for the existence of God and then ambiguously resurrects God from the spirit of practical reason, "only on account of the police." And so it continues: Fichte as Napoleon; Schelling the philosopher of nature as a materialist in disguise; finally Hegel himself as the lightning that precedes the dreadful thunder of a frightful German revolution. Philosophy is only the dry husk of a "blood-red" revolution. Among the gods who amuse themselves with nectar and ambrosia on Olympus there is only one who "always wears a coat of mail, a helmet on her head and keeps her spear in her hand. She is the goddess of wisdom."[21]

What both fascinates and disturbs Heine are the energies that lie hidden in even the most transparent folds of logically consistent philosophical thought. The hatred that battered Heine as a Jew and an intellectual all his life made him well aware of the double-edged nature of a nationalism that came into the world as a republican-cosmopolitan idea but was then afflicted with "all sorts of boils and sores." Heine was suspicious of the fanatical and narrow-minded, the deeply antimodern and particularist qualities of the Germanophile Jacobins, who confused xenophobia with love of one's native land, who burned books and were prepared to set national unity above the emancipatory content of bourgeois individual liberties. Again and again Heine pressed for a differentiation of the two aspects, one of which adopted the principles of the "French doctrine of freedom" under the banner of "humanity, cosmopolitanism, and the rationality of the younger generation," and the other of which made short shrift of the unenlightened masses of the people with the slogan "the fatherland, Germany, the beliefs of our fathers."

It *was* the suspiciousness of a representative of the Enlightenment that led Heine to react so vehemently to the teutomanic features of populism. How radically Heine differed from the reception of the Enlightenment in Germany, which defused it and smoothed off all the rough edges, is shown unmistakably in his defense of the honor of the bookseller Nicolai, who even after 1945 was being paraded before us schoolchildren as the frightful symbolic figure of the "Enlightener." It is the obscurantists, says Heine, who ridiculed him to death. Despite the remarkable misjudgments that Nicolai was guilty of, as in his satire of Werther, he was never wrong on the main issues: "It cannot be denied that many a blow directed against superstition unfortunately struck poetry itself. Nicolai fought, for instance, against the rising partiality for old German folksongs. But essentially he was once more in the right. Despite all their excellence, the songs did contain many recollections that were anything but up-to-date—these ancient strains of the Alpine cowherds of the Middle Ages could not lure the hearts of the people back into the stables of a day gone forth."[22] To appreciate the explosive force of this sentence, one has to know with what rapture Heine himself had spoken of *Des Knaben Wunderhorn,* Brentano's collection of folksongs, how enthusiastically he had praised the *Nibelungenlied,* how romantically he painted the creative force of the "folk spirit" for his French readers in speaking of the traveling apprentices from Halberstadt.[23]

And here, I think, lies the thorn that chafes German readers, the thing for which they have not forgiven Heine. They might have forgiven Heine, the radical representative of the *Enlightenment* for defending the honor of that comical screwball Nicolai; but they could not forgive him for the argument he used in doing so—they have not forgiven Heine the *Romantic* for rescuing their Romantic heritage from a deadly nationalistic idealization, from false historicizing, from a transfiguring sentimentality, and restoring it to its own radical origins. They have not forgiven him for linking the "party of flowers and nightingales" with the party of the revolution, for liquidating the opposition that the Restoration of the now old and pious

Romantics had itself constructed, the opposition between Romanticism and Enlightenment.

This thorn sticks in German flesh on the Left as on the Right. The atheistic coloring given the mystical expectation that God awaits His redemption through the self-emancipation of humanity may still be acceptable on this side of the barricades; but that this emancipation should encompass not only a people deprived of happiness but happiness itself, "genius scorned and beauty ravished," irritates even virtuous revolutionaries.[24] The hedonistic democracy that Heine defends against the Puritans of a revolution carried on at the cost of beauty is marked by an exuberant materialism of happiness: "You demand simple clothing, reserved manners, and unspiced delicacies; we on the other hand demand nectar and ambrosia, robes of royal purple, expensive perfumes, voluptuousness and luxury, nymphs dancing and laughing, music and comedies—do not be annoyed by this, you virtuous republicans."[25] Heine referred back to this passage ten years later, in 1844, just after he had met Dr. Marx. Like Heine, this Marx of the *Paris Manuscripts* was engaged in a progressive revision of the motifs of the early Romantic movement; but only in Heine's hands were those motifs transformed into the motivating impulses of a libertarian socialism that will not plow up the laurel trees to make potato fields, will not make wrapping paper out of the *Book of Songs,* and will indeed protect "all those quaint and fantastic whims that are so dear to the poet."[26] Heine turns to radical purposes the Romantic movement he has misappropriated— which was even more unforgivable than the radical Enlightenment itself.[27]

2. The Weimar intellectuals could do nothing with this Heine—neither those on the Left, who subordinated themselves to the party apparatus, nor those on the Right, who wanted to advance the National Revolution. In his famous radio speech of April 1933, Gottfried Benn took to task all the intellectuals who had ever spoken out for intellectual freedom and unrestricted gratification. Once more he contrasted them with the "thinkers," those who from Nietzsche on had embodied "the new biological type." In a single sentence, his closing one, Benn negated everything that Heine wrote for: "Don't

waste your time on arguments and words, be lacking in reconciliation, shut the gates, build the state."[28] Not everyone, of course, thought like Benn, like Jünger, Heidegger, and Carl Schmitt—neither Hermann Hesse nor Thomas Mann, not Max Weber and not Georg Lukács. Why even for *them* Heine could not become a model as an intellectual figure, nor even a guide, cannot be explained by the radical *content* of his writings. Here, rather, it is mentalities that clash with one another, premises that get on people's nerves. I will discuss the two premises on which an understanding of the intellectual's role is based in order to show why Heine could not become a model for the intellectuals who did not want to be intellectuals.

(a) Far off in Helgoland, Heinrich Heine experienced the July Revolution in Paris as a media event and later also celebrated it as such: he speaks of "wild rays of sunlight wrapped in print" and in his journal entry for the 10th of August reports excitedly that "this morning another pack of newspapers" arrived, with touching details that occupied him, like a child, far more than the whole that was so important. On this day the "weapons of the poet" that will later play a role in *Germany, A Winter's Tale* acquire a singular reality: "Give me my lyre, that I may sing a battle-hymn. . . . Words like flaming stars that have shot from heaven to burn palaces and illumine hovels! . . . Words like bright javelins. . . ."[29] The poet fights at the side of the revolutionary crowd, but with *his own* weapons. What does this conception of the militant poet intervening in the events of the day mean for the relationship between poetry and politics, mind and power?

Heine developed great sensitivity to the mode in which literary products exert their influence, a mode reflected through the medium of the bourgeois public sphere and both refracted and accelerated by the daily and weekly press: with the condensed journalistic form of communication, art and scholarship had changed the manner and tempo of their working. This modern awareness is also expressed in Heine's aesthetic attitude, which is oriented toward the work's reception. He was concerned with the social and political significance of the Romantic School, with the effective history of religion and philosophy in Germany. He was already analyzing the composition of the reading public from a sociological perspective and the dissemination of cultural products from the perspective of media analysis. And he grasped the July Revolution as the point at which the overall situation of the public sphere changed—the point at which a political public sphere emerged from the literary public sphere (even if, in Germany, at first only temporarily). Heine observed how this structural transformation affected the poet's attitude toward his work and toward the public, how it entered into the author's aesthetic self-understanding and even into the aesthetic form itself.

It was only in the Classical period immediately preceding his own that literature and art—whose production and consumption shifted in the course of the eighteenth century from patrons to the market—had attained their autonomy. Heine calls this the "art period." Literary and artistic activity had become differentiated—as had scholarly and scientific activity—to the point where culture on a professional level could become transparent in its inner structure and laws and could set itself off from everyday life, from politics and society. This autonomy was reflected in the classical aesthetics of the work of art, and in Humboldt's idea of the university. But if writers and scholars were not drawn into the wake of movements for emancipation, if they established a relationship to the vibrating center of the public sphere and addressed themselves to it, if they were already producing some of their works with the intention of having a political effect and they understood words as potential deeds—would not art (and scholarship), which had just become established as a "second, independent world," once again forfeit thereby their autonomous inner logic and become instruments of external ends, whether political or social? So it seems, when Heine praises the "writers of the contemporary Young Germany movement," who "wish to make no distinction between life and writing, who never separate politics from science, art, and religion, and who are simultaneously artists, tribunes, and apostles."[30]

This in any case is the premise on which the nonpolitical writers and the mandarins of the German university in the 1920s proceeded; under this premise, they understood the "politicization of the mind" as a betrayal of the autonomy of intellectual structures. In 1918, Hermann Hesse waxed indignant about poets who called themselves journalists: "They hadn't been writers for a long time; they were journalists and wheelers and dealers and clever talkers. . . . As though their crime consisted in previously having been too little concerned with politics, having thought too little . . . about so-called reality! My God, . . . for a long time they had been forcing themselves to do the only thing a poet exists for, namely the holy service of a world that is more than real, that is eternal."[31] The same premise, with its sign reversed, recurs in those, like Max Weber, who are oriented to *Realpolitik*. They too think of the writer and philosopher who becomes involved in the public sphere only as the promoter of a dedifferentiation of mind and power, a political dilettante who in his naive enthusiasm conflates the two spheres and violates their inner logic. The politically committed writer jeopardizes both: the autonomy of art and scholarship on the one hand and the rationality peculiar to political activity on the other.

Both these reproaches, I believe, are based on the same error: a fetishization of mind and a functionalization of power. The two ideas mesh to exclude the concept of a political public sphere, the only sphere in which the intellectual could play a genuine role. For the literary masters and the mandarins of Weimar, culture presented itself as a continent accessible only to the elites, sufficient unto itself and maintaining no ongoing connection to politics or society. Their opposite numbers, conversely, thought of politics as a functionally specified realm of action that needs its own experts who are qualified to participate in a power struggle organized as an ongoing activity. Between the culture of the one group and the politics of the other, there is no room for the political public sphere and the intellectual in it; for the intellectual commits himself on behalf of public interests as a sideline, so to speak (something that distinguishes him from both journalists and dilettantes), without giving up his professional involvement in contexts of meaning that have an autonomous logic of their own, but also without being swallowed up by the organizational forms of political activity. From the point of view of the intellectual, art and scholarship remain autonomous, certainly, but not altogether esoteric; for him, political will-formation is certainly related to the system dominated by professional politicians, but it is not controlled exclusively by it.

This was also Heine's view. He always defended the autonomy of art and literature, but he did not fetishize them. Some well-known statements of his seem to contradict this: "The deed is the child of the word, and the beautiful words of Goethe are childless." But this famous statement is directed not against the independence of the "second world," the world of aesthetic illusion presented in Goethe's work; it opposes only the quietistic conclusions that Goethe's followers drew from his work in opposition to every kind of politically committed literary activity: "The Goetheans allowed themselves to be misled into proclaiming the supremacy of art and turning away from the demands of that original real world, which, after all, must take precedence."[32] Nor does the famous remark that belongs in this context mean anything different: Heine's remark about the childlessness of the relationship between Pygmalion and the statue he awakened into life with his kisses. How else could one explain Heine's horror and fear of a future rule of the iconoclasts who would smash "all the marble figures of my beloved art world" "with their red fists."[33]

The book Heine wrote attacking Börne demonstrates unmistakably that he rejected the "men of the movement" who merely put the "art interest" to work for the political interests of the day. He explains defiantly why on the day of his arrival in Paris he hurried not to the graves of Voltaire and Rousseau but to the Bibliothèque Royale to be shown the Manesse Manuscript [a famous manuscript collection of Middle High German songs]. At the same time, Heine opposed the false alternative between fetishizing the mind and making art a political instrument. Heine scornfully cites a statement of Börne's: "For the person for whom form is the highest thing, as it is for him (Heine), it must also remain the only thing; for as soon as he crosses the boundary, he flows out into the unbounded, and the sand swallows him up."[34] Heine ridicules the opponent who wants to dismiss him from politics and put him out to pasture on Parnassus—only because he, Heine, has refused to sacrifice the inner logic of aesthetic illusion to political activity. For

Heine, the autonomy of art and scholarship remains a necessary condition if the locked granaries that the intellectual wants to open for the people are not to be empty.[35]

(b) In the dispute with Börne the other theme is also discussed, the theme of the concept of politics by which the politically committed writer Heine is guided. In opposition to Börne, Heine insists that the weapons of the poet cannot be those of the professional revolutionary, or of the professional politician. Admittedly, Heine's tenor often creates a different impression; the Young Hegelian pathos of the philosophy of the deed is not alien to Heine: "Take note of this, you proud men of action. You are nothing but unconscious handymen for the men of thought who, often in the humblest quiet, have prescribed with the utmost precision all your actions."[36] And Heine sees himself sitting at his desk at night—a muffled figure with the executioner's axe behind him. During his winter journey he meets this shadow again, at night in the Cathedral Square in Cologne. He addresses him and receives the answer:

I'm of a practical nature, sir,
and it is time you knew it.
So listen: what you have thought out in your mind,
I carry it out, I do it.[37]

Is Heine thinking here of the intellectual in the double role of a "man of thought" who also, as his own henchman, achieves practical effectiveness?

That corresponds in any case to the image that the activists among the writers designed for themselves in the 1920s. In 1919, Wilhelm Herzog published the appeal "Let Us Organize the Army of the Spirit at Last." In the tone of the times, he demands the "solidarity of all the torchbearers of the spirit: against those who despise the spirit, against those who defame the revolution, for a new world order that knows no death penalty and no slavery, for a classless community of all men."[38] Once again these idealists stand opposed to the more realistic party people, who subordinate themselves to the imperatives of the organization but think no less of their mission for it: "The head-workers are concerned above all with whether the proletarian revolution will come with all the horrors of civil war, amid the thunderings of Judgment, or whether it can prevail like a gentle autumn wind that shakes the ripe fruit from the trees. . . . The question is, whether they are up to the historical role that is allotted them."[39] Whether the Hegelian-Marxist understanding of theory and practice is diverted into inflated idealism or flattened out in Leninist fashion, power and mind are put into a relationship that is both elitist and instrumental—like the relationship between the henchman and their men of thought.

But Heine's conception of the interplay between poetic thought and political movements is completely different. For the image of Robespierre as the bloody hand of Rousseau's ideas evokes nothing but aversion in him: "If I held all the ideas of this world in my hand—I would perhaps beg you to cut off my hand immediately. . . ."[40] And the dream in Cologne also comes to a surprising resolution: It is only the skeletons of the Three Holy Kings in their sarcophagi, it is the *spiritual* power of a chimerical past over a present that has already been condemned that the poet wants to destroy with his words. And ultimately even his servant has no weapons at his disposal but those of the poet:

He came up close and with that axe
he smashed to pieces those pretty
but fleshless superstitions, he struck
without a trace of pity.[41]

Thus the intellectual is to redeem the present from the false hybrid, "part Gothic madness, part modern lies,/that's neither flesh, fish, nor fowl,"[42] solely through the reflective power of thought. Heine's distance from Börne and the early socialist craftsmen in Paris, his fear of both right- and left-wing politicians, his ambivalent relationship to Marx, to the "godless self-gods" and their leveling revolution, is based on evaluations that certainly do not stand up to criticism in every respect; I see the secret center of his antipathy, however, in the fact that Heine could see no simple instrumental connection between word and deed, that he distrusted the tribunalization of art and the doctrinalization of scholarship and did not want to skip over the mediations between the enlightenment of a public capable of judgment and the introduction of an organized struggle for political power. Heine would have brought this reserve of an intellectual whose influence is directed not to brains and hand but to opinions to bear on the institutionalized activity of the professional politician just as energetically as he did on the revolutionary movement (which in his eyes was certainly necessary).

III

With all that, Heine did *not* become a model for the Weimar intellectuals. Only since 1945 has Heine's intellectual self-understanding worked to create a tradition in Germany. Only in the Federal Republic has a stratum of intellectuals who accept themselves as such developed. Now the step that France took with the Dreyfus Affair, the step to the normalization of the public political involvement of writers, and increasingly of scholars and scientists as well, is being accomplished. With the welfare state compromise and the pacification of the class struggle, with the expansion of the educational sector, including higher education, with electronic media and a culture industry that has shifted from word to image, with highly bureaucratized political parties becoming autonomous vis-à-vis members and voters, with the monitoring of public opinion, with ideology planning and the commercial creation of mass loyalty, another structural transformation of the public sphere has taken place. Against this background, everything seems to me to depend on one thing alone: the mentalities characteristic of the educated German bourgeoisie, the pattern of thought that was still dominant during the Weimar period, had to be visibly corrupted to a great extent by the Nazi regime before Heine's painful and profound distantiation from his own identity and his cultural tradition could find a place in Germany. Without this detachment the intellectual's critical activity, which is at the same time dependent on self-criticism, is not possible. Only the revelations of the Nazi crimes have opened our eyes to the monstrous and sinister things that Heine saw brooding even within our best, our most cherished traditions. The Jewish emigré in Paris was separated by a political-geographical and also by a cultural distance from the homeland he loved as ambivalently as passionately—and thus from himself. Only after 1945 were we able to transform the spatial distance that lay between Heine and the arena in which he intended his work to have its effect into a historical distance, into a reflexively disrupted relationship to the traditions and intellectual forms that have shaped our identity. Now what is most our own, once become problematic, no longer needs to remain shielded from the estranging intellectual gaze.

Impressionistic Epilogue on the Federal Republic of Germany

The institutionalization of the role of the intellectual is not, however, following a straight course in the Federal Republic.

The most recent period in the history of the German intellectuals is badly documented[43]; I will limit myself to some key points from the selective memory of a contemporary who played a partisan role in it.

After Germany's defeat in World War I, political culture lagged behind the level of constitutional norms, which were in any case practiced only halfheartedly. Uncertainties within the political culture remained the case after 1945 as well. But because this time military defeat was connected with the revelation of a moral catastrophe, constitutional institutions not only took root more firmly in actual constitutional practice; the political culture too was characterized from the beginning by the intellectuals' distrust of false continuities. By the end of the 1950s a stratum of intellectuals had become established with an alternative program to the mentality of the broad population and the restoration-minded government, a mentality focused on reconstruction and security. It was primarily politically committed writers like the Group 47 who entered the public sphere, but also professors like Jaspers, Kogon, or Adorno, who had had to keep silent during the Nazi period or had been imprisoned or forced to emigrate. Unlike the Dreyfus Affair, through which the role of the intellectual first became accepted in France, the Spiegel affair of 1962 only confirmed the fact that the role had already been successfully established.*

In comparison with the Weimar period, the intellectuals' self-understanding had now changed in two respects. The theme of "mind and power" did, it is true, retain a sentimental note; the mutual lack of understanding of intellectuals and government parties yielded only with the social-liberal (SPD/FDP) coalition, with Gustav Heinemann and Willy Brandt. But the Weimar premises—the fetishization of mind and the purely instrumental understanding of power—had been withdrawn from circulation even earlier. If one thinks of figures like Heinrich Böll or Alexander Mitscherlich, who since the 1960s have symbolized the new influence of intellectuals on a public sphere that in the meantime has shifted to television, what I mean will be clear to everyone involved. The "spirit" embodied in such people, a spirit that had become both egalitarian and fallible, had cast off both the elitist cultural humanism and the emphatic concept of truth held by a philosophical tradition that was still Platonist. The intellectuals had also adopted the normative self-understanding of democratic will-formation: even when to do so was to fly in the face of the facts, they trusted the power of social integration of a public sphere in which attitudes were to be changed through arguments.[44]

The names Böll and Mitscherlich, of course, appear again in a different context: in 1975 Helmut Schelsky devoted to them a particularly harsh excursus on the theme "Class Conflict and the Priestly Rule of the Intellectuals."[45] Reading this pamphlet, one feels oneself back in the milieu of the Weimar period—anti-intellectualism that claims a theoretical grounding. What had happened?

In the meantime, the spirits of Weimar, strangely transformed, had experienced a ghostly resurrection. For in the course of the student protest movement the debate that Lukács had started about the intellectuals' position in the class struggle had been taken up again and given a social-psychological turn. Identification with the leaders of the nationalist revolutionary

The editor of *Der Spiegel* was arrested for publishing an article that was alleged to violate national security; protests led to Defense Minister Franz Joseph Strauss's fall from office. (translator's note)

struggles in Vietnam, China, Cuba, and South America allowed the students in revolt to transpose the "autonomous class betrayal of the bourgeois intellectual," and with it the ideal image of the professional revolutionary, from the 1920s to the 1960s. The politics of symbolic action became a "praxis of self-transformation" carried on collectively.[46] This pseudorevolutionary self-understanding slipped like a shadow of the past across a stage that was soon occupied by other forces lured out by the antiauthoritarian actions. A critique of the left-wing intellectuals made its appearance. It too drew on the armory of the Weimar period. For the critique of the intellectuals current in the 1970s was decisively inspired by the work of Arnold Gehlen, a disappointed supporter of the national revolution who since the beginning of the 1960s had been readying Joseph Schumpeter's Weberian sociology of intellectuals[47] for use in contemporary politics.[48]

Gehlen explains what he describes as the socially critical aggressiveness and the overwrought state of hypermoralistic intellectuals as due to the disparity between the information that floods in from a worldwide communication network on the one hand, and on the other hand the absence of possibilities for practical intervention on the part of a profession that is out of touch with reality, engaged only in manipulating opinions, and free from the constraints of objective exigencies. The opinion makers and the "fellows with glib tongues" are not equal to the complexity of a highly differentiated society that operates through a division of labor and on whose systemically controlled processes they can have no influence. Thus in their convictions they are discharging the animosity of the intellectual spectator who is condemned to passivity, and they do so in the forms of an "ethics of solidarity that is hostile to tradition because it is all-inclusive," that has no impact on reality and is suited only to aimless agitation. Heine had celebrated the autonomous ethics of the Enlightenment developed by Rousseau and Kant. Gehlen now calls that ethics a "humanitarianistic ethics of conviction" and sees it as a mere reflection of the intellectual enclosed within the "world traffic in consciousness"—free-floating, cut off from reality, objectively lacking in responsibility, and having no jurisdiction. Max Weber's opposition between the irresponsible dilettantism that follows an ethics of conviction and the virtue of the competent professional politician who is in touch with reality and ready to take on responsibility returns here—now, however, generalized to refer to *all* those practically involved in economics, administration of any kind, associations and unions, even the learned professions.[49] For the intellectuals who were Gehlen's original target were not politically engaged scholars and scientists but only political journalists and writers.

That changed in the course of the 1970s, as the terrorism of the Red Army Faction offered both the occasion and the pretext for enriching Gehlen's critique of the intellectual with another piece redeemed from the discussion of the 1920s, Carl Schmitt's theory of the domestic enemy, and extending it to left-wing intellectuals in the universities. The descendants of the mandarins of old had been provoked by the protest movement. From their ranks were recruited the counterintellectuals who, like Schelsky and Sontheimer,[50] took up Gehlen's critique of the intellectual and worked it up into a Theory of the New Class—the "class" of the mediators of meaning. The *Tendenzwende*, the "ideological shift" in German politics, had produced a new type, that of the counterintellectual. This counterintellectual not only takes the form of a political opponent, as right-wing intellectuals have done since the days of the Action Française; he not only criticizes the opponent's negative traits, like the Weimar intellectuals who battled with one another; rather, he tries to explain why the already institutionalized role of the intellectual represents a social pathology. The counterintellectual works with the means of the intellectual to show that the intellectual should not even exist. For in this version it is the intellectual himself who is the sickness he tries to demonstrate in a society that without him would function well. And he has a place only in these theories, which warn of "overpoliticization," which would like to diminish the burden of legitimation to which government is subject, and which see social rationality as embodied only in subsystem-specific objective dynamics, not, any longer, in a democratic public sphere.[51]

But after three decades the intellectuals were clearly already so firmly established in the Federal Republic that the counterintellectuals could no longer stop the process of normalization. That became clear in the fall of 1977, [known as the "German autumn"], when for a short time the conservative parties wanted to exploit a critical mood aroused by terrorism, especially the abduction and murder of the industrialist Hans-Martin Schleyer, for a pogrom against left-wing intellectuals. As the *Letters in Defense of the Republic*, edited by F. Duve, Heinrich Böll, and R. Staeck, or the film series *Germany in Autumn*, initiated by Alexander Kluve, indicate, the intellectuals rose to the defense quickly and decisively. The activities of the ideological shift had a disconcerting effect on the other side as well: the rebellion against the normalization of a role that the neoconservative intellectuals themselves had meanwhile assumed rebounded, ironically, against its originators. Our right-wing intellectuals have stopped disavowing themselves and since then have been making use of the role they initially denounced, by no means without success. Today they are already planning a "move into the public sphere" when, encouraged by a Christian Democratic senator, they set about founding an academy of science and scholarship.[52] In the process the neoconservative, of course, always runs into the temptation to betray the intellectual he is to the ideology planner he would like to be. In the meantime, Heine too has been rehabilitated. The most elegant testimony to this is the answer Golo Mann gave on a similar occasion to the question, "To whom does Heine belong"?: "Heine belongs to no one. Better yet, he belongs to all who love him."[53] If the figure of Heine has been a shadow image of the German intellectual, then with a Heine who belongs to everyone the role of the intellectual must have become unproblematic, even in Heine's fatherland—must have become, in fact, so mundane that the Left no longer has to claim a monopoly on it.

Notes

1. Cited in M. Stark, ed., *Deutsche Intellektuelle 1910–1933* (Heidelberg, 1984), p. 94.

2. Max Weber, *From Max Weber: Essays in Sociology*, Hans Gerth and C. Wright Mills, eds. (New York, 1958), p. 115.

3. Heinrich Heine, *Germany, A Winter's Tale*, tr. Herman Salinger (New York, 1944), p. 10.

4. Peter Uwe Hohendahl, *Literarische Kultur im Zeitalter des Liberalismus 1830–1870* (Munich, 1985).

5. W. Hädecke, *Heinrich Heine* (Munich, 1985), especially pp. 7–28.

6. De Gaulle is said to have made this remark with respect to Sartre: see Régis Debray, *Voltaire verhaftet man nicht: Die Intellektuellen und die Macht in Frankreich* (Cologne, 1981).

7. Dietz Bering, *Die Intellektuellen* (Stuttgart, 1978), p. 43ff.

8. Bering, p. 263ff.

9. In M. Stark, *Deutsche Intellektuelle*, p. 363.

10. Theodor W. Adorno, *Eingriffe* (Frankfurt, 1963), p. 32.

11. This phrase and the ones that follow are taken from Otto Flake, "Von der jüngsten Literatur" (1915), in Stark, p. 79ff.

12. Thomas Mann, *Reflections of a Nonpolitical Man* (New York, 1983), p. 40.

13. See Fritz K. Ringer, *The Decline of the German Mandarins: The German Academic Community 1890–1933* (Cambridge, MA, 1969); and my review of it in Jürgen Habermas, *Philosophisch-politische Profile* (Frankfurt, 1981), p. 458ff. (This essay is not included in the English translation of *Philosophisch-politische Profile*.)

14. R. Becher, "Partei und Intellektuelle," in Stark, p. 299.

15. W. Stapel, "Der Geistige und sein Volk" (1930), p. 315.

16. Theodor W. Adorno, "Die Wunde Heine," in *Noten zur Literatur* I (Frankfurt, 1958), p. 145.

17. Adorno, "Die Wunde Heine," p. 145f.

18. Heine, preface to *Germany, a Winter's Tale*, in *The Complete Poems of Heinrich Heine*, tr. Hal Draper (Boston, 1982), p. 482.

19. In his *Aufklärung heute* (Frankfurt, 1985), p. 139ff., here p. 148, Hans Mayer calls attention to the most radical of Heine's *New Poems*, published in 1944, "Seraphine," in *Complete Poems*, p. 332: "Upon this rock we'll build a church/ All suffering transcended,/ The Church of the third New Testament,/ The days of pain are ended./ Annulled the great Antithesis/ That held us along deluded;/ The stupid torments of the flesh/ Are over now, concluded."

20. Heine, "Briefe über Deutschland," *Sämtliche Schriften*, ed. K. Brieglub (Munich, 1968ff.), Vol. V, p. 196ff.

21. Heine, "Religion and Philosophy in Germany," in *Selected Works* (New York, 1973), p. 420.

22. "Religion and Philosophy in Germany," p. 354.

23. Heine, "The Romantic School," in *Selected Works*, p. 223.

24. In the otherwise accurate analysis by M. Windfuhr, "Zum Verhältnis von Dichtung und Politik bei Heinrich Heine," *Heine Jahrbuch* 24 (1985), p. 103ff., insufficient attention is paid to the radical motifs of a libertarian and hedonistic socialism, which explain Heine's distance both from Börne and from Marx and Ruge.

25. Heine, *Sämtliche Schriften*, Vol. III, p. 670.

26. Heine, preface to "Lutetia," in *Sämtliche Schriften*, Vol. V, p. 232.

27. In his poems, Heine develops the intentional refraction of the Romantic legacy to the point of virtuosity. It becomes almost routine for him to contradict the gentle tenor with which he at first ingratiates himself into the reader's horizon of expectations, a horizon established by Romanticism, negating it in the last line. See, for example, in the *New Poems*, "Seraphine" or "Yolante and Marie." Because of this, the most moving passages also acquire a functionalist quality; they are characterized by the glossiness of something that is beautiful in the instrumental sense. Adorno's reservations about Heine's poetry, to which he prefers the prose, are to be explained on this basis. We hear the echo of Karl Kraus's verdict when Adorno says, "Heine's poems were ready mediators between art and an everyday reality bereft of meaning. The experiences with which they dealt became raw material to be written about, as for the feuilletonist; they made the nuances and values they discovered interchangeable at the same time, delivered them over to a ready-made language." Adorno, "Die Wunde Heine," p. 147.

28. Gottfried Benn, "Der neue Staat und die Intellektuellen," in Stark, p. 336.

29. Heine, letter of August 10, 1930, in *The Poetry and Prose of Heinrich Heine*, Frederic Ewen, ed. (New York, 1948), p. 394.

30. Heine, "The Romantic School," in *Selected Works*, p. 242.

31. Hermann Hesse, "Phantasien," in Stark, p. 184.

32. Heine, "The Romantic School," p. 168.

33. Heine, preface to "Lutetia," p. 232.

34. Heine, "Ludwig Börne," in *Sämtliche Schriften*, Vol. IV, p. 133.

35. Heine, "Religion and Philosophy in Germany," p. 275.

36. Heine, "Religion and Philosophy in Germany," p. 366.

37. Heine, *Germany, A Winter's Tale* (New York, 1944), p. 30.

38. W. Herzog, "Unabhängigkeits-Erklärung des Geistes," in Stark, p. 200.

39. E. Hoernle, "Die Kommunistische Partei und die Intellektuellen," in Stark, p. 255.

40. Heine, "Religion and Philosophy in Germany," p. 367.

41. Heine, *Germany, A Winter's Tale* (New York, 1944), p. 36.

42. Heine, *Germany, A Winter's Tale*, p. 79.

43. Cf. H. Glaser, *Bundesrepublikanische Lesebuch, Drei Jahrzehnte geistiger Auseinandersetzung* (Munich/Vienna, 1978).

44. On these observations, see Hauke Brunkhorst, "Im Schatten der Wahrheit. Notizen über Philosophie und Denken mit öffentlichem Anspruch," in *Neue Rundschau* 95 (1984), p. 120ff.

45. The subtitle of Helmut Schelsky's *Die Arbeit tun die Anderen* (Opladen, 1975).

46. A. Steil, "Selbstverwandlung und Ich-Opfer. Zur Ethik des Klassenverrats," in *Düsseldorfer Debatte* 10 (1985), p. 27ff.

47. Joseph Schumpeter, *Capitalism, Socialism, and Democracy* (New York, 1950), pp. 145–155.

48. Arnold Gehlen, "Das Engagement der Intellektuellen gegen den Staat," in his *Einblicke* (Frankfurt, 1978), p. 253ff.

49. Gehlen, p. 255.

50. Kurt Sontheimer, *Das Elend unserer Intellektuellen. Linke Theorie in der Bundesrepublik Deutschland* (Hamburg, 1976), p. 263ff.

51. Helmut Dubiel, *Was ist Neokonservatismus?* (Frankfurt, 1985). Recently the *Frankfurter Allgemeine Zeitung*'s feuilleton section has been using guest columnists from other countries to support the polemic of the domestic anti-intellectuals. Using Günter Grass as an example, Hilton Kramer complains (in the *FAZ*, April 11, 1986), that opposition intellectuals have become an "obstacle to democracy."

52. *Denkschrift für die Gründung einer Akademie der Wissenschaften zu Berlin*, p. 15. See also the *Streitschrift gegen die Akademie der Wissenschaften zu Berlin* published by the Alternative Liste Berlin (Berlin, 1986).

53. Golo Mann, "Heine, wem gehört er?" in *Neue Rundschau* 83 (1972), reprinted in G. Busch and J. H. Freund, eds., *Gedanke und Gewissen* (Frankfurt, 1986), p. 465ff.

4

The Idea of the University: Learning Processes

I

In the first issue of *Die Wandlung* [*The Transformation*], a journal founded shortly after World War II by Karl Jaspers and Alfred Weber, Dolf Sternberger and Alexander Mitscherlich, one can read the text of an address delivered by Jaspers, who was returning from inner emigration to reassume his chair in philosophy, at the reopening of the University of Heidelberg in 1945: Karl Jaspers, "The Renewal of the University." With an emphasis appropriate to the new beginning of which the contemporary historical situation held out the prospect, Jaspers took up the central theme of his book *The Idea of the University*, which had first appeared in 1923 and was reprinted in 1946. Fifteen years later, in 1961, a revised edition of the book appeared. In the intervening period Jaspers had seen his expectations disappointed. Impatiently, almost imploringly, he wrote in the preface to the revised version: "Either we will succeed in preserving the German university through a rebirth of its idea in the decision to create a new organizational form, or the university will end up in the functionalism of giant institutions for the training and development of specialized scientific and technical expertise. This is why it is crucial to envision . . . the

In the summer of 1986 the Heidelberg Municipal Theater organized a lecture series in celebration of the six-hundredth anniversary of the founding of the University of Heidelberg. This lecture was given as part of that series, in the city in which Habermas began his teaching career with Gadamer and Löwith.

possibility of a renewal of the university on the basis of its idea."[1]

Jaspers was still unabashedly proceeding from premises derived from the implicit sociology of German Idealism. Institutions are forms of objective spirit. An institution remains capable of functioning only as long as it embodies in living form the idea inherent in it. As soon as the spirit leaves it, an institution rigidifies into something purely mechanical, as an organism without a soul decomposes into dead matter.

Once the unifying bond of its corporative consciousness disintegrates, the university too ceases to form a whole. The functions the university fulfills for society must preserve an inner connection (via a web of intentions), as it were, with the goals, motivations, and actions of the members cooperating in its division of labor. In this sense the university is to embody institutionally and anchor motivationally a form of life, in fact an exemplary form of life, in which its members share intersubjectively. What since Humboldt has been called "the idea of the university" is the project of embodying an ideal form of life. Further, this idea is to be distinguished from other foundational ideas in that it refers not to only one of the many particular forms of life found in the occupationally stratified early bourgeois society, but rather—thanks to its intimate connection with science, scholarship, and truth—to something universal, something prior to the plurality of social life forms. The idea of the university refers to the formative principles in accordance with which *all* forms of objective spirit are structured.

Even if we disregard this extravagant claim to exemplary status, isn't the very premise that a vast structure like the modern university system should be permeated with and sustained by a way of thinking common to its members unrealistic? "Only someone who carries the idea of the university in himself can think and act appropriately on behalf of the university," wrote Jaspers.[2] Couldn't he have learned from Max Weber that the organizational reality into which the functionally specific subsystems of a highly differentiated society settle and take shape rests on completely different premises? The capacity of such operations and institutions to function depends precisely on the detachment of organizational goals and functions from the motivations of their members. Organizations no longer embody ideas. Those who would bind them to ideas would have to restrict the scope of their operations to the comparatively narrow horizon of the lifeworld intersubjectively shared by their members. One of the many articles of tribute with which the *Frankfurter Allgemeine Zeitung* indulged the University of Heidelberg on the six-hundredth anniversary of its founding thus came to the sobering conclusion: "Allegiance to Humboldt is the life-lie of our universities. They have no idea."[3] From this perspective, all the university reformers who, like Jaspers, have appealed, and with ever weaker voices still appeal, to the idea of the university belong to the defensive minds whose cultural criticism is rooted in hostility to modernization.

Jaspers was certainly not free from the idealistic tendencies of an educationally elitist bourgeois cultural pessimism to which sociology was alien, that is, from the background ideology of the German mandarins. But he was not the only one, nor even the most influential of those who, in arguing in the 1960s for a long overdue reform of the university, had recourse to the ideas of the nineteenth-century Prussian university reformers. In 1963, two years after the revised edition of Jaspers's book appeared, Helmut Schelsky entered the discussion with a book bearing the unequivocal title *Solitude and Freedom*. And two years later, the final version of an SDS position paper originally presented in 1961 appeared under the title *The University in a Democracy*. Three works on reform, from three generations with three different perspectives. Each marks an increasing distance from Humboldt, and a growing social-scientific disenchantment with the idea of the university. Yet despite the distance between the generations and the intellectual reorientation that has taken place, none of these three parties is able to completely abandon the notion that the central issue remains a critical renewal of that very idea: "University reform today," Schelsky wrote, "is a re-creation and transformation of its normative models, thus a recapitulation in contemporary terms of the task Humboldt and his contemporaries accomplished for the university."[4] And the preface I wrote at that time for the SDS position paper closes with the statement:

"This work may seem provocative to those who propose to simply continue a great tradition *without disruption*. But this critique is so merciless only because it derives its criterion from the better spirit of the university. The authors"—at that time students in Berlin, now established and well-known professors like Claus Offe and Ulrich Preuss—"identify themselves with what the German university once claimed to be."[5]

Today twenty years and an organizational reform of the university that was carried out halfheartedly and has in part already been rescinded separate us from these attempts to give the university new form in the light of a renewal of its idea. Now that the dust of the polemics over the group university set up during this period has settled, we are resigned to seeing a polarized university landscape. What can we learn from these twenty years? It looks as though the realists who, as Jaspers noted, were already saying after World War I, "The university is dead! Let us abandon the illusions! Let us not pursue fictions!"[6] were right. Or did we simply misunderstand the role that such an idea could play, now as then, in the self-understanding of learning processes organized in university form? Did the university, as it gained in functional specificity within a system of science and scholarship [*Wissenschaftssystem*] that was differentiating itself with increasing rapidity,* have to discard what was once called its idea, like an empty shell? Or is the university form of organized scientific and scholarly learning processes dependent even today on a *bundling* of functions that requires if not a normative model still a certain commonality in the self-interpretations of the members of the university—the residue of a corporative consciousness?

II

Perhaps a look at the *external* development of the university will suffice to answer these questions. The expansion of education after World War II was a worldwide phenomenon that

---

*"*Wissenschaft*," as Habermas will remark later in this essay, has a broad range of meaning. It covers any organized branch of knowledge, thus including the humanities and social sciences as well as the physical or natural sciences. I have usually translated it as "science and scholarship." (translator's note)

led Talcott Parsons to speak of an "educational revolution." In the German Reich the number of students was halved between 1933 and 1939, dropping from 121,000 to 56,000. In 1945, only fifteen universities were still in existence in the area later to become the Federal Republic of Germany. By the mid-1950s, however, fifty universities were accommodating about 150,000 students. At the beginning of the 1960s, a planned expansion of the tertiary sector was begun. Since then the number of students has once again quadrupled. Today over a million students are being educated at ninety-four universities.[7] These figures, of course, reveal their significance only in the context of international comparisons.

In almost all the industrial societies of the West, the trend toward expanding formal education began after 1945 and continued in intensified form until the end of the 1970s; in the developed socialist nations, the same expansion phase was concentrated in the 1950s. UNESCO figures show that in the period between 1950 and 1980 the rate of secondary school attendance in all industrial countries increased from 30 to 80 percent, and the rate of university enrollment went from barely 4 percent to 30 percent. The parallels in the educational expansion of various industrial societies become even clearer if one compares, as does the Max Planck Institute for Educational Research's forthcoming second report on education, the selectivity of the educational system in the Federal Republic with that of the United States, Great Britain, France, and East Germany. Although the national educational systems of these countries are structured very differently, and despite distinctions in their political and social systems, the figures show the same orders of magnitude for the highest levels of qualification. If one measures the educational elite in terms of higher academic degrees (usually the completion of a dissertation), it comprises between 1.5 and 2.6 percent of those born in a given year; if one defines it in terms of completion of the most important forms of extended academic study (the bachelor's degree, the master's degree, state examinations), it represents between 8 and 10 percent of a given age group. The authors of the second *Report on Education* extended this comparison into areas of qualitative differentiation and found, for example, that publications and scholarly productivity, as estimated by external indicators, showed a surprisingly high degree of correspondence internationally in individual fields—completely independently of whether the national university systems were more openly structured or more strongly oriented to selectivity and the formation of elites.[8]

For all their stubborn resistance to government-mandated reforms, furthermore, it is not only in the quantitative dimensions that German universities have changed. The most salient features of a specifically German heritage have been stripped away. Antiquated hierarchies were dismantled with the university of the *Ordinarius* professor; and with a certain leveling of status the mandarin ideology also lost its basis. External and internal differentiation have caused teaching and research to become more separate. In sum, even in their internal structures the mass universities of the Federal Republic have come to resemble the universities of other industrialized nations.

From the distance provided by the international comparisons of educational sociology, then, a picture emerges that makes a functionalist interpretation compelling. According to this interpretation, the general patterns of social modernization also determined the development of the university, a development that began a decade later in the Federal Republic than it did in East Germany or in other Western countries. During the period of greatest acceleration, educational expansion generated ideologies that conformed to it. During that period the debate between the reformers and the defenders of a status quo that had become untenable seems to have been conducted on both sides under the false premise that the issue was whether to renew the idea of the university or to preserve it in its current form. In these ideological forms, a process intended by neither of the two parties took place—a process which rebelling students in turn opposed as "technocratic university reform." It seems that the only thing that took place in Germany under the aegis of reform was a new phase in the differentiation of the system of science and scholarship, which, here as everywhere, has become functionally autonomous, and which is less and less in need of normative integration in the minds of professors and students the more it comes to be steered by systemic mechanisms and oriented to the environments of the economy and administrative planning through the production by the individual disciplines of technically usable information and professional qualifications. The pragmatic recommendations of the *Wissenschaftsrat* [Science Advisory Council], which call for a shift in emphasis toward systemic control, disciplinary autonomy, and the differentiation of research and teaching, fit in with this picture.[9]

But the *Wissenschaftsrat*'s reserve when it comes to questions of intellectual politics leaves room for other interpretations. Their cautious recommendations do not necessarily imply a functionalist reading in line with the currently widespread neoconservative pattern of interpretation. On the one hand, that interpretation favors a functionally differentiated system of science and scholarship for which the integrative normative force of an ideal center anchored in a corporative self-understanding would only be a hindrance; on the other hand, university jubilees like the one we are now celebrating are used as rhetorical occasions to spread over the university's autonomy, now congealed into a system, the traditional mantle of an autonomy that was once understood in a completely different way, namely normatively. Under this veil, information flowing between subsystems that have become functionally autonomous, between the universities and the economic-military-industrial complex, can be coordinated all the more inconspicuously. Viewed from a sociological perspective, of course, this neoconservative interpretation could itself be merely a reflection of a cycle in the educational sector that follows its own course—unmoved by the policies or the themes and theories that it helps to ascendancy at any given time.

Until the end of the Grand Coalition, the activist educational policy set in motion in West Germany during the course of an overdue push for modernization at the beginning of the 1960s rested on a viable consensus among all parties; during Brandt's first administration, the Federal Republic experienced a boom in the area of educational policy—and the beginning of polarization. The downswing finally begin in 1974; since that time educational policy has been affected from both directions by the economic crisis that set in: those just finishing their studies have faced more difficult conditions in the labor market, while with respect to costs and financing universities have been affected by the government's fiscal crisis.[10] Thus, what to the neoconservatives currently appears as a realistic reorientation of educational policy can also be understood as a phenomenon of the recession in educational planning, to be explained primarily in terms of economics and politics.[11] But if upswings and downswings in the educational sector cut through themes and theories, then the functionalist interpretation dominant today should not simply be taken at face value either. Processes of differentiation that have accelerated over the last two decades do not *have to* be described in terms of systems theory, and they do not *have to* lead to the conclusion that universities have now left the horizon of the lifeworld behind completely.

The traditional bundling of different functions under the roof of one institution, and the awareness that in that institution the process of acquiring scientific knowledge is intertwined not only with technical development and preparation for the academic professions but also with general education, the transmission of culture, and enlightenment in the public political sphere, might be of vital importance for research itself. Empirically, it seems to be an open question whether the impetus behind scientific and scholarly learning processes would not ultimately become paralyzed if those processes became specialized exclusively for the function of research. Scientific and scholarly productivity might be dependent upon university forms of organization, dependent, that is, on the internally differentiated complex that includes the training of future scientists and scholars, preparation for the academic professions, and participation in processes of general education, cultural self-understanding, and the formation of public opinion.

The universities are still rooted in the lifeworld through this remarkable bundling of functions. Of course, *within* the university the general processes of socialization, cultural transmission, and social-integrative will-formation, through which the lifeworld reproduces itself, are carried on only under the highly artificial conditions of academic learning processes programmed for the acquisition of knowledge. As long as this complex has not been completely torn apart, the idea of the university cannot be completely dead. The complexity and inner differentiation of this complex, however, should not be underestimated. When the classical German university was born, the Prussian reformers sketched an image of the university that suggests an oversimplified connection between scientific and scholarly learning processes and forms of life in modern societies. Taking the perspective of an idealist philosophy of reconciliation, they attributed to the university a power of totalization that necessarily overburdened this institution from the beginning. The idea of the university in Germany owes its fascination—which extended on into the 1960s—not least to this impulse. How much of its force it has lost in the meantime can be seen in the location of this lecture series. The fact that it is the Heidelberg Municipal Theater that has taken the praiseworthy step of sponsoring it suggests that new life can be breathed into the idea of the university only from outside its walls.

In order to clarify the complexity of the connection between the university and the lifeworld, I would like to separate the essential core of the idea from the shell of its oversimplifications. I will begin by going back to the classical idea in Schelling, Humboldt, and Schleiermacher, and then examine the three variants of its renewal offered by Jaspers, Schelsky, and the SDS reformers.

III

Humboldt and Schleiermacher connect two notions with the idea of the university. First, they are concerned with the problem of how modern science and scholarship, released from the tutelage of religion and the church, can be institutionalized without their autonomy being threatened from another quarter—whether by the commands of the state authority that makes the external existence of science and scholarship possible or by influence from bourgeois society, which has an interest in applying the results of scientific and scholarly work. Humboldt and Schleiermacher see the solution to the problem in a state-organized autonomy of science and scholarship that would shield institutions of higher learning from both political intervention and societal imperatives. At the same time, Humboldt and Schleiermacher—and this is the second notion—also want to explain why it is in the interest of the state itself to guarantee the university the external form of an internally unlimited freedom. A *Kulturstaat* of this kind is to be desired for the beneficial consequences that the unifying, totalizing power of science and scholarship institutionalized as research would necessarily have. If scientific and scholarly work were left to the inner dynamics of the research process, and if the principle of "regarding science as something that has not yet been and never will be completely discovered"[12] were maintained, then, both were convinced, the moral culture, indeed the whole spiritual life of the nation would come to be concentrated in the institutions of higher learning.[13]

These two notions merged to form the idea of the university, and they explain some of the more striking features of the German university tradition. They make comprehensible (1) the affirmative relationship of university scholarship, which thinks of itself as apolitical, to the state; (2) the defensive relationship of the university to professional practice, especially to educational requirements that could jeopardize the principle of the unity of teaching and research; and (3) the central position of the philosophical faculty within the university and the emphatic significance attributed to science and scholarship for culture and society as a whole. In German, in fact, the word *"Wissenschaft"* has accumulated such rich connotations that there is no simple equivalent for it in English or French. Thus the idea of the university produced on the one hand an emphasis on the autonomy of science and scholarship, which fosters development because it points to the functional independence of the system of science and scholarship. This autonomy, of course, was to be made use of only in "solitude and freedom," at a distance from bourgeois society and the political public sphere. From the idea of the university there also comes, on the other hand, the general culture-shaping power of a science in which the totality of the lifeworld was to be concentrated in reflexive form. In order to maintain its defensive relationship to bourgeois society and its internal relationship to the lifeworld as a whole, of course, such a science, which was envisioned as a philosophical fundamental science, has to fulfill very special conditions.

The reformers of that period were able to think of the scientific process as a narcissistically self-enclosed circular process of research and teaching because the philosophy of German Idealism by its very nature required a *unity of teaching and research*. Whereas today a discussion of the current status of research in a certain area and a presentation of the same material for instructional purposes are two different things, Schelling, in his *Lectures on the Methodology of Academic Study*, demonstrated that the form in which a philosophical idea is transmitted pedagogically arises out of its construction. To the mere "historical presentation" of finished results he opposes the constructive unfolding "of the whole of a science from inner living intuition."[14] In a word, this type of theory required a constructive form that was equivalent to the curriculum of its presentation.

In the same way, according to Schelling, the university's inner connection to the lifeworld was due to the totalizing power of science and scholarship. The reformers attributed to philosophy a unifying power with regard to what we now call cultural tradition, socialization, and social integration. First, the philosophical fundamental science was structured *encyclopedically*, and as such was able to ensure both unity in the multiplicity of scientific and scholarly disciplines and the unity of science and scholarship with art and criticism on the one hand and law and morality on the other. Philosophy presented itself as a reflexive form of culture as a whole. Second, its basic *Platonist* character was to assure the unity of research processes with the processes by which a person acquired general education. For when ideas are comprehended they are simultaneously incorporated into the knower's ethical character, and they free it of any onesidedness. This elevation to the absolute opens the way for the full development of individuality. Because involvement with this kind of science makes one rational, the "nurseries of science" can at the same time be "institutions of general education."[15] Finally, the fact that all theory formation was *grounded in the philosophy of reflection* promised a unity of science and scholarship with enlightenment. Whereas today philosophy has become a subject that attracts the esoteric interest of specialists, a philosophy that was based on the epistemological subject's relationship to himself and that developed cognitive contents through the reflective movement of thought could satisfy the specialist's esoteric interest in science at the same time as the lay person's exoteric interest in self-understanding and enlightenment.[16] By grasping its age in thought, as Hegel was to say, philosophy was to replace the integrative social force of religion with the reconciling force of reason. Thus Fichte could see the university, which merely institutionalized a science of this kind, as the birthplace of an emancipated society of the future, even as the locus of the education of the nation. For philosophy, which provides training in reflection, creates clarity not only about things that remain alien to us, but about the innermost root of our life: "Every scientific body must desire to be surrounded by this clarity, on the basis of self-interest, and must promote it with all its might; thus, once it has achieved more self-consistency it must proceed irresistibly to the organization of the education of the nation, as its proper ground, to clarity and freedom of the spirit, and thus prepare and make possible the renewal of all human relationships."[17]

One does not realize just how daring and improbable the idea of the university defined in these famous founding documents was until one realizes the conditions that would have had to be fulfilled for such a science to be institutionalized—a science that is to make possible and to ensure, solely on the basis of its internal structure, the unity of research and teaching, the unity of the scientific and scholarly disciplines, the unity of science and scholarship with general education, and the unity of science and scholarship with enlightenment.

Strictly speaking, the unity of research and teaching means that teaching and learning will take place only in the manner required for the innovative process of scientific progress. Science and scholarship are to be able to reproduce themselves in the additional sense that professors are to train their own successors. The future researcher is the sole goal for the sake of which a university composed of teaching scholars takes on the tasks of instruction. This restriction of academic professional preparation to the nurturing of the next generation of scientists and scholars did in fact retain a certain plausibility, at least for the philosophical faculty, as long as university professors still replenished their ranks from the circle of *Gymnasium* teachers they had trained.

Further, the unity of the scientific and scholarly disciplines could be put into effect only if the upper faculties that held the leadership in science and scholarship were subordinated to a completely restructured arts faculty, and if philosophy, whose seat was in the arts faculty, did in fact advance to the status of the primary science on which the combined natural sciences and *Geisteswissenschaften* were based. This is the meaning of the polemic against "bread and butter" sciences, against the dispersal of the scientific and scholarly disciplines into organized schools, against the merely derivative character of faculties whose "unity [lies] not directly in knowledge but rather in an external occupation." The demand that the philosophical faculty assume leadership followed from this as a logical but from the outset counterfactual conclusion, "because all members of the university, no matter what faculty they are part of, must be rooted in philosophy."[18]

The unity of science and scholarship with general education had as its institutional precondition the unity of teachers and learners: "The relationship of teacher and student becomes completely different than before. The former does not exist for the sake of the latter; both exist for the sake of science."[19] This cooperatively structured and in principle egalitarian complementary relationship was to be realized in the discursive forms of the seminar. It was incompatible with the personnel structure that soon developed in the hierarchically organized institutes of a research practice modeled on the experimental natural sciences.

Finally, the idea of the unity of science and scholarship with enlightenment was extravagant in that it burdened the autonomy of the scientific and scholarly disciplines with the expectation that within its walls the university could anticipate in microcosm a society of free and equal citizens. The science of philosophy seemed to combine in itself the universal competences of the human species in such a way that the higher academic institutions were for Humboldt not only the pinnacle of the whole educational system but also the "apex of the moral culture of the nation." From the outset, however, it remained unclear how this mission of enlightenment and emancipation was to accompany the abstention from politics that was the price the university had to pay for state authorization of its freedom.

These institutional preconditions for the implementation of the fundamental idea of the German university were either nonexistent from the beginning or became increasingly less susceptible of fulfillment as the nineteenth century wore on. First, a differentiated occupational system required scientific and scholarly training for more and more academic professions. Technical colleges, business schools, teachers colleges, and art schools could not remain permanently outside the university. Second, the empirical sciences that sprang from the womb of the philosophical faculty pursued a methodological ideal of procedural rationality that doomed to failure any effort to situate their contents encyclopedically within an all-encompassing philosophical interpretation.[20] This emancipation of the empirical sciences sealed the disintegration of coherent metaphysical worldviews. In the midst of a plurality of beliefs, philosophy also lost its monopoly on the interpretation of culture as a whole. Third, science advanced to the status of an important productive force in industrial society. With Liebig's institute in Giessen in mind, for instance, the Baden state government emphasized as early as 1850 the "extraordinary importance of chemistry for agriculture."[21] The natural sciences gave up the role of providing a worldview for the sake of producing technically usable knowledge. Working conditions for research organized in the form of institutes were designed less to serve the functions of general education than to serve the functional imperatives of the economy and administration. Finally, academic education in Germany served to define the social stratum of the educated bourgeoisie, on the model of the upper-level civil servant.[22] The establishment of an occupational differentiation between popular and academic education, however, served as an acknowledgment of class structures that effectively gave the lie to the universalist content of the idea of the university and the promise it had held for the emancipation of society as a whole.[23]

As awareness of these countervailing developments grew, the idea of the university had to be asserted in ever greater opposition to the facts—it degenerated into the ideology of a professional class with a high level of social prestige. In the humanities and social sciences, Fritz K. Ringer dates the decline of the culture of the German mandarins to the period from 1890 to 1933.[24] In the inwardness of these mandarins, sheltered by official power, the neohumanist ideal of education had taken the distorted form of the intellectually elitist, apolitical, and bureaucratically conformist self-understanding of an educational institution that was removed from practice, internally autonomous, and intensively research oriented.[25] Of course one must also look at the positive side. In both its forms—as idea and as ideology—the idea of the university had contributed to the brilliance and the success, unparalleled elsewhere, of German university science and scholarship in the nineteenth century and even up into the 1930s. With state-organized scientific autonomy, responsibility for the differentiation of the scientific and scholarly disciplines was transferred to the unfettered internal dynamics of the research process itself. Under the aegis of a merely superficially adopted educational humanism, the natural sciences quickly won their autonomy and for all their positivism became, with their research work organized in institute form, a fruitful model even for the humanities and social sciences, where scholarly activity had originally been organized in seminar form.[26] At the same time, the ideology of the German mandarins provided the university with a strong corporative self-consciousness, with support from the *Kulturstaat,* and with a recognized position within society. And last but not least, the moment of utopian extravagance inherent in the idea of the university preserved a critical potential that was in accord with the fundamental convictions of Western rationalism and could be revived periodically in the service of a renewal of the institution of the university.

IV

This, at any rate, was the belief of the reformers of the early 1960s. The first impulses toward renewal after 1945 had been insufficient. Along with material depletion there was an exhaustion of the corporative consciousness. The idea of the university, in the traditional form of mandarin consciousness, had survived even the Nazis; but by virtue of its demonstrated impotence in the face of, or even complicity with, the Nazi regime, it stood convicted in all eyes of a lack of substance. Nevertheless, after 1945 the traditionalists representing the Humboldtian idea of the university remained strong enough, even on the defensive, to stave off well-intended attempts at reform and to reach an agreement with the pragmatists on the *Wissenschaftsvat,* which was established in the late 1950s. Thus the unavoidable quantitative growth of the universities took place in the form of an expansion within structures that remained otherwise unchanged. Looking back, Thomas Ellwein described this lack of decision as an expansion without reconstruction, a maintenance of the internal hierarchical structure of the university and the tertiary sector of education as a whole—with the universities at the head of it.[27]

This is the situation in which Jaspers once again returned to Humboldt; Schelsky and the SDS students attempted a critical reappropriation of the same heritage from a certain social-scientific distance by prefacing their proposals for reform with a sober diagnosis of the structural changes the university had undergone in the meantime. Formulating these changes as "the societalization of the university along with the scientization of professional practice," they explored the differentiation of academic subjects, the institutionalization of research, the bureaucratization of academic training, the loss of the functions of science and scholarship for general education and enlightenment, the change in personnel structure, and so forth. The international comparisons made by educational sociologists, the needs analyses produced by educational economists, and the civil rights postulates of the educational policy-makers were already present in the background. Schelsky summarized all this in the term "inherent dynamics," for these processes have a systemic character and produce structures detached from the lifeworld. They undermine the corporative consciousness of the university and shatter the fictional unities that Humboldt, Schleiermacher, and Schelling had tried to establish through the totalizing force of scientific and scholarly reflection. Interestingly, Schelsky was no more in favor of a simple adaptation on the part of the universities to those "inherent dynamics" than were the reformers on the Left; he did not opt for the kind of ongoing technocratic reform that has since become established practice. This is the option one would have expected him to choose, given the theory of technocracy he developed around the same time. Instead, drawing on the store of Humboldtian ideas, Schelsky calls for a "shaping" of the inherent dynamics: "The crucial point is that these inherent developmental tendencies are one-sided . . ., that a re-connection and formative countervailing forces must come into play; they cannot be taken for granted but only produced through creative efforts."[28] A differentiated system of science and scholarship should not simply merge with the economy, technology, and administration but rather should *remain* rooted in the lifeworld through the traditional bundling of its functions. And this bundling of functions, in turn, is to be explained in terms of the structure of science itself.

Thus, the theoretically ambitious reform initiatives of the early 1960s once again took as their point of departure the conception of a science that one could still credit with some kind of unifying power; and once again the university was conceived as being merely the external organizational form of this power. In the meantime, however, the position of philosophy vis-à-vis the scientific and scholarly disciplines had changed, so that it no longer formed the center of the differentiated scientific and scholarly fields. But what was to move into the place it had left vacant? Was it really necessary to hold onto the idea of the unity of the scientific and scholarly disciplines? Certainly the totalizing power of the scientific process could no longer be thought of as a synthesis and grounded in a metaphysical connection to the absolute or to the world as a whole. Theories that had recourse to totality—whether directly or by way of the scientific disciplines—were no longer up for discussion.

Jaspers offers a comparatively conventional answer. He admits that the rationalism of the empirical sciences, which do not have predetermined goals and are defined solely by methodology, is wholly procedural and can no longer provide a basis for substantive unity in a canon of disciplines that differentiate themselves unpredictably. But Jaspers still wants to reserve a special role for philosophy, which he had initially moved to the periphery and given the tasks of illuminating *Existenz* and analyzing a nonobjectifiable *Umgreifendes* ["the encompassing"], vis-à-vis the now emancipated scientific and scholarly disciplines. The scientific and scholarly disciplines, according to Jaspers, are even in need of the guidance of philosophy, because only philosophy, through its reflection on the presuppositions of research and its confirmation of the key ideas of research, can ensure the motivation of an unconditional desire for knowledge and the habitus of scientific thinking. Thus philosophy retains at least its role as guardian of the idea of the university—and the mission of setting the pace for reform.

Schelsky's reflections are less idealistic; he replaces philosophy with a theory of science. He proceeds from a threefold division of the scientific disciplines into the natural sciences, the social sciences, and the humanities. Individual disciplines develop autonomously, but each of the three groups of disciplines with its specific form of knowledge is functionally intermeshed with modern society in a different way. The disciplines as a body can no longer be encompassed by philosophical reflection; rather, philosophy now migrates into the various sciences and settles in each of them as its corresponding form of self-reflection. Thus there emerges an equivalent to the now fictitious unities of the Humboldtian university: "In that it *emerges from* the scientific disciplines and transcends them critically by taking them as its object, philosophy indirectly regains the whole of scientific civilization as its object. By investigating the limits and the conditions of the individual sciences, it keeps them open . . . in the face of their narrowing *relations to the world*."[29]

During the same period I advocated a material critique of science and scholarship that was to illuminate the interrelationships of methodologies, global background assumptions, and objective contexts of application.[30] I had the same hope as Schelsky—that in this dimension of scientific self-reflection it would be possible to make the connections of research processes to the lifeworld transparent in terms of those processes themselves, and not only their connections to the application of scientific and scholarly information but also and especially their connection to culture as a whole, to general processes of socialization, to the continuation of traditions, and to the enlightenment of the political public sphere.

Yet another element of the Humboldtian legacy was revived in these reform initiatives: the exemplary significance accorded the autonomy of science and scholarship, above and beyond the constitutional guarantee of freedom of teaching and research. Jaspers understood the autonomy of science and scholarship to mean the realization of an international communication network that would protect the free state from the totalitarian state.[31] Schelsky gave this a personalistic, existentialist twist: scientific autonomy would mean a detachment, practiced in obligatory solitude, from, and a moral sovereignty over both the pressures for action and the systemic reifications that result from the inherent dynamics of modern society that are in need of "shaping."[32] As for the authors of the SDS position paper on the university, the leftist reformers in general, although what we defended at the time as the "democratization of the university"[33] was not linked with the transference of models of will-formation on the national level to the university, nor with the formation of a state within the state, it was indeed linked with the expectation of a capacity for political action in the form of participatory self-management that was certainly intended to be exemplary.

This is not the place for a complete evaluation of the organizational reforms that were actually carried out; I will only say that the goals whose conceptions were derived from a critical appropriation of the idea of the university were not realized. Nor can I discuss the individual reasons for this that one can see in retrospect in attempting to explain the failure of this aspect of the reform initiatives. In a postscript to his book, added in 1970, Schelsky explains the failure of the reforms by the fact that under the pressure of increasing complexity the system of science and scholarship had become extremely differentiated and thus "could no longer be held together in its various functions by a shared guiding image."[34] The revealing expression "guiding image" points to premises that were perhaps truly too naive to keep pace with the dynamics of differentiation in research. It was clearly unrealistic to assume that a form of reflection not engendered by the logic of research itself could be implanted in research activity that was organized in terms of the differentiated disciplines. The history of the modern empirical sciences teaches us that *normal science* is characterized by routines and by an objectivism that shields the everyday practice of research from problemizations. Crises set off bursts of reflection, but even then the suppression of degenerating paradigms by new ones takes place quasi-naturally rather than through a reflective process. Where, in contrast, reflection on fundamental issues and the critique of science are ongoing, they become established—like philosophy itself—as one discipline among others. No less unrealistic was the expectation that collegial self-management in the universities would be filled with political vitality and attain the capacity for political action solely through the functionally organized participation of the groups involved, especially when the reforms had to be mandated administratively against the will of the professors.

But if the inner integrity of the university can no longer be saved even under these premises, should we not admit that this institution can get along perfectly well without the fond idea it once had of itself?

V

In the choice of its basic concepts, social-scientific systems theory makes a prior judgment: it assumes that all domains of social action are held together beneath the level of normative orientations by value-neutral control mechanisms such as money or administrative power. For systems theory, the integrative force of ideas and institutions belongs a priori to the more or less functional superstructure of a substratum of flows of action and communication that are tuned to one another as a system and do not require the addition of norms. I consider this prior judgment, which is purely methodological, to be premature. Norms and value orientations are *always* embedded in the context of a lifeworld; however differentiated the lifeworld may be, it remains a background totality, and it thus draws all processes of differentiation back into its totalizing vortex. The functions of the lifeworld—the reproduction of culture, socialization, and social integration—may become differentiated into special domains of action, but in the last analysis they *remain* enclosed within the horizon of the lifeworld and intertwined with one another. It is this very circumstance that systems theorists turn to their advantage: theoretical approaches, they say, that still take the integrative force of ideas and institutions seriously—the idea of the university, for example—fail to grasp social complexity. For in modern societies autonomous subsystems have formed that are not interlocked in any way and that are specialized for precisely one function and one kind of activity.

It is the spectacle of an economy steered by money or a state administrative system regulated by power relations that makes this assertion seem obvious. What is problematic in the assertion is its generalization to *all* systems of action—it is from this that systems theory derives its primary assertion. It suggests that every domain of social action, if it is to remain *au courant* in terms of social modernization, has to adopt the form of functionally specialized subsystems decoupled from one another and differentiated through steering media. It does not first ask whether that can be true for all domains of action, as for example cultural systems of action like scientific and scholarly activity, the nucleus of which has to this point always been lodged within a system of institutions that *bundles functions*—in universities, which have by no means outgrown the horizon of the lifeworld as have capitalist business enterprises or international agencies. We do not yet know whether large-scale and basic research activities that have moved out of the university will be able to detach themselves completely from the generative process of university-organized science and scholarship—

whether they will be able to stand completely on their own feet or will remain parasitical. It is at least plausible to suppose that the development of a scientific or scholarly field separated from university forms, and thus also from research, would suffer. For the present, the experience that Schelsky describes as follows speaks against this overgeneralization on the part of systems theory: "The unique aspect of the institutional development of the modern university resides in the fact that in this case functional differentiation occurs *within* the same institution, and there is scarcely any loss of function through transfer of tasks to other agencies. On the contrary, one can speak rather of an enrichment of functions, at least of an increase in significance and a broadening of the university's areas of functioning over the last hundred years of its development."[35]

Thus in his book on the American university,[36] which is still the definitive work on the sociology of higher education, Talcott Parsons proceeds on the assumption that the system of higher education fulfills *four* functions *at the same time:* The core function (a) of research and the training of new scientists and scholars goes hand in hand with (b) academic preparation for the professions (and the production of technically usable knowledge) on the one hand and (c) the tasks of general education and (d) contributions to cultural self-understanding and intellectual enlightenment on the other hand. In the system of higher education in the United States, which is more highly differentiated institutionally, Parsons can assign the first three functions listed to different institutions: the graduate schools, the professional schools, and the colleges. But each of these institutions is again so differentiated internally that it branches off (with varying emphasis, depending on the case) into all domains of function. Only the fourth function has no institutional vehicle of its own. It is fulfilled through the professors' role as intellectuals. if one considers that in this fourth function Parsons includes not only the externally directed work of enlightenment, which is addressed to the public, but also the reflection of the scientific and scholarly disciplines on their own role and on the relationship of the cultural spheres of value—science and scholarship, morality, and art—to one another, then one realizes that this catalogue of functions reproduces, in a different form, precisely what the Prussian university reformers once envisioned as "unities": the unity of research and teaching, the unity of science and scholarship with general education, the unity of science and scholarship with enlightenment, and the unity of the scientific and scholarly disciplines.

Of course, the significance of this last idea has changed substantially, for the openly differentiated multiplicity of the scientific and scholarly disciplines no longer represents as such the medium that can tie all those functions together. As before, however, the learning processes that take place within the university not only enter into an exchange with the economy and administration but also stand in an inner relationship to the functions through which the lifeworld reproduces itself. These learning processes extend beyond professional preparation to make a contribution to general processes of socialization by providing training in the scientific mode of thought, that is, in the hypothetical attitude toward facts and norms; they go beyond the production of expert knowledge to make a contribution to intellectual enlightenment with their informed political stands on concrete issues; they go beyond reflection on fundamental issues and questions of methodology to contribute to the hermeneutic continuation of tradition through the humanities, and to the self-understanding of the scientific and scholarly disciplines within the whole of culture through theories of science and scholarship, morality, art, and literature. It is the organization of scientific and scholarly learning processes in university form that continues to root the differentiated specialized disciplines in the lifeworld by fulfilling these various functions *simultaneously*.

The differentiation of the specific fields requires, of course, a correspondingly sharp differentiation within the university. That is a process that is still going on, as in the establishment of the postgraduate centers recommended by the *Wissenschaftsrat*, for example. Different groups with different vantage points within the university perceive the various functions as having different degrees of importance. In this way the corporative consciousness becomes diluted to an intersubjectively shared awareness that while some do different things than others, as a group all of them, insofar as they are engaged in one form of science or another, fulfill not just one but rather a whole complex of functions. These functions remain enmeshed with one another through the division of labor involved in the scientific process. Today, however, the fact that the functions remain tied together can hardly still be attributed, as Schelsky thought, to the binding force of the normative ideal of the German university. And would that even be desirable?

It is certainly valuable to use the six-hundred-year jubilee of the founding of a university to call to mind the idea of the university and what remains of that idea. The corporative consciousness of the members of the university, however diluted it may be, may even be strengthened by such a reminder—but only if the work of remembering itself takes on the form of a scientific analysis and does not remain a mere ceremony designed to compensate for the technocratic daily life of the university with pious sentiment. The corporative self-understanding of the university would be in trouble if it were anchored in something like a normative ideal, for ideas come and go. The ingenious thing about the old idea of the university was that it was supposed to be grounded in something more stable: the permanently differentiated scientific process itself. But if science can no longer be used to anchor ideas in this way, because the multiplicity of the disciplines no longer leaves room for the totalizing power of either an all-encompassing philosophical fundamental science or even a reflective form of material critique of science and scholarship that would emerge from the disciplines themselves, on what could an integrative self-understanding of the corporative body of the university be based?

Schleiermacher has already provided the answer: "The first law of all efforts directed toward knowledge [is] communication; and in the impossibility of producing anything at all without language, even if only for itself alone, nature herself has proclaimed this law quite clearly. From the drive for knowledge alone, then, . . . all the connections necessary for its practical satisfaction, the various forms of communication and the various forms of association among activities must develop of themselves." This is one of Schleiermacher's *Gelegentliche Ge-danken über Universitäten im deutschen Sinne* [*Reflections on Universities in the German Sense*],[37] and I refer to it without sentimentality, because I seriously believe that in the last analysis it is the communicative forms of scientific and scholarly argumentation that hold university learning processes in their various functions together. Schleiermacher considers the idea that "any scientific person could live shut off by himself in solitary labors and undertakings" to be an "empty illusion"; however much that person might seem to work alone in the library, at his desk, or in the laboratory, his learning processes are inevitably embedded in a public communication community of researchers. Because the enterprise of the cooperative search for truth refers back to these structures of public argumentation, truth—or even the reputation achieved within the community of investigators—can never become the mere steering medium of a self-regulating subsystem. The scientific and scholarly disciplines were constituted within specialized internal public spheres, and they can maintain their vitality only within these structures. The specialized internal public spheres come together and branch off again in the university's organized public events. The old-fashioned title of *ordentlicher öffentlicher Professor* [literally, ordinary public professor] serves to remind us of the public character of lectures, seminars, and scientific and scholarly cooperation among working groups at institutes affiliated with the university. What Humboldt said about the communicative relationship of professors with their students holds true not only for the ideal form of the seminar but also for the normal form of scientific work: "If they (students and younger colleagues) did not of themselves gather around him," the teacher would "seek them out in order to better achieve his ends by joining his powers, which are trained and for that very reason less vital and more inclined to become one-sided, to theirs, which are weaker and still strike out courageously and impartially in all directions."[38]

I can assure you that this sentence describes the more tightly organized activities of a Max Planck Institute just as faithfully as those of a philosophy seminar. Even outside the university, scientific and scholarly learning processes retain something of their original university form. They are all sustained by the stimulating and productive forces of a discursive debate that carries with it the promissory note of the surprising argument. The doors stand open; at any moment a new viewpoint may emerge, a new idea appear unexpectedly.

I do not want to repeat the mistake of characterizing the communication community of researchers as something exemplary. The egalitarian and universalistic content of its forms of argumentation expresses only the norms of scientific and scholarly activity, not those of society as a whole. But they share emphatically in the communicative rationality in whose forms modern societies, that is, societies which are not fixed once and for all and which have no guiding images, must reach an understanding about themselves.

Notes

1. Karl Jaspers and K. Rossman, *Die Idee der Universität* (Heidelberg, 1961).

2. Jaspers and Rossmann, p. 36.

3. K. Reumann, "Verdunkelte Wahrheit," in the *Frankfurter Allgemeine Zeitung*, March 24, 1986.

4. Helmut Schelsky, *Einsamkeit und Freiheit* (Hamburg, 1963), p. 274.

5. W. Nitsch, U. Gerhardt, Claus Offe, and Ulrich K. Preuss, *Hochschule in der Demokratie* (Neuwied, 1965), p. vi.

6. Jaspers and Rossmann, p. 7.

7. This does not include an additional 94 technical schools and 26 art schools. See H. Köhler and J. Naumann, "Trends der Hochschulentwicklung 1970 bis 2000," in *Recht der Jugend und des Bildungswesens* 6:32 (1984), p. 419ff. An overview can be found in Max Planck Institut für Bildungsforschung, *Das Bildungswesen in der Bundesrepublik* (Hamburg, 1984), p. 228ff.

8. Max Planck Institut für Bildungsforschung, *Bildungsbericht II*.

9. Wissenschaftsrat, *Empfehlungen und Stellungnahmen*, 1984; *Empfehlungen zum Wettbewerb im deutschen Hochschulsystem*, 1985; *Empfehlungen zur Struktur des Studiums*, 1985; *Empfehlungen zur klinischen Forschung*, 1985.

10. K. Hüfner, J. Naumann, H. Köhler, and G. Pfeffer, *Hochkonjunktur und Flaute:*

Bildungspolitik in der BRD (Stuttgart, 1986), p. 200ff. See also K. Hüfner and J. Naumann, *Konjunkturen der Bildungspolitik in der BRD* (Stuttgart, 1977).

11. An indication of this is the uneven developments in educational reform proposals from one country to the next. Thus last year, for example, fifty professors at the Collège de France presented the President of that country with recommendations for educational reform that in their goals and tenor were very reminiscent of the reform climate in the Federal Republic during the 1960s. The recommendations, inspired by Pierre Bourdieu, appeared in *Neue Sammlung* 3:25 (1985).

12. Wilhelm von Humboldt, "Über die innere und äussere Organisation der höheren Wissenschaftlichen Anstalten" (1810), in E. Anrich, ed., *Die Idee der deutschen Universität* (Darmstadt, 1959), p. 379.

13. "In any case a decent and noble life is no more possible for the state than it is for the individual, as long as one fails to attach a general meaning to proficiency in a specific area of knowledge, which is always limited. The state as well as the individual makes it a natural and necessary presupposition for all this knowledge that it be grounded in science and that it can be properly reproduced and perfected only through science." Friedrich Schleiermacher, "Gelegentliche Gedanken über Universitäten im deutschen Sinn" (1808), in Anrich, p. 226.

14. F.W.J. Schelling, "Vorlesungen über die Methode des akademischen Studiums" (1802), in Anrich, p. 20.

15. Schelling, in Anrich, p. 21.

16. E. Martens and Herbert Schnädelbach, *Philosophie-Grundkurs* (Hamburg, 1985), p. 22ff.

17. Johann G. Fichte, "Deduzierter Plan einer in Berlin zu errichtenden höheren Lehranstalt," in Anrich, p. 217.

18. Schleiermacher, in Anrich, p. 259f.

19. Humboldt, in Anrich, p. 378.

20. On the reactions of German philosophy to this new situation, see Herbert Schnädelbach, *Philosophie in Deutschland 1831–1933* (Frankfurt, 1983), p. 118ff. (English translation, *Philosophy in Germany 1831 to 1933*, Cambridge, Eng., 1984, p. 91ff.)

21. J. Klüwer, *Universität und Wissenschaftssystem* (Frankfurt, 1983), p. 1985.

22. L. von Friedeburg, "Elite—elitar?" in G. Becker et al., eds., *Ordnung und Unordnung* (Weinheim, 1986), p. 23ff.

23. Thomas Ellwein, *Die deutsche Universität* (Königstein, 1985), p. 124ff.

24. Fritz K. Ringer, *The Decline of the German Mandarins* (Cambridge, MA, 1969).

25. See my review of Ringer's book *The Decline of the German Mandarins* in Jürgen Habermas, *Philosophisch-Politische Profile* (Frankfurt, 1981), p. 458ff.

26. For a discussion of this thesis, see J. Klüwer, *Universität und Wissenschaftssystem*.

27. Ellwein, p. 238.

28. Schelsky, p. 275.

29. Schelsky, p. 290.

30. Jürgen Habermas, "Vom sozialen Wandel akademischer Bildung" and "Universität in der Demokratie—Demokratisierung der Universität," in his *Kleine Politische Schriften I–IV* (Frankfurt, 1981), p. 101ff. and 134ff.

31. Jaspers and Rossman, p. 33ff.

32. Schelsky, p. 299: "The danger [is] that man will expend himself only in outer action that transforms the environment and maintain and deal with everything, other men as well as himself, on this object level of constructive action. This new form of human self-alienation, which can rob man of the inner identity of himself and others, this new metaphysical temptation, is the danger that the creator will lose himself in his work, the constructor will lose himself in his construction. People are horrified at the thought of transferring themselves completely into self-produced objectivity, and yet they labor unceasingly to further this process of scientific-technical self-objectivation."

33. See note 30.

34. Schelsky, *Einsamkeit und Freiheit*, 2nd ed. (Hamburg, 1970), p. 243.

35. Schelsky, *Einsamkeit und Freiheit* (Hamburg, 1963), p. 267.

36. Talcott Parsons and Gerald M. Platt, *The American University* (Cambridge, MA, 1973); see the appendix to chapter 2, p. 90ff.

37. In Anrich, p. 224.

38. Humboldt, in Anrich, p. 378.

5

The Horrors of Autonomy: Carl Schmitt in English

It is difficult to think of Carl Schmitt in the context of Anglo-Saxon discussions. Both the intellectual profile and the political destiny of this man belong to a very German tradition, even where his Catholic mentality stands in contrast to the Protestant complexion of his environment, the university of the German mandarins.

Carl Schmitt was a year older than Adolf Hitler, the man who determined his fate. He died last year in his Westphalian birthplace, Plettenberg, at the age of ninety-seven. The impassioned tone of the obituaries bears witness to the fact that even today Schmitt represents a division in the intellectual world.

An Expressionist Concept of the Political

In 1932, Schmitt's *The Concept of the Political* [*Der Begriff des Politischen*] appeared, a famous work in which Schmitt takes issue in passing with Harold Laski's pluralistic theory of the state, among others. The author was familiar, of course, with the pertinent definitions of Max Weber. But he was no social scientist and had no interest in an analytic concept of political power. Like a traditional philosopher, Schmitt inquired into the "nature" of the political. From an Aristotelian standpoint, to be sure, the answer Schmitt offered reads more like an answer to the question of the nature of the strategic. The

This review for the *Times Literary Supplement* was occasioned by the publication in 1986 of the first English translation of two early works by Carl Schmitt: *Political Theology* and *The Crisis of Parliamentary Democracy*.

political does not reveal itself, for instance, in the binding character of decisions made by a state authority; instead, according to Schmitt, it manifests itself in the collectively organized self-assertion of a "politically existing" people against external and internal enemies. Schmitt was fascinated by the First World War's "storms of steel," to use the title of Ernst Jünger's war diary *In Stahlgewittern*. A people welded together in a battle for life and death asserts its uniqueness against both external enemies and traitors within its own ranks. The political "extreme case" is characterized in terms of the phenomenon of defining one's own identity in the struggle against the alienness of an enemy who threatens one's very existence, and thus in terms of the situation of war between peoples or civil war. In either case, it is the "real possibility of physical killing" that defines the state of political emergency. And an event should be called political only if it refers, at least implicitly, to this extreme situation: all politics is essentially foreign affairs. Domestic affairs too should be conceived in terms of the dangers posed by an enemy who threatens one's very existence. Thus, in the expressionistic style of his time, Carl Schmitt constructs a dramatic concept of the political in the light of which everything normally understood by the word must seem banal.

Schmitt's *Political Theology* of 1922 [*Politische Theologie*], which continued on from his book on dictatorship, was intended to revive the concept of sovereign power in its full counterrevolutionary significance. *The Crisis of Parliamentary Democracy* [*Geistesgeschichtlichen Grundlagen des Parlamentarismus*], published in 1923, took up motifs from his book *Political Romanticism* [*Die Politische Romantik*, 1919] and mercilessly disposed of liberalism. The decisionist theory of the state that Schmitt propagates in the later book flows directly from his critique in the earlier book of a political thought founded on natural law. The abysslike character of these two early works can be seen more clearly in the light of Schmitt's chief work, a study of Hobbes which, like his other books, is fairly short. There Schmitt summarizes his philosophy of the state. That book, *Leviathan*, which dates from 1938 and was published in the middle of the Nazi period, also leads us to the political center of Schmitt's intellectual world.

The Myth of Leviathan

Schmitt both admires and criticizes Hobbes. He celebrates in Hobbes the only major political theorist to have recognized in sovereign authority the decisionist substance of state politics. But he also deplores in Hobbes the bourgeois theoretician who shrank from drawing ultimate metaphysical conclusions and who became against his will the ancestor of a constitutional state based on positive law.

As a political theologian, Carl Schmitt sees his ambivalent evaluation confirmed by the "significance and failure of a political symbol," as he subtitled his book. The reference is to the Old Testament image of Leviathan, the giant, fiendish dragon that no power on earth could withstand. Leviathan rises from the sea and overwhelms Behemoth, the land power. To the Jews this battle of the monsters had always seemed a fearsome and hateful image of the heathen life force. Because he was unfamiliar with this subversive interpretation, Schmitt says, Hobbes erred in his choice of a symbol. Hobbes's own intention, which aimed in the opposite direction, succumbed to the deadly power of the mythical image. For in the centuries that followed, the substance of the modern state, as represented by this image, was misunderstood as something abnormal and contrary to nature: "The image was not adequate to the system of thought with which it was linked. . . . The traditional Jewish exegesis rebounded against the Leviathan of Hobbes."

Schmitt fills in this mythological framework with two theses drawn from intellectual history. First, he projects back onto Hobbes the idea of sovereignty he developed in his *Political Theology* in 1922. Just as it is only in vanquishing Behemoth that Leviathan can be the power he is, so it is only in suppressing revolutionary opposition that the state can assert itself as a sovereign power. The state consists of the ongoing prevention of civil war. Its dynamic consists of the crushing of revolt, the containment of a chaos inherent in the evil nature of individuals. Individuals press for their autonomy and would perish in the terrors of their emancipation if they were not rescued through the facticity of a power that overcomes every other power. He who decides in the exceptional situation is the one who is sovereign. And because the subversive forces always appear under the name of truth and justice, the sovereign who wishes to guard against the exceptional situation will also reserve the power to define what is publicly held to be true or just. His decision power is the source of all validity. The state alone determines the public creed of its citizens.

But with regard to religious creeds, Schmitt argues, Hobbes makes a logical error with important consequences: he distinguishes "faith" from "confession" and declares the state neutral with respect to its citizens' confession, their private religious beliefs. Only public worship is subject to state control. Carl Schmitt bases his second thesis on this allegedly illogical distinction. In Schmitt's view, the space Hobbes reserved for private religious belief is the gate through which the subjectivity of bourgeois conscience and private opinion make their entrance and gradually unfold their subversive forces. For this private sphere is turned inside out and extends to become the bourgeois public sphere; in that sphere bourgeois society makes itself felt as a rival political power and finally, with the authorization to legislate through parliament, topples Leviathan from the throne. This scenario, however, completely disregards the fact that *from the beginning* Hobbes had developed his concept of sovereignty in connection with the development of positive law. In terms of its very concept, positive law requires a political legislator who can no longer be tied to the superordinate norms of natural law—and to this extent is sovereign. Thus Hobbes's idea of a sovereign legislator who is bound to the medium of positive law already contains the seed of the development of the constitutional state that Carl Schmitt sees as a great disaster—and that he tries to derive from the neutralization of state power vis-à-vis the powers of private religious belief, Weber's "gods and demons."

The Total State and Its Enemies

This version of Schmitt's theory once again draws on his earlier ideas, developed in *The Crisis of Parliamentary Democracy,* on the
This version of Schmitt's theory once again draws on his earlier ideas, developed in *The Crisis of Parliamentary Democracy,* on the

crisis of the constitutional state. A state with a parliamentary legislature had come into being in Germany only after the First World War, under conditions of organized capitalism and in the forms of a mass welfare state democracy. At that time Carl Schmitt thought of this interventionist state as a system of legality that had been captured by the "social powers." This is the meaning of the preface to the second edition, in 1933, of the *Political Theology*, in which Schmitt hastens to develop the decisionist form of juristic thought into the "institutionalist" form.

Schmitt's *Leviathan* shows how well this adaptation succeeded with the Prussian *Staatsrat*, which stood under the protection of Hermann Göring. This is especially true of the way Schmitt developed the thesis already mentioned, the idea that the Jewish interpretation ultimately rebounded against the Leviathan, in terms of the history of ideas: Schmitt constructed an anti-Semitic genealogy of the enemies of Leviathan. It begins with Spinoza, who as a Jewish philosopher approached the state religion from the outside and opened up a dangerous breach in it for individual freedom of thought; it continues with Moses Mendelssohn and with "the restless spirit of the Jews" in the Freemason and Illuminati orders of the late eighteenth century, who undermined state power "with a sure instinct . . . for the crippling of the alien and the emancipation of their own Jewish people"; it leads, finally, to the emancipated Jews Heine, Börne, and Marx, who made subversive use of their "fields of operation" in journalism, art, and science. All of them together accomplished the "intellectual paralysis" of Leviathan, the state as myth.

Carl Schmitt's Influence in the Federal Republic

A few years ago the first edition of Schmitt's *Leviathan* was reissued in Germany—with a postscript by the editor, a disillusioned activist of the late 1960s who has withdrawn his libido from Fidel Castro and transferred it to Carl Schmitt. Admittedly, Günther Maschke does not want to play down Schmitt's portrait gallery of Jewish ancestors of the enemies of the total state as mere lip service—as George Schwab (the translator of the *Political Theology*) had done in his book *The Challenge of Exception*—but he would nevertheless like to see it derived from the format of documents of a "classic Catholic anti-Semitism." For the rest, Maschke makes every effort to see Carl Schmitt's situation during the Nazi tyranny through Schmitt's own eyes, as best that can be done. For Schmitt, without a word of self-criticism, had presented himself as the "Benito Cereno of European international law." This is an allusion to the unfortunate captain in Herman Melville's novel of the same name, whom all believe to be the master of the pirate ship on which in fact, as a hostage, he had to risk his life.

In the United States and England people will wonder why a man like Carl Schmitt still exercises considerable intellectual influence in the Federal Republic forty years later. The reasons lie, first, in the quality of his work. As his brilliant *Constitutional Theory [Verfassungslehre]* of 1928 shows, Carl Schmitt was a competent constitutional lawyer, who was taken seriously as a sharp-witted adversary by even the most influential jurists of the Weimar period: by Richard Thoma, Hermann Heller, and Rudolf Smend. Furthermore, Schmitt was a good writer who could combine conceptual precision with surprising and ingenious associations of ideas. (This art of formulation does not, unfortunately, come through in the English translation.) Furthermore, Schmitt was an intellectual, who up into the 1920s applied his expertise in diagnoses of his time that displayed a high degree of sensitivity. And finally, for all the clarity of his language he retained the bearing of a metaphysician who descends into the depths and at the same time unmasks a base reality. It has been hollowed out by positive law and robbed of the substance of its authority. This was the result of a process, extending over centuries, of disenchantment of a state power that had once been sacred and that even in modern times had been able to maintain its true sovereignty only as a unity of secular and spiritual power. This unity had first dissolved into the dualism of state and society and then splintered into the pluralism of social powers. As "indirect powers," political parties, trade unions, and associations ultimately become totalitarian, although in a nonpolitical form: they want power without responsibility, they still have opponents but no longer have enemies, and they evade the dangers of genuinely political self-assertion. Of the political power to make decisions they retain only the binding character of orders issued by the state, not the existential risk of a life-and-death struggle for self-assertion.

Schmitt's book on Hobbes develops the point of view in terms of which these arguments from the 1920s fit together. Weimar was seen as the period of decline; the remnants of a state that was conceived halfheartedly, even by Hobbes himself, disintegrated into a nonpolitical "self-organization of society." The crisis could be overcome only through temporary dictatorial use of the emergency paragraph forth-eight of the Weimar constitution; in the long run, however, it could be overcome only through the "total state." Here Schmitt at first had Mussolini and Italian fascism in mind. After the Nazi seizure of power he was opportunistic enough to give his construction of the state the little twist necessary so that the *Führer*'s decisionsim would no longer have to be understood in purely Hobbesian terms but could be seen instead as the sovereign tip of the "concrete orders" of the people.

These qualities alone, to be sure, would not have outweighed the discrediting effect of his crude anti-Semitism and his toadying to the Nazi authorities had not other factors come into play. Schmitt had, and still has, important disciples, and disciples of disciples—all the way up into the Federal Constitutional Court. With Ernst Forsthoff, Schmitt exercised an influence over the controversy that went on in the 1950s among constitutional lawyers about the relationship between the constitutional state and the social-welfare state. And for a long time afterwards the old man conducted a successful policy of working with subsequent generations from his private residence; scholarly works by well known jurists, historians, and philosophers were personally inspired by him.

Even this constellation of factors would not have sufficed, however, if the Young Conservative mentality did not remain as fascinating as ever. To look back: in the 1920s, when Max Weber's sociological enlightenment had stripped state authority of its aura of kinship with reason and religion, the demise of right-wing Hegelianism left a painful void. At that time people wanted to put the loss of the aura behind them, but they could not reconcile themselves to the banality generated by an administrative state governed by party democracy. On the one hand, people had become cynical, and they saw through the purely mechanical nature of the enterprise; on the other hand, the substance and mystery of a dilapidated sovereignty were to be restored—even if it had to be through an unprecedented act of exaltation.

A Carl Schmitt, drawing on the same experiences as his contemporaries Martin Heidegger, Gottfried Benn, and even Ernst Jünger, could satisfy this vague yearning. With their pseudorevolutionary answers, all of them spoke to this nostalgia for something really old in something really different, which always came down to the same old thing. Nor has this message lost its appeal even today, especially in certain forgotten subcultures of formerly left-wing provenance.

The Contemporary Relevance of the Intellectual Motifs

In contemporary French philosophy the major German thinkers Nietzsche and Heidegger, whom André Glucksmann invokes in opposition to Hegel and Marx, tend to play a confusing role. But I do not think that Carl Schmitt will have a similar power of contagion in the Anglo-Saxon world. If the case were otherwise, one would need to call attention to a study, inspired by Helmuth Plessner, comparing Carl Schmitt with Ernst Jünger and Martin Heidegger: the 1958 dissertation by Christian von Krockow (Stuttgart), which is still worth reading. Outside the politically charged German context, I see the opportunity for a discussion, ahistorical perhaps, but unbiased, of a number of stimulating and objectively important ideas. Even today, the themes of Carl Schmitt's thought may cause a stir.

In 1970, Schmitt himself returned to his *Political Theology* [*Politische Theologie II*, Berlin] in order to link it to two contemporary discussions to which it is in fact relevant. For in the 1960s the *Political Theology* had been taken up by theologians like Johann Baptist Metz and Jürgen Moltmann under the influence of Ernst Bloch, thus from a completely different point of view; and since then, dogmatic controversies over post-Conciliar currents of thought have also given new relevance to the liberation theology influential in South America. Parallels with the third and fourth chapters of the *Political Theology* of 1922 are obvious, even if a half century later their author claimed to have been interested at the time only in analogous conceptualizations in theological and legal doctrine. In fact, the Spenglerian exposition of morphological similarities in the intellectual motifs of theology and political philosophy was by no means an end in itself for him. The comparison, for instance, between the role of the miracle in theology and the exceptional circumstance in political philosophy was intended to lend a dimension of profundity to Schmitt's theory of sovereignty. Schmitt wanted to bring into play the political philosophy of the counterrevolution, which was directly religiously motivated—in particular the doctrines of Donoso Cortes, who disposed of the oversolicitous legitimism of the July monarchy after 1848 and opposed to the discussion-filled rule of the liberal bourgeoisie a dictatorship justified on religious-existential grounds. What is the link between this kind of counterrevolutionary theology and Liberation Theology? And what does it mean that the theses of Cardinal Ratzinger [official Vatican spokesperson on matters of church doctrine], which fit better within the framework of a theology of the counterrevolution, can currently be advanced in the name of a critique of *all* political theology, almost along the lines of Karl Barth?

This touches on the context of the second discussion in which the political theology of a Carl Schmitt belongs today: the debate about the legitimacy, or the autonomy, of the modern era. Can modernity stabilize itself in the knowledge that it derives its normative orientations from within itself, or must it allow itself, as an ungrounded product of a disintegrative process of secularization, to be drawn back within the horizon of eschatology and cosmology? In the 1980s, tendencies toward a return to metaphysics have become unmistakable. Symptomatic is the intellectual evolution of the Catholic philosopher Robert Spaemann, whose point of departure was Carl Schmitt's decisionism and who has now arrived at Plato. Perhaps it is this reflection on tradition in a spirit critical of modernity that explains the initially puzzling interest of American followers of Leo Strauss and Michael Oakeshott in introducing Carl Schmitt posthumously to the Anglo-Saxon world.

Interest in this short book could also be based on Carl Schmitt's relationship to Hugo Ball, a Dadaist who from the Café Voltaire in Zurich returned to the bosom of the only road to salvation, the Catholic Church. For Carl Schmitt's polemical discussion of political Romanticism conceals the aestheticizing oscillations of his own political thought. In this respect, too, a kinship of spirit with the fascist intelligentsia reveals itself. The last chapter of *The Crisis of Parliamentary Democracy* bears the title "Irrationalist Theories of the Direct Use of Force." In that chapter Schmitt draws a line from Donoso Cortes through Sorel to Mussolini and makes the insightful prognosis that the myth of the general strike will be supplanted by the myth of the nation. But above all it is the aesthetics of violence that fascinates him. Interpreted on the model of the *creatio ex nihilo*, sovereignty acquires a halo of surrealistic meanings through its relationship to the violent destruction of the normative as such. That both calls for comparison with Georges Bataille's concept of sovereignty and also explains why at that time Carl Schmitt felt impelled to congratulate the young Walter Benjamin on his essay on Sorel.

The Normative Bases of Democracy

To be sure, seen against the Anglo-Saxon background of an empiricist understanding of democratic will-formation that simply associates democracy with the reconciliation of interests, majority rule, and the formation of elites, Carl Schmitt's reflections seem provocative. But one does not *have to* adhere, as Carl Schmitt and later Arnold Gehlen did, to an institutionalism along the lines of Harriou and believe in the *creative* force of ideas to attribute a not inconsiderable actual significance to the *legitimating* power of the self-understanding of an established practice. In this more trivial sense one can also understand an interest in the foundations in intellectual history of the rule of parliamentary law. The normative bases of democracy continue to be debated, because on democracy's self-understanding depend not only the stability of an existing practice but also the criteria for its critical evaluation.

Carl Schmitt, however, gives such an idealistic turn to the ideas that he sees as explaining the parliamentary system that in the absence of further argument they seem to the reader to lose their basis in reality. The way he goes about providing this idealistic edge and making the ideas ridiculous is instructive, now as before—instructive, furthermore, for the left-wingers in the Federal Republic and, especially now, in Italy, who drive out the Devil with Beelzebub by filling the gap left by a non-existent Marxist theory of democracy with Carl Schmitt's fascistic critique of democracy.

The medium Schmitt ridicules, that of public discussion guided by arguments, is in fact essential to any democratic justification of political authority. And the rule of the majority can also be interpreted as a procedure intended to make possible realistic approximations to the idea of forming as rational a consensus as possible under the pressure to make a decision. Schmitt draws his caricature by ignoring, even on the level of democracy's theoretical self-understanding, three things. In the first place, the assumptions of rationality which participants in discursive will-formation are obliged to make *in actu* are necessary but as a rule counterfactual presuppositions. All the same, it is only in the light of such *assumptions* of rationality that one can grasp the function and meaning of rules of parliamentary procedure. Further, practical discourses are concerned with the universalizability of interests; consequently one cannot, as Schmitt does, set up an antithesis between the contest for the better argument and competition among underlying interests. And finally, one cannot simply completely eliminate negotiations aimed at reaching compromise from this model of public will-formation; of course, it is again only discursively that one can check whether compromises have come about under fair conditions.

The really problematic move that Carl Schmitt makes, however, is the separation of democracy from liberalism. Schmitt restricts the procedure of public discussion to its role in parliamentary legislation and decouples it from democratic will-formation in general, as though liberal theory had not always included the notion of a general formation of opinion and will in the notion of the political public sphere. What is democratic is the condition that all participate with equal opportunity in a legitimation process conducted through the medium of public discussion. Schmitt's reasons for wanting to separate democracy, which he conceives in terms of identity, from public discussion, which he attributes to liberalism, are transparent. He wants to lay the conceptual groundwork for detaching democratic will-formation from the universalist presuppositions of general participation, limiting it to an ethnically homogeneous substratum of the population, and reducing it to argument-free acclamation by immature masses. Only thus can one envision a caesaristic and ethnically homogeneous *Führerdemokratie*, a democracy under a *Führer*, in which such a thing as "sovereignty" would be embodied. Carl Schmitt, incidentally, thereby provided the concept of democracy that his colleagues who had emigrated to the United States would later use for their theory of totalitarianism.

Today Carl Schmitt's objection to the "general significance of the belief in discussion" has once again become relevant. At this point his critique touches the core of Western rationalism. That his tune is the same as it was once before is reason enough to pale at it.

6

Work and Weltanschauung: The Heidegger Controversy from a German Perspective

Prefatory Note

This text was originally written as the foreword to the German edition of Victor Farias's book, *Heidegger et le Nazisme* (1988). I believe a separate publication is warranted because certain aspects of the general issue have not been sufficiently distinguished in previous discussion. The moral judgment of a later generation, which in any case is called forth more strongly by Heidegger's behavior after 1945 than by his political engagement during the Nazi period, must not be allowed to cloud our view of the substantial content of his philosophical work. But just as little should the legitimate distinction between person and work cut off the question of whether—and, if so, to what extent—that work itself may be affected, in its philosophical substance, by the intrusion of elements from what we Germans call *Weltanschauung*—an ideologically tinged worldview. This question takes a clearer shape in light of the historical investigations of Farias and Hugo Ott. But it cannot be answered with the methods of historical analysis alone.

I

In his excellent critical bibliography of Heidegger's writings, Winfried Franzen introduces the section on "Heidegger and Nazism" with these words: "Meanwhile, the Federal Republic has also produced a whole series of pertinent discussions of the 'case of Heidegger'; . . . A genuinely open and unhindered discussion, however, has not yet taken place in Germany, notably not in the 'camp' of the Heidegger school itself." That was in 1976.[1] The situation has since changed. Discussion has been sparked by, among other things, the publication in 1983 of notes in which Heidegger sought to vindicate, from the point of view of 1945, his political conduct in 1933–34. (A reprint of the "Rektoratsrede," Heidegger's inaugural address as rector of the University of Freiburg, is also included.)[2] Most important, the work of the Freiburg historian Hugo Ott[3] and of the philosopher Otto Pöggeler, himself associated with Heidegger for decades,[4] have brought new facts to light, as did Karl Löwith's report (set down in 1940) of a 1936 meeting with Heidegger in Rome.[5] In addition, the ongoing publication of the *Gesamtausgabe*, the complete edition of Heidegger's works, has shed light on the lectures and writings from the thirties and forties, themselves still not published in their entirety.[6] It required, however, the efforts of a Chilean professor in Berlin to make, at last, a political biography of Heidegger available in Germany—by way of its French translation, however, and with recourse to the Spanish original. This detour through the viewpoint of a foreigner may provide the most appropriate response to the cramped discussion Franzen noted in Germany; the resulting distance of Farias's work, which must ultimately speak for itself, from the current German context may justify my attempt to relate the two.

From the perspective of a contemporary German reader, one consideration is particularly important from the start. Illumination of the political conduct of Martin Heidegger cannot and should not serve the purpose of a global depreciation of his thought. As a personality of recent history, Heidegger comes, like every other such personality, under the judgment of the historian. In Farias's book as well, actions and courses of conduct are presented that suggest a detached evaluation of Heidegger's character. But in general, as members of a later generation who cannot know how *we* would have acted under conditions of a political dictatorship, we do well to refrain from moral judgments on actions and omissions from the Nazi era. Karl Jaspers, a friend and contemporary of Heidegger, was in a different position. In a report that the denazification committee of the University of Freiburg requested at the end of 1945, he passed judgment on Heidegger's "mode of thinking": it seemed to him "in its essence unfree, dictatorial, uncommunicative."[7] This judgment is itself no less informative about Jaspers than about Heidegger. In making evaluations of this sort Jaspers, as can be seen from his book on Friedrich Schelling, was guided by the strict maxim that whatever truth a philosophical doctrine contains must be mirrored in the mentality and life-style of the philosopher. This rigorous conception of the unity of work and person seems to me inadequate to the autonomy of thought and, indeed, to the general history of the reception and influence of philosophical thought.[8] I do not mean by this to deny all internal connection between philosophical works and the biographical contexts from which they come—or to limit the responsibility attached to an author, who during his lifetime can always react to unintended consequences of his utterances.

But Heidegger's work has long since detached itself from his person. Hebert Schnädelbach is right to begin his presentation of philosophy in Germany with the comment that our "contemporary philosophy has been decisively shaped by . . . Ludwig Wittgenstein's *Tractatus logico-philosophicus* (1921), Georg Lukács's *Geschichte und Klassenbewusstein* [*History and Class-Consciousness*] (1923) and Martin Heidegger's *Sein und Zeit* [*Being and Time*] (1926)."[9] With *Being and Time*, Heidegger proved himself, almost overnight, to be a thinker of the first rank. Even philosophers at some remove, such as Georg Misch, immediately recognized the "indefatigability" and "craftsmanship" of a leading philosopher. In *Being and Time*, Heidegger did nothing less than meld and recast, in an original way, the competing intellectual movements of Diltheyan hermeneutics and Husserlian phenomenology, so as to take up the pragmatic themes of Max Scheler and bring them into a postmetaphysical, historicizing overcoming of the philosophy of subjectivity.[10] This new venture in thought was all the more amazing because it seemed to allow the impassioned themes of the Kierkegaardian dialectic of existence to engage the classical Aristotelian philosophical problematic. From today's standpoint, Heidegger's new beginning still presents probably the most profound turning point in German philosophy since Hegel.

While the *detranscendentalizing* of the world-constituting ego carried through in *Being and Time* was unprecedented, the *critique of reason* that set in later and built on Nietzsche was the idealist counterpart—somewhat delayed—to a materialist critique of instrumental reason that was itself indebted to Hegel while productively combining Marx with Weber. Heidegger paid for the wealth of his later insights, which among other things revealed the ontological premises of modern thought, with a narrowing of his view to the dimension of a resolutely stylized history of metaphysics. This abstraction from the contexts of social life may be one reason for Heidegger's reliance on whatever interpretations of the age happened by, unfiltered by any knowledge of the social sciences. The more real history disappeared behind Heideggerian "historicity," the easier it was for Heidegger to adopt a naive, yet pretentious, appeal to "diagnoses of the present" taken up ad hoc.

With his detranscendentalizing mode of thought and his critique of metaphysics, Heidegger, whose work was of course criticized but whose position remained uncontested during the thirties and forties, had an *uninterrupted* impact on German universities. This academic, school-founding impact continued until the late sixties. Its importance is well documented in a collection of essays keyed to "perspectives on the interpretation of his work," which Pöggeler edited for Heidegger's eightieth birthday.[11] The Heideggerian school retained its dominant position during the long incubation of the Federal Republic, to the beginning of the sixties; when analytical philosophy of language (with Wittgenstein, Rudolf Carnap, and Karl Popper) and Western Marxism (with Max Horkheimer, Theodor Adorno, and Ernst Bloch) then regained footing in the universities, that was really only a delayed return to normalcy.

Still more significant than its academic influence on several generations of scholars and students is the inspirational glow of Heidegger's work on independent minds who selected particular themes and made them fruitful in systematic contexts of their own. The early Heidegger, to begin with, had influence on the existentialism and phenomenological anthropology of

Jean-Paul Sartre and Maurice Merleau-Ponty. In Germany something similar holds for the philosophical hermeneutics of Hans-Georg Gadamer. Productive developments continue into my generation as well, for example, with Karl-Otto Apel, Michael Theunissen, and Ernst Tugendhat.[12] Heidegger's critique of reason has been taken up more strongly in France and the United States, for example, by Jacques Derrida, Richard Rorty, and Hubert Dreyfus.

Questionable political conduct on the part of a thinker certainly throws a shadow on his work. But the Heideggerian oeuvre, espically the thought in *Being and Time,* has attained a position of such eminence among the philosophical ideas of our century that it is simply foolish to think that the substance of the work could be discredited, more than five decades later, by political assessments of Heidegger's fascist commitments.

So what interest, apart from the detached one of historical and scientific concern, can examination of Heidegger's political past claim today—especially in the Federal Republic? I think that these matters deserve our attention primarily from two points of view. On the one hand, Heidegger's attitude to his own past after 1945 exemplifies a state of mind that persistently characterized the history of the Federal Republic until well into the sixties. It is a mentality that survives up to the present day, as in the so-called historian's debate about revisionistic interpretations of German war crimes.[13] In order to ferret out what is symptomatic of deeper matters in Heidegger's refusal to change his mind and in his unwavering practice of denial,[14] we must inform ourselves of what Heidegger, to his death, repressed, glossed over, and falsified. On the other hand, in Germany *every* tradition that served to make us blind to the Nazi regime needs a critical, indeed a distrustful, appropriation. That certainly holds for a philosophy that, even in its rhetorical means of expression, absorbed impulses from the ideologies of its epoch. One cannot bring the truth-content of a philosophy into discredit by associating it with something external to it; but no more can—or may—one make a complex, tradition-shaping form of objective spirit into an object of conservation like a national park, immunizing it against the question of whether issues of substance have been confused with those of ideology.[15] What was always acceptable in Germany with respect to Stalinism must also be acceptable with regard to fascism.

Manfred Frank has recently expressed the opinion, with reference to the variations on the Heideggerian critique of reason currently disseminated in France, that the question of refurbishing a constellation of *Weltanschauungen* of German (that is, Young-Conservative) origin has not yet been laid to rest in Germany: "The new French theories are taken up by many of our students like an evangel. . . . It seems to me that young Germans are here eagerly sucking back in, under the pretense of opening up to what is French and international, their own irrationalist tradition, which had been broken off after the Third Reich."[16] I would like here to supplement Farias's investigation with a few remarks, taking up a question I previously broached in another place[17]: whether there was in *internal* connection between Heidegger's philosophy and his political perception of the world-historical situation.[18]

II

In 1963, Otto Pöggeler presented the "path of thought of Martin Heidegger" in a version that, authorized by Heidegger himself, mirrored Heidegger's own self-understanding. It is this faithful collaborator to whom, twenty years later, doubts came: "Was it not through a definite orientation of his thinking that Heidegger fell—and not merely accidentally—into the proximity of National Socialism without ever truly emerging from this proximity?" (*HPT*, p. 272). Pöggeler has since presented a point of view that brings the history of Heidegger's works closer together with that of his life than was previously done.

He distinguishes, in the first instance, the religious crisis into which Heidegger personally fell around 1917 from the general mood of crisis of 1929, into which Heidegger was drawn politically. As Heidegger, in 1919, withdrew at his own request from the philosophical training for Catholic theologians, he explained the step by saying that for him "epistemological insights . . have made the system of Catholicism problematic and unacceptable to me—but not Christianity and metaphysics (these, of course, in a new sense)" (*HPT,* p. 265). When we connect this with Heidegger's growing interest in Martin Luther and in Søoren Kierkegaard, as well as with his intense communication with Rudolf Bultmann in Marburg, we can understand the point of view from which the problem of mediating historical thought and metaphysics must have posed itself for Heidegger; the attitude of methodical atheism did not yet require closing off the authentically Christian domain of experience. Heidegger pursued at that time a "phenomenology of life" that was grounded in boundary experience of personal existence. The experience of history, therefore, arose in contexts of self-reassurance on the part of concrete individuals in their current situations. This (a) suggested a hermeneutical interpretation of Husserl's phenomenological method, (b) required an interpretation of the metaphysical question of Being from the horizon of the experience of time, and (c) called forth the pathbreaking transformation of the generative achievements of the transcendental ego into the historically situated life-projection of a factical being that finds itself in the world—Dasein. The connection between (b) and (c) explains, finally, why Heidegger's interest *remained* fixed on the constitution of human existence as such, and required a clear differentiation of existential ontology from the then contemporary enterprise of existentialism (Jaspers). The "analytic of Dasein" carried through in *Being and Time* remained, however, rooted in concrete experiences, a *theory* of Being-in-the-world as such. This explains the contrast, remarked many times, between a pretension of radical historical thinking and the fact that Heidegger rigidly maintained the abstraction of historicity (as the condition of historical existence itself) from actual historical processes.

The pathbreaking achievement of *Being and Time* consists in Heidegger's decisive argumentative step towards overcoming the philosophy of consciousness.[19] This achievement may be *illuminated* by the motivational background of a personal life crisis, but is not *impeached* by it. Naturally the spirit of the times, with which our author was already imbued, shows itself in this central work. The prevailing critique of mass civilization finds expression particularly in the connotations of his analysis of "das Man"; elitist complaints about the "dictatorship of public opinion" were common currency to the German mandarins of the twenties, and similar versions are to be found in Jaspers, E. R. Curtius, and many others. Indeed, the ideology inscribed in the "hidden curriculum" of the German Gymnasium has affected entire generations—on the Left as well as the Right. To this ideology belong an elitist self-understanding of academics, a fetishizing of *Geist,* idolatry for the mother tongue, contempt for everything social, a complete absence of sociological approaches long developed in France and the United States, a polarization between natural science and the *Geisteswissenschaften,* and so forth. All these themes are unreflectively perpetuated by Heidegger. More specific to him are the remarkable connotations with which he already at the time loaded terms like "fate" [*Schicksal*] and "destiny" [*Geschick*]. The pathos of heroic nihilism binds Heidegger to Young Conservatives, such as Oswald Spengler, the Jünger brothers, Carl Schmitt, and the circle connected with the journal *Die Tat.* But Pöggeler correctly dates the real invasion of such ideological motifs into Heidegger's self-understanding and, in fact, into the heart of his philosophical thought only from 1929—the time of the world economic crisis and the downfall of the Weimar republic.

If we understand the ideology of the German mandarins in the sense of Fritz Ringer,[20] we may see connections between the mandarin consciousness of the German professor Heidegger and certain *limitations* from which the argumentation of *Being and Time* cannot free itself. But even from the point of view of the sociology of knowledge one would hardly discover more than what immanent critique has already shown anyway. To put it in a nutshell: with his steady focus on the invariant structures of Dasein, Heidegger from the start cuts off the road from historicity to real history.[21] Attributing a merely derivative status to Mitsein (Being-with others) he also misses the dimension of socialization and intersubjectivity.[22] With the interpretation of truth as disclosure, Heidegger further ignores the aspect of unconditionality that attaches to a validity-claim, which, *as a claim,* transcends all merely local standards.[23] Heidegger's methodical solipsism prevents him, finally, from taking seriously normative validity-claims and the meaning of moral obligations.[24] From all this it is already apparent why "the philosophy of *Being and Time* obviously cannot, whether for Heidegger or for a whole series of colleagues and students who stand near him, possess critical potential vis-à-vis Fascism."[25] Franzen, too, comes to the judgment that "much of what Heidegger said and wrote in 1933–34, if it did not necessarily follow from what was in *Being and Time,* was at least not incompatible with it" (*E,* p. 80).

I would like to close the gaps this negative explanation leaves open with the thesis that from around 1929 on, Heidegger's thought exhibits a *conflation* of philosophical theory with ideological motifs. From then on themes of an unclear, Young-Conservative diagnosis of the time enter into the heart of Heidegger's philosophy itself. Only then does he wholly open up to the antidemocratic thought that had found prominent Right-wing advocates in the Weimar republic and had attracted even original minds.[26] The defects that immanent textual criticism can detect in *Being and Time* could not be seen *as* deficits by Heidegger because he shared the widespread anti-Western sentiments of his intellectual environment and held metaphysical thinking to be more primordial than the vapid universalism of the Enlightenment. Concrete history remained for him a mere "ontical" happening, social contexts of life a dimension of the inauthentic, propositional truth a derivative phenomenon, and morality merely another way of expressing reified values. Blind spots in Heidegger's innovative *Being and Time* can be explained in this way. But only after *Being and Time* would the "anticivilizational" undercurrent of German tradition (Adorno) erode that approach itself.[27]

III

Pöggeler is surely correct to emphasize the biographical turning point of 1929. Three things came together at that time. First, Friedrich Hölderlin and Nietzsche came into view as the authors who were to dominate the following decades. This paved the way for the *neopagan turn* that pushed Christian themes into the background in favor of a mythologizing recourse to the archaic; even at the end of his life, Heidegger placed his hopes in "a" god who can save us. Pöggeler asks himself:

Was there . . . a road from Nietzsche to Hitler? Did not Heidegger attempt, from 1929 on, with Nietzsche, to find his path, by way of the creativeness of the great creators, back to the tragic experience of life and thus to an historical greatness, in order then to win back for the Germans the beginnings of Greek thought and a horizon transposed by myth.[28]

Second, Heidegger's understanding of his role as a philosopher changed. During his encounter with Ernst Cassirer at Davos (March 1929), he expressed brusque dismissals of the world of Goethe and German Idealism. A few months later, after his July inaugural address as a professor in Freiburg, Heidegger completed the break with his teacher Husserl. At the same time, he returned to a theme he had just engaged ten years previously: he lectured on the "essence of the university and on academic studies." He seems at that point to have carried out a conscious break with academic philosophy, in order thenceforth to philosophize in another, nonprofessional way— in immediate confrontation with problems of the time perceived as urgent. As can be shown from the "Rektoratsrede" of 1933, Heidegger perceived the university as the preferred institutional locus for a spiritual renewal, to be brought about with unconventional means.

Third, Heidegger also opened himself up to Young-Conservative diagnoses of the times, even in his classroom.[29] In his lectures for the 1929–30 winter semester on "Basic Concepts of Metaphysics," he relates himself to writers such as Spengler, Ludwig Klages, and Leopold Ziegler, and swears by the heroism of audacious Dasein against the despised normality of bourgeois misery: "Mystery is lacking in our Dasein, and with it the inner horror which every mystery bears with it and which gives Dasein its greatness."[30] In the following years Heidegger studies the writings of Ernst Jünger: *War and Warrior* (1930) and *The Worker* (1932).

The invasion of the philosophy of *Being and Time* by ideology is not merely to be explained, however, by an awareness of the contemporary crisis that made Heidegger receptive to Nietzsche's critique of metaphysics; that also suggested the role of a savior in the moment of highest necessity for a philosophy freed from academic chains and for its site, the university; and that, finally, opened the doors to pickup critiques of civilization. The invading forces came together with a problematic that arose from the uncompleted opus itself, *Being and Time*.

Existential ontology had followed the transcendental approach so far that the structures it laid bare had to be attributed to Dasein *as such;* they had retained the character of being above history. This was not consistent with Heidegger's aim of subjecting the basic concepts of metaphysics to a radically temporalized analysis. Two works from 1930–31 (which are however available only in a later revised version) attempt to make good on that claim.

In the lectures "On the Essence of Truth" and "Plato's Doctrine of Truth," the existentials change from basic constitutional features of Dasein into the products of a process coming from afar. They come forth from an idealistically deified history, which is supposed to have completed itself in the medium of changes in ontological frames, metaphysics, *behind* or *above* real history. The dialectic of revelation and concealment is no longer conceived as an interplay of invariant possibilities of Being that continually holds open to the individual the perspective of authenticity, but as the story of a fall, which begins with Plato's metaphysical thought and proceeds in epochal fashion through different "peoples." With this shift, Heidegger gains a dimension within which the analytic of Dasein can illuminate the conditions under which it itself arose. Theory becomes reflexive in a way similar to that of the Hegelian Marxism of Lukács—though with the essential difference that Lukács's social theory conceives of its own genesis in terms of a concrete historical context that is accessible to social-scientific research, while existential-ontological thought transcends itself towards a sublime, primordially operative domain that is removed from all empirical (and ultimately all argumentative) grasp. In this domain, philosophy rules alone; it can therefore contract a dark alliance with scientifically unexamined diagnoses of the times. Heidegger's reconstruction of an unfolding of metaphysics that lies before all history is guided by the consciousness of crisis of the present moment to which he continually appeals, that is, by a conservative/revolutionary interpretation of the German situation at the beginning of the thirties.

Interpreters of his thought today follow Heidegger's retrospective self-interpretation in holding that he completed his turn from existential ontology to the thinking of the history of Being with the two texts from 1930–31. But this is not wholly correct, for those essays merely open up a path that ultimately leads, in several stages, to the "Letter on Humanism" of 1947. The pathos of bondage and letting-be, the quietistic understanding of man as the shepherd of Being, the thesis that "language is the house of Being in which man ek-sists by dwelling, in that he belongs to the truth of Being, guarding it"[31]— all this is only the later result of the deliverance of philosophical thinking over to a "World-destiny" that, between 1930 and 1945, prescribed various twists and turns to a philosopher who was quite ready to go along.

At the beginning of the thirties, not only the word but the very concept of the "history of Being" is missing. What changes at that time in Heidegger's philosophical conception is not the activist demand for resoluteness and projection, but rather Heidegger's way of taking authenticity as the standard for the responsible acceptance of one's own life history. This standard is liquidated and along with it the critical moment of *Being and Time* provided by the *individualistic* heritage of existential philosophy. The concept of truth is then transformed so that historical challenge through a collective fate takes over. Now it is a "people" and no longer the individual, which ek-sists. Not we as individuals, but *We* with a capital *W* see ourselves exposed to the "need of turning" and the "prevailing of the mystery." But this does not yet free us from decision: "By leading him astray, errancy dominates man through and through. But, as leading astray, errancy at the same time contributes to a possibility that man is capable of drawing up from his ek-sistence— the possibility that, by experiencing errancy itself and by not mistaking the mystery of Da-sein, he *not* let himself be led astray."[32]

After 1929 we see a "turning" only in the sense that Heidegger (a) relates the analytic of Dasein reflectively to a movement of metaphysical thought conceived in terms of a history of the Fall (from Being); in that (b) he allows ideological motifs from a scientifically unfiltered diagnosis of crisis to filter into his present-oriented reconstruction; and in that (c) he dissociates the dialectic of truth and untruth from the individual's care for his own Dasein and interprets it as a happening, which challenges the people to a resolute confrontation with a common historical fate.[33] With this, the switches are set for a national/revolutionary interpretation of what in *Being and Time* was a self-heeding and self-assertion sketched in existential terms. Thus Heidegger, who had opted for the Nazi party before 1933, could explain Hitler's successful power-grab in terms of concepts *retained* from his own analytic of Dasein.[34] But he adds something: the nationalistic privileging of the *German* fate, the conflation of the collectivistically interpreted category of "Dasein" with the Dasein of the German people, and those mediating figures, the "guides and guardians of the German destiny," who can shape necessity and create the new, if only their followers keep themselves in hand.

The leaders [*Führer*] are, then, the great creators, who put truth to work.[35] But the relation of leader to followers only concretizes the decision, as formal now as it was previously, "whether the entire people chooses its own Dasein, or whether it rejects it." In Heidegger's agitation for the Führer and "the complete transformation of our German Dasein," the old semantics of *Being and Time* can still be recognized—though it is now obscenely recolored. For example, in the speech Heidegger gave to the election rally of German scholars and scientists held at Leipzig on November 11, 1933, we hear that from "a coordinated readiness to follow in regard to the unconditional demand of responsibility-for-self, there first arises the possibility of mutually taking each other seriously . . . . What sort of event is this? The people win back the truth of its will to exist, for truth is the manifestation of that which makes a people secure, lucid, and strong in its knowing and acting. From such truth stems the real desire to know."[36]

With *this* as background, the acceptance of the rectorship at Freiburg and the "Rektoratsrede" are not only compatible with Heidegger's earlier work but result from his dismissal of academic philosophy, from his elitist understanding of the German university, from his unbounded fetishizing of *Geist,* and from the missionary view of himself that allowed him to see the role of his own philosophy only in contexts of an eschatological world destiny. It is doubtless a specifically German *déformation professionelle* that gave Heidegger the idea of leading the Leader, Hitler. There is today no longer any controversy over the details of Heidegger's behavior at that time.

IV

The lectures and writings that mark Heidegger's philosophical development during the Nazi period have not yet been completely published. Nonetheless, a careful reading of the two volumes on Nietzsche could teach us that Heidegger did not rid himself, even to the end of the war, of his original political option for the Nazis. The work of Franzen (1975–76) and Pöggeler (1983, 1985, and 1988) confirms the impression "that in the thirties, Heidegger himself placed the decision about the truth of Being as he sought it in a political context" (*HPT,* p. 278). The orientation of his thought, through which he "fell into the proximity of National Socialism," kept him from "ever truly emerging from this proximity" (*HPT,* p. 272).[37] Heidegger's philosophical trajectory between 1935 and 1945 shows itself to be a process of working through a series of disappointments, without any real insight, so as to *continue* the "turn" introduced with the texts of 1930—31. Three aspects must here be distinguished: (a) the development of the critique of reason through the history of metaphysics; (b) the essentially unchanged, nationalistic estimation of the Germans as the "heart of all peoples"; and (c) the position with regard to National Socialism. Only from this third aspect is the significant reconfiguration revealed, through which the concept of a "history of Being" first gains its definitive form.

A. Instigated by an increasingly intense confrontation with Nietzsche—also the authoritative point of reference for official Nazi philosophy—Heidegger works up an approach under which the "destruction of metaphysics," which he had in view early on, merges completely with the known themes of his critique of the times. The thought of Plato—forgetful of Being, theoretically objectifying—hardens (in several stages) into the modern thought of subjectivity. Heidegger's analyses of "representational thought," though enlightening on several matters, now have as their target the ontological premises on which the determining spiritual powers of modernity, natural science and technology, rely. In the context of a history of metaphysics, "technology" is the expression for a will to will, which in practice makes itself felt in the phenomena of positivistic science, technological development, industrial labor, the bureaucratized state, mechanized warfare, the management of culture, the dictatorship of public opinion, and generally of urbanized mass civilization. Traits of totalitarian politics find their way into this template for the age of the masses, Nazi racial politics included. In spite of Heidegger's sustained relationship with one of the leading Nazi theoreticians of race, he was himself no racist; his anti-Semitism, so far as it can be confirmed at all, was rather of the usual, culturalistic breed. However that may be, *after* 1935 Heidegger subsumed political and social practice hastily under a few stereotypical code words without even an attempt at nuanced description, to say nothing of empirical analysis. His ontologizing talk of "technology" itself as a destiny that is at once mystery, security, and danger reaches globally, and with strongly essentialistic conceptions, through the foreground domains of the ontical. Even within the frame of this *Weltanschauung*, Heidegger pursues critical insights about reason that have not been superseded even today.

B. The crude nationalism Heidegger openly sustained even after 1933 remains, in a form more or less sublimated through Hölderlin, an invariant feature of his thought. The basic schema of interpretation is established by 1935. In the *Introduction to Metaphysics* the German people, heir to the Greeks, is privileged as the metaphysical people from which alone a turning of the planetary fate can be expected. In the wake of an ideology of the "country of the middle," itself developed long ago, the Germans' Central European location is the key to their world-historical vocation: Heidegger expects "the peril of world darkening . . . to be forestalled" only "if our nation in the center of the Western world is to take on its historical mission" (*IM*, p. 50). Thus Heidegger relates "the question of being to the destiny of Europe, where the destiny of the earth is being decided—while our own historic being-there proves to be the center for Europe itself" (*IM*, p. 42). And further: "Europe lies in a pincers between Russia and America, which are metaphysically the same, namely in regard to their world character and their relation to the spirit" (*IM*, p. 45). Because Bolshevism stems from Western Marxism, Heidegger sees in it only a variation on something worse—Americanism. Pöggeler reports a passage in a lecture manuscript that Heidegger, tastefully, did not actually deliver. It relates to Carnap, who had emigrated in the meantime: "his philosophy manifests 'the most extreme flattering and uprooting of the traditional theory of judgement under the guise of mathematical-scientific method'. . . . It is no accident that this kind of 'philosophy' is both 'internally and externally connected' with 'Russian communism' and celebrated its triumph in America" (*HPT*, p. 276). Heidegger repeats his interpretation again in the Parmenides lectures of 1942—43 and the Heraclitus lectures of the 1943 summer semester, when he sees the planet already "in flames," the "world slipping its moorings": "Only from the Germans can world historical meditation come—provided that they find and defend what is German."[38]

C. After leaving the rectorate in April 1934, Heidegger is disillusioned. He is convinced that this historical movement was as if intended for himself and his philosophy; and he remains convinced of the world-historical importance and of the metaphysical meaning of Nazism to the bitter end. In the summer of 1942, he again speaks unmistakably, in a lecture on Hölderlin, of the "historical uniqueness of National Socialism."[39] For Nazism is privileged by its particularly intimate relation to the nihilism of the time—and it remains so, even after Heidegger, apparently under the impact of the events of the war, learned to reevaluate the *position* of Nazism with respect to the history of Being.

In the first instance—in 1935—Heidegger's talk of the "inner truth and greatness" of the Nazi movement (*IM*, p. 199) betrays a distancing from certain phenomena and practices that are supposed to have nothing to do with the spirit of the thing itself. The philosopher, anyhow, knows better: *he* knows the metaphysical status of the national revolution. All is not yet lost, though the political leaders are allowing themselves to be deceived about their *true* mission by false philosophers such as Ernst Krieck and Alfred Bäumler. Walter Bröcker, who heard that lecture, recalls that Heidegger actually spoke of the inner truth and greatness of "the" movement, and not—as the published text has it—of "this" movement: "With the term 'the movement' the Nazis, and *only* they, meant their own party. That is why Heidegger's 'the' was for me unforgettable."[40] If that is right, then Heidegger's identification with the Nazis cannot exactly have been broken by 1935. Pöggeler reports as well on a passage in the Schelling lecture of the summer of 1936, which was struck from the published version of 1971 (supposedly without Heidegger's knowledge): "the two men who, each in his own way, have begun a countermovement to nihilism, Mussolini and Hitler, have both learned from Nietzsche, in essentially different ways. This does not mean, however, that Nietzsche's true metaphysical domain has come in this into its own."[41] The same image thus comes again, and is also consonant with Löwith's report of an encounter in Rome at the same time: the leaders of fascism know their own calling; but they must heed the philosopher in order to know its exact meaning. Only he could explain to them what it means, in terms of the history of metaphysics, to overcome nihilism and put truth to work. He at least sees the goal clearly before him: how the fascist leaders, if only they succeed in awakening the heroic will to Dasein of their peoples, could overcome the "bleak frenzy of unleashed technology and the rootless organization of the normal human being."

I do not know exactly when the next stage of working through his disillusionment began: perhaps after the beginning of the war, perhaps only after the depressing knowledge of inevitable defeat. In the notes on "Overcoming Metaphysics" (from the years after 1936, especially from the wartime), Heidegger is increasingly impressed by the totalitarian traits of an age that ruthlessly mobilizes all reserves of strength. Only now does the messianic mood of basic change of 1933 become an *apocalyptic* hope of salvation: now, *only* in the greatest need does the saving force also grow. World-historical tragedy alone sounds the hour for overcoming metaphysics: "Only after this decline does the abrupt dwelling of the Origin [*Anfang*] take place for a long span of time."[42] With this change of mood, the evaluation of National Socialism changes again. Heidegger's working through his disillusionment after 1934 had led to a differentiation between the unfortunate superficial forms of Nazi practice and its essential content. Now he undertakes a more radical revaluation, which has to do with the "inner truth" itself of the Nazi movement. He resolves on a recasting of the roles in the history of Being. Whereas previously national revolutions with their leaders at the head represented a *countermovement* to nihilism, now Heidegger thinks that they are a particularly characteristic *expression* of it, and thus are a mere symptom of that fateful destiny of technology against which they were formerly supposed to be working. Technology, now the signature of the epoch, expresses itself in the totalitarian "circularity of consumption for the sake of consumption," and

"leader natures" are those who allow themselves to be put in the service of this procedure as its directive organs on account of their assured instincts. They are the first employees within the course of business of the unconditional consumption of beings in the service of the guarantee of the vacuum of the abandonment of Being. ["OM," p. 107]

Untouched by this is the nationalistic privileging of the Germans as that "humanity" that "is suited to bring about unconditional nihilism in a historical manner" ("OM," p. 103). It is in this that the "uniqueness" of National Socialism consists, while "the Nazi power holders are in a way stylized into chief functionaries of the abandonment of Being" (*E,* p. 99).

For the *internal* connection between Heidegger's political engagement and his philosophy, it seems to me of the greatest importance that only his hesitant—indeed in comparison with other intellectual fellow travelers of the regime astonishingly *protracted*—detachment from and reevaluation of the Nazi movement leads to a revision, which Heidegger's postwar concept of the history of Being finally grounds. As long as Heidegger could imagine that national revolution could, with its projection of a new German Dasein, find an answer to the objective challenge of technology, the dialectic of claim [of Being] and correspondence [to that claim] could still be conceived in harmony with the basically activist tendency of *Being and Time,* precisely in terms of national revolution. Only after Heidegger gave up this hope and had to demote fascism and its leaders into symptoms of the disease they were originally supposed to heal—only after this change of attitude did the overcoming of modern subjectivity take on the meaning of an event that is *only* to be undergone. Until then, the decisionism of self-assertive Dasein, not only in the existential version of *Being and Time* but also (with certain changes of accent) in the national/revolutionary version of the writings from the thirties, had retained a role in disclosing Being. Only in the final phase of working through his disillusionment does the concept of the history of Being take on a fatalistic form.[43]

V

The fatalism of the history of Being already exhibited clear contours in, for example, the 1943 afterword to "What Is Metaphysics?" After the end of the war, Heidegger's apocalyptically darkened mood changes yet again. An "apocalypse" is conditioned by the expectation of coming catastrophe. That was averted for the moment by the entry of French troops into Freiburg, but this was only a postponement for the time being. The victors were America and Russia, alike in their essence, who now divided up world hegemony. So the Second World War, in Heidegger's view, had decided nothing *essential.* That is why the philosopher prepared, after the war, to persevere *quietistically* in the shadows of a still-unconquered destiny. In 1945 there remained for him only retreat from the disappointing history of the world. But this only underscores his continuing conviction that the history of Being is articulated in the words of essential thinkers—and that this thinking is eventuated by Being itself. Heidegger had allowed his thought to be engaged for over a decade and a half by political events. The "Letter on Humanism" of 1947 reflects this development, but only in such a way as to obscure its context of origin and— once historically displaced—to detach it from all relation to surface historical reality.

In the "Letter on Humanism," the traces of nationalism are effaced. The *Daseinsraum* of the people is sublimated into the *Heimat,* the natural home: "the word is thought here in an essential sense, not patriotically or nationalistically but in terms of the history of Being" (LH," p. 217). The world-historical mission of the people in the heart of Europe is retained only on a grammatical level: it lives on in the metaphysical privileging of the German language, in which Heidegger (now as before) sees the only legitimate successor to Greek. In his late interview with the German magazine *Der Spiegel* it is still clear: one must speak German in order to understand Hölderlin. The middle realm of the "demigods," of the creative leaders, disappears without a trace. The leaders are sublimated into poets and thinkers; the philosopher achieves an immediate relation to Being. What once held for political adherence is now generalized for all into obedience to the destiny of Being: only such submission "is capable of supporting and obligating" (LH," p. 238).

With the help of an operation that we might call "abstraction via essentialization," the history of Being is thus disconnected from political and historical events. This, again, allows for a remarkable self-stylization by Heidegger of his own philosophical development. From now on he emphasizes the continuity of his problematic and takes care to cleanse his concept of the history of Being from telltale ideological elements by projecting it back onto the never-completed *Being and Time.* Heidegger's "turn," supposedly completed by 1930, "is not a change of standpoint from *Being and Time*" ("LH," p. 208).[44]

Heidegger dealt with the theme of humanism at a time when the images of the horror that the arriving allies encountered in Auschwitz and elsewhere had made their way into the smallest German village. If his talk of an "essential happening" had any meaning at all, the singular event of the attempted annihilation of the Jews would have drawn the philosopher's attention (if not already that of the concerned contemporary). But Heidegger dwells, as always, in the Universal. His concern is to show that man is the "neighbor of Being"—not the neighbor of man. He directs himself, undisturbed, against "the humanistic interpretations of man as *animal rationale,* as 'person,' as spiritual-ensouled-bodily being," because "the highest determinations of the essence of man in humanism still do not realize the proper dignity of man" ("LH," p. 210). The "Letter on Humanism" also explains why moral judgments in general must remain beneath the level of essential thinking proper. Hölderlin had already left behind "the mere cosmopolitanism of Goethe." Heidegger's philosophizing, now become commemorative, strikes right through "ethics" and reaches, instead, the "destined": "Whenever thinking, in historical recollection, attends to the destiny of Being, it has already bound itself to what is fitting for it, in accord with its destiny." In writing this sentence, the memory of the "unfittingness" of the National Socialist movement must have struck the philosopher, for he immediately adds: "To risk discord in order to say the Same"—Being is always only itself—"is the danger. Ambiguity threatens, and mere quarreling" ("LH," p. 241).

Heidegger has nothing more than this to say about his own error. That is hardly inconsistent. For the place of all essential thinking with respect to the eventuating of Being transposes the thinker into error. He is absolved from all personal responsibility, because error itself objectively befalls him. A mistake could be ascribed only to an intellectual, an unessential thinker. In the "case of the rectorate [in] 1933/34," which "in itself" was "unimportant," Heidegger sees, even after the war, only "a sign of the metaphysical state of the essence of science" ("R," p. 497). For him, "it is as unimportant as the barren rooting in past attempts and measures taken, which in the context of the entire movement of the planetary will to power are so insignificant that they may not even be called tiny" ("R," pp. 498–99).

Some insight into Heidegger's retrospective assessment of his own conduct is given by the "Facts and Thoughts" that he noted down in 1945, and the interview with *Der Spiegel,* also published only posthumously, in which he essentially repeats the testimony of 1945.[45] It is precisely under the premises of the objective irresponsibility of essential thinking, and of the moral indifference of personal entanglements, that the palliative character of this self-presentation is so astounding. Instead of giving a sober account of the facts, Heidegger simply whitewashes himself. The "Rektoratsrede" he understands as already an "opposition," his entrance into the Nazi party under spectacular circumstances as a "matter of form" ("R," pp. 490, 493). For the following years, he claims, "the opposition that had begun in 1933 had continued and grown more vigorous" ("R," p. 500). Silenced in his own country, he saw himself as sacrificed to a "witch hunt." True, he mentions a "Clean Up Drive"[46] during his rectorship, "which often threatened to exceed its goals and limits: ("R," p. 492). But there is only one mention of guilt—the guilt of others, "who even then were so endowed with the gift of prophecy that they foresaw all that came" yet nevertheless waited "almost ten years before opposing the threatening disaster" ("R," p. 486). For the rest, Heidegger resists those who today wrongly understand his words of the time: "'Armed Service,' however, I mentioned neither in a militaristic, nor in an aggressive sense, but understood it as defense in self-defense" ("R," p. 487).[47] The investigations of Hugo Ott and Victor Farias do not leave many details of these excuses standing. But it was not only in his posthumously published self-justifications that Heidegger resorted to falsification.

In 1953 Heidegger published his lectures from 1935 on the *Introduction to Metaphysics.* I was, as a student, at that time so impressed with *Being and Time* that reading these lectures, fascist right down to their stylistic details, actually shocked me. I discussed this impression in a newspaper article—mentioning especially the sentence about the "inner truth and greatness of the Nazi movement." What shocked me most was that Heidegger had published in 1953, without explanation or comment, what I had to assume was an unchanged lecture from 1935. Even the foreword made no reference to what had happened in between. So I directed to Heidegger the question: "Can even the planned mass murder of millions of people, about which all of us know today, be made understandable in terms of the history of Being, as a fateful error? Is it not the factual crime of those who were responsible for carrying it out—and the bad conscience of an entire people?"[48] It was not Heidegger, but Christian E. Lewalter who answered.[49] He read the lecture with eyes completely different from mine. He understood it as documenting that Heidegger had in 1935 seen the Hitler regime, not as an "indication of new wellbeing" but as a "further symptom of decline" in the whole story of the decline of metaphysics. In this, Lewalter relied on an addition to the text, in parentheses, which characterized the Nazi movement as "the encounter between global technology and modern man" (*IM*, p. 199). Lewalter read this as saying that "the Nazi movement is a symptom for the tragic collision of man and technology, and as such a symptom it has its 'greatness,' because it affects the entirety of the West and threatens to pull it into destruction."[50] Surprisingly, Heidegger then expressed himself in a letter to the editor concerning Lewalter's article: "Christian E. Lewalter's interpretaion of the sentence taken from my lecture is accurate in every respect. . . . It would have been easy to remove that sentence, along with the others you have mentioned, from the printed version. I have not done this, and will not do it in the future. On the one hand, the sentence historically belongs to the lecture; on the other, I am convinced that the lecture itself can clarify it to a reader who has learned the craft of thinking."[51]

We may well suspect that Heidegger did not keep to this later, but struck politically offensive passages without indicating the omissions. (Or did Heidegger know nothing of this publication procedure?) More notable is the circumstance that Lewalter's interpretation, which falsely projected a later self-understanding back to 1935, was explicitly condoned by Heidegger even though it rested solely on a clause that Heidegger himself had added to the manuscript in 1953. In fact, Heidegger had, in the "Prefatory Note" of the book, explicitly declared that this clause was part of the original lecture, and he maintained this deception even in the interview with *Der Spiegel;* but, little by little, the truth has come to light. In 1975, Franzen, after a careful examination of the text, substantiated doubts that "Heidegger really meant what in 1953 he claimed he had"

(*E*, p. 93). In 1983, Pöggeler reported that the page of the manuscript with the controversial passage was missing from the Heidegger archives. He too considered the parenthetical remark to be a later addition, but did not consider the possibility of an intentional manipulation (*HPT*, pp. 277–78). After publication of the French version of Farias' book, Rainer Marten, a close associate of Heidegger, portrayed the incident as follows: Heidegger, in 1953, had refused the advice of his three collaborators that the insidious sentence be struck out and had added in parentheses the contentious commentary, on which Lewalter's interpretation and Heidegger's chronologically misleading self-presentation were then based.[52]

Interestingly enough, in 1953 the real issue was lost in the conflict of philosophical opinions. On the question of his position with regard to the Nazi mass crimes, Heidegger never, then or later, gave any answer. We may suspect, with solid grounds, that the answer as usual would have been very general. In the shadow of the "universal rule of the will to power within history, now understood to embrace the planet," everything becomes one and the same: "today everything stands in this historical reality, no matter whether it is called communism, or fascism, or world democracy" ("R," p. 485). That is how it was in 1945, and that is how Heidegger always repeated it: abstraction by essentialization. Under the leveling gaze of the philosopher of Being even the extermination of the Jews seems merely an event equivalent to many others. Annihilation of Jews, expulsion of Germans—they amount to the same. On May 13, 1948, Herbert Marcuse answered a letter in which Heidegger had maintained just that:

You write that everything I say about the extermination of the Jews holds equally for the Allies, if instead of "Jew" we write "Eastern German." With this sentence, do you not place yourself outside the realm in which a conversation among humans is possible at all—outside the logos? For only from fully beyond this "logical" dimension is it possible to explain, adjust, "comprehend" a crime by saying that others did the same thing too. More: how is it possible to place the torture, mutilation, and annihilation of millions of people on the same level as the forcible resettlement of groups in which none of these misdeeds has occurred (save perhaps in a few exceptional cases)?[53]

VI

Heidegger's entanglement with National Socialism is one thing, which we can safely leave to the morally sober historical judgment of later generations. Quite another is Heidegger's apologetic conduct after the war, his retouchings and manipulations, his refusal publicly to detach himself from the regime to which he had publicly adhered. That affects us as his contemporaries. Insofar as we share a life-context and a history with others, we have the right to call one another to account. Heidegger's letter to Marcuse, in which he takes up a manner of settling accounts that even today is widespread in academic circles, was his reply to the following challenge from Marcuse, a former student: "Many of us have long waited for a word from you, a statement that you would clearly and definitively free yourself from this identification, a statement that expresses your real current attitude to what has happened. You have made no such statement—at least none has escaped the private sphere."[54] In this regard, Heidegger remained bound by his generation and his time, the milieu of the Adenauer era of repression and silence. He acted no differently from others, was one of many. The excuses that came from his circle are hardly convincing: that Heidegger had to defend himself against slander, that any new admission would be taken for a further adaptation, that Heidegger was struck dumb by the inadequacy of any possible explanation, and so on. The image of his character that is gradually coming to the fore makes most plausible the report of a friend that Heidegger saw no occasion for a "trip to Canossa" because he had not been a Nazi; and because he feared that such a move would deter young people from reading his books.[55]

A self-critical attitude, an open and scrupulous comportment to his own past, would have demanded from Heidegger something that would surely have been difficult for him: the revision of his self-understanding as a thinker with a privileged access to truth. After 1929, Heidegger veered farther and farther away from the circle of academic philosophy; after the war he actually strayed into the regions of a thinking *beyond* philosophy, *beyond* argumentation itself. This was no longer the elitist self-understanding of an academic corporate guild. It was the consciousness of a mission cut to the form of one's own person, with which the admission of a few mistakes, to say nothing of guilt, was incompatible.

As a contemporary, Heidegger is thrown into an ambiguous light, overtaken by his own past because when everything was finished and done he could not adequately relate to it. His behavior remained, even according to the standards of *Being and Time,* ahistorical. But what makes Heidegger into a manifestation, typical for his time, of a widely influential postwar mentality concerns his person—not his work. The conditions of reception for an oeuvre are largely independent of the behavior of its author. That holds, at least, for the writings up to 1929. Up to *Kant and the Problem of Metaphysics,* Heidegger's philosophical work is faithful enough to the stubborn logic of his problematic that those portions of it explainable in terms of the sociology of knowledge and relating to the context in which it arose do not prejudice the context of justification. One does Heidegger a favor when one emphasizes the autonomy of his thought during this most productive phase—in 1929 he was already forty years old—particularly against Heidegger's later self-stylizations, against his overemphasis on continuity.

Even after the beginning of the process of ideological infiltration— a process that, at first insidious, eventually burst forth so spectacularly—Heidegger remained the productive philosopher he had previously been. Even his critique of reason, which begins with the Plato interpretation of 1931 and is developed between 1935 and 1945, especially in his confrontation with Nietzsche,[56] is responsible for *lasting* insights. These insights, which reach a high point in the influential Descartes interpretation, became points of departure for interesting developments and inspired extremely productive new approaches. An example of this is the philosophical hermeneutics of Hans-Georg Gadamer, one of the most important philosophical innovations of the postwar period. Further visible testimony to the effect of the Heideggerian critique of reason, undistorted by his worldview, are, in France, the phenomenology of the late Merleau-Ponty and Michel Foucault's analysis of forms of knowledge; in America, Rorty's critique of representational thought and Dreyfus's investigation of life-world practice.[57]

No short circuit can be set up between work and person. Heidegger's philosophical work owes its autonomy, as does every other such work, to the strength of its arguments. But then a productive relation to his thinking can be gained only when one engages those *arguments*—and *takes them out* to their ideological context. The farther the argumentative substance sinks into the unchallengeable morass of ideology, the greater is the demand on the critical force of an alert and perceptive appropriation. This hermeneutical commonplace loses its triviality especially when the later generations appropriating a work stand in the same tradition from which it has drawn its themes. In Germany, therefore, the critical appropriation of a thought that has been supportive of Nazism can only succeed when we learn from Heidegger to take into account the *internal* relations that exist between his political engagement and the changes in his attitude towards fascism, on the one hand, and the arguments of his critique of reason, which was also politically motivated, on the other.

The indignant tabooing of this set of problems is counterproductive. We must divest ourselves of the self-understanding, the postures, and the claims that Heidegger connected with his *role* before we can get to the substance of the matter. Hedging the authority of the great thinker—only he who thinks greatly can err greatly[58]—can only inhibit the critical appropriation of his arguments in favor of merely socializing people into an unclarified language game. The conditions under which *we* can learn from Heidegger are incompatible with the anti-Occidental frame of mind deeply rooted in Germany. Fortunately, we broke with this after 1945. It should not be resurrected with a mimetically assimilated Heidegger. I refer above all to Heidegger's pretension that "there is a thinking more rigorous than the conceptual" (LH," p. 235). This attitude is connected, first, to the claim that a few people have a privileged access to truth, may dispose of an infallible knowledge, and may withdraw from open argument. Further, connected with the same attitude are concepts of morality and truth that detach the validity of knowledge from intersubjective examination and recognition. The same attitude suggests, finally, detaching philosophical thinking from the egalitarian business of science, severing the emphatically extraordinary from its roots in ordinary, everyday experience and practice, and destroying the principle of equal respect for all.

Response to the French publication of the present book was lively. In Germany, professional philosophers held back from taking positions. With some justification, it was pointed out that the topic of "Heidegger and Nazism" has been treated often in the Federal Republic, from Georg Luckács and Karl Löwith via Paul Hühnerfeld, Christian von Krockow, Theodor Adorno, and Alexander Schwan, to Hugo Ott—while in France Heidegger was instantly denazified and even given the status of a resister.[59] But in Germany also, the effect of the critique was minor. Neither Franzen's critical presentation of Heidegger's philosophical development nor the newer points established by Ott and Pöggeler on Heidegger's political engagement have become anything more than specialists' affairs.

Notes

1. Winfried Franzen, *Martin Heidegger* (Stuttgart, 1976), p. 78; all translations from German texts are mine unless a previous English translation could be found—TRANS.

2. Heidegger, *Die Selbstbehauptung der deutschen Universität, Rede, gehalten bei der feierlichen Übernahme des Rektorats der Universität Frieburg i. Br. am 27. 5. 1933*, and *Das Rektorat 1933–34. Tatsachen und Gedanken* (Frankfurt am Main, 1983); trans. Karsten Harries, under the title "The Self-Assertion of the German University: Address, Delivered on the Solemn Assumption of the Rectorate of the University Freiburg," and "The Rectorate 1933/34: Facts and Thoughts," *Review of Metaphysics* 38 (Mar. 1985): 467–502; quotations from "The Rectorate" are hereafter abbreviated "R."

3. Hugo Ott, "Martin Heidegger und die Universität Freiburg nach 1945," *Historisches Jahrbuch* 105 (1985): 95–128. See also Ott, "Martin Heidegger und der Nationalsozialismus," in *Heidegger und die praktische Philosophie*, ed. Annemarie Gethmann-Siefert and Otto Pöggeler (Frankfurt am Main, 1988), pp. 64–77.

4. See Pöggeler, "Den Führer führen? Heidegger und kein Ende," *Philosophische Rundschau* 32 (1985): 26–67, and Pöggeler, "Heideggers politisches Selbstverständnis," in *Heindegger und die praktische Philosophie*, pp. 17–63.

5. Karl Löwith, *Mein Leben in Deutschland vor und nach 1933. Ein Bericht* (Stuttgart, 1986), p. 57.

6. See Nicolas Tertulian, "Heidegger—oder: die Bestätigung der Politik durch Seins-geschichte. Ein Gang zu den Quellen. Was aus den Texten des Philosophen alles sprudelt," *Frankfurter Rundschau,* 2 Feb. 1988.

7. Ott, "Martin Heidegger und der Nationalsozialismus," p. 65.

8. Refraining from political and moral evaluation of Heidegger's conduct from that time ought to include renouncing comparisons that are only too easily set up in an endeavor to balance accounts. We can learn this lesson even from the circumspect Pöggeler, who not only compares Heidegger's engagement with Hitler to Ernst Bloch's and Georg Luckács's option for Stalin, but adduces as well a review in which Theodor Adorno, completely misunderstanding the situation in 1934, thought himself able to survive the nightmare in Germany. See Pöggeler, "Den Führer führen? Heidegger und kein Ende," p. 28. When in 1963 Adorno was confronted (in the pages of the Frankfurt student newspaper *Diskus*) with that review from 1934, he responded with a completely open letter; his words could not contrast more impressively with the shameful silence of Heidegger. See Adorno, *Gesammelte Schriften,* ed. Rolf Tiedemann, 22 vols. (Frankfurt am Main, 1973—78), 19:635–39. In these pages, one will find Tiedemann's editorial afterword, Adorno's letter, and a statement by Max Horkheimer.

9. Herbert Schnädelbach, *Philosophie in Deutschland 1831–1933* (Frankfurt am Main, 1983); trans. Eric Matthews, under the title *Philosophy in Germany 1831–1933* (Cambridge, Eng., 1984), p. 1.

10. For pragmatic themes in Heidegger, see C. F. Gethmann, "Vom Bewußtsein zum Handeln. Pragmatische Tendenzen in der Deutschen Philosophie der ersten Jahrzehnte des 20. Jahrhunderts," in *Pragmatik: Handbuch pragmatischen Denkens,* ed. Herbert Stachowiak, 2 vols. (Hamburg, 1986–87), 2:202–32.

11. See *Heidegger: Perspektiven zur Deutung seines Werks,* ed Pöggeler (Cologne, 1969).

12. An intensive engagement with the early Heidegger left its marks on my own work as well, up to *Knowledge and Human Interests,* trans. Jeremy J. Shapiro (Boston, 1971). See also the bibliographical references in Franzen, *Martin Heidegger,* p. 127. The Heideggerian Marxism of the young Herbert Marcuse fascinated me: see Alfred Schmidt, "Existential Ontologie und historischer Materialismus bei Herbert Marcuse," in *Antworten auf Herbert Marcuse,* ed. Habermas (Frankfurt, 1968), pp. 17 ff.

13. Hans-Ulrich Wehler, *Entsorgung der deutschen Vergangenheit? ein polemischer Essay zum "Historikerstreit"* (Munich, 1988). Even in the work of the historian Andreas Hill-gruber, one could find in 1986 the same comparison of the German crimes with the expulsion of Germans from the Eastern territories, a comparison that Marcuse objected to in an open letter to Heidegger in 1948; on this correspondence, see below pp. 163–64.

14. Jaspers and Archbishop Gröber even demanded, or expected, from their friend Heidegger in 1945 a "genuine rebirth" and a "spiritual reversal" (Ott, "Martin Heidegger und der Nationalsozialismus," p. 65).

15. Even Richard Rorty misses the point that the problem is not the relation between person and work, but the amalgamation of work and worldview. See Rorty, "Taking Philosophy Seriously," a review of *Heidegger et le Nazisme,* by Victor Farias, *The New Republic,* 11 Apr. 1988, pp. 31–34.

16. Manfred Frank, "Philosophie heute und jetzt," *Frankfurter Rundschau,* 5 Mar. 1988.

17. Habermas, *The Philosophical Discourse of Modernity: Twelve Lectures*, trans. Frederick Lawrence (Cambridge, Mass., 1987), pp. 155–60.

18. Unfortunately, I was at that time unacquainted with the pertinent investigation by Franzen, *Von der Existentialontologie zur Seinsgeschichte* (Meisenheim am Glan, 1975), part 3, pp. 63–101 (hereafter abbreviated *E*), and with the afterword to the second edition of Pöggeler, *Der Denkweg Martin Heideggers* (Pfullingen, 1983), pp. 319–55; trans. Daniel Magurshak and Sigmund Barber, under the title *Martin Heidegger's Path of Thinking* (Atlantic Highlands, N.J., 1987); hereafter abbreviated *HPT*.

19. Habermas, *The Philosophical Discourse of Modernity*, pp. 141 ff. On the controversial prehistory of *Being and Time*, see the following contributions in *Dilthey-Jahrbuch für Philosophie und Geschichte der Geisteswissenshaften* 4 (1986–87): Hans-Georg Gadamer, "Erinnerungen an Heideggers Anfänge," pp. 13–26; Gethmann, "Philosophie als Vollzug und als Begriff. Heideggers Identitäts-philosophie des Lebens in der Vorlesung vom Wintersemester 1921/22 und ihr Verhaltnis zu *Sein und Zeit*," pp. 27–53; and Theodor Kisiel, "Das Entstehen des Begriffsfeldes 'Faktizität' im Frühwerk Heideggers," pp. 91–120.

20. Fritz K. Ringer, *The Decline of the German Mandarins: The German Academic Community 1890–1933* (Cambridge, MA, 1969); see my review of this book in Habermas, *Philosophischpolitische Profile* (Frankfurt am Main, 1971), pp. 239–51. See also H. Brunkhorst, *Der Intellektuelle im Land der Mandarine* (Frankfurt am Main, 1987).

21. See *E*, pp. 47 ff. Adorno, by the way, had already noted this in his inaugural lecture of 1931. See Adorno, "The Actuality of Philosophy," *Telos* 31 (Spring 1977): 120–33.

22. See Michael Theunissen, *Der Andere: Studien zur Sozialontologie der Gegenwart* (Berlin, 1977), p. 182; trans. Christopher Macann, under the title *The Other: Studies in the Social Ontology of Husserl, Heidegger, Sartre, and Buber* (Cambridge, MA, 1984)

23. See Ernst Tugendhat, "Heideggers Idee von Wahrheit," in *Heidegger: Perspektiven zur Deutung seines Werks*, pp. 286–97. See also Karl-Otto Apel, *Transformation der Philosophie*, 2 vols. (Frankfurt am Main, 1973), vol. 1, part 2.

24. Gethmann, "Heideggers Konzeption des Handelns in *Sein und Zeit*," in *Heidegger und die praktische Philosophie*, pp. 140–76.

25. Ibid., p. 142.

26. Kurt Sontheimer, *Antidemokratisches Denken in der Weimarer Republik: die politischen Ideen des deutschen Nationalismus zwischen 1918 und 1933* (Munich, 1962). See also Christian von Krockow, *Die Entscheidung: eine Untersuchung über Ernst Jünger, Carl Schmitt, Martin Heidegger* (Stuttgart, 1958).

27. Heidegger's French apologists get things backwards when they seek to explain his commitment to National Socialism by saying that the thought of *Being and Time* is still too rooted in "metaphysical thinking" and still too bound up with the fate of nihilism. See Philippe Lacoue-Labarthe, *La Fiction du politique: Heidegger, l'art et la politique* (Paris, 1987). For a critical treatment see Luc Ferry and Alain Renaut, *Heidegger et les modernes* (Paris, 1988).

28. Pöggeler, "Den Führer führen? Heidegger und kein Ende," p. 47.

29. See the early essay by Marcuse—still one of the keenest analyses of this relation-

ship—"The Struggle against Liberalism in the Totalitarian View of the State," *Negations: Essays in Critical Theory* (Boston, 1968), pp. 3–42. See especially p. 41 for references to Heidegger's article in the Freiburg student newspaper, *freiburger Studentenzeitung,* 10 Nov. 1933.

30. Heidegger, *Die Grundbegriffe der Metaphysik,* ed. Friedrich-Wilhelm von Herrmann, vol. 29/30 of *Gesamtausgabe* (Frankfurt am Main, 1983), p. 244. For an analysis of the whole of section 38 of this work, see Franzen, "Die Sehnsucht nach Härte und Schwere," in *Heidegger und die praktische Philosophie,* pp. 78–92.

31. Heidegger, "Letter on Humanism," trans. Frank A. Capuzzi, J. Glenn Gray, and David Farrell Krell, *Basic Writings,* ed. Krell (New York, 1977), p. 213; hereafter abbreviated "L.H."

32. Heidegger, "On the Essence of Truth," trans. John Sallis, *Basic Writings,* p. 136.

33. Some interpreters of Heidegger are inclined to view the final chapters of *Being and Time,* especially the talk of "fate" and "destiny," in a collectivistic sense. This way of reading, however, only repeats Heidegger's own retrospective self-portrait. See my remarks in *The Philosophical Discourse of Modernity,* pp. 403–4 n.41.

34. Johannes Gross, a trustworthy witness, has communicated, in the sixty-second installment of the new series of his "Notizbuch" in the magazine of the *Frankfurter Allgemeine Zeitung,* the content of a letter from Heidegger to Carl Schmitt of August 22, 1932 (!). The last paragraph runs: "Today I would just like to say that I am very much counting on your resolute collaboration in rebuilding the entire faculty of law from the inside out, both as to research and as to teaching. Everything is unfortunately very gloomy here. It becomes even more urgent to gather together the spiritual forces that can bring about what is to come. For today I close with friendly greetings. Heil Hitler. Yours, Heidegger."

35. This figure of thought stands in the center of Heidegger's lectures on the "Introduction to Metaphysics" of 1935. See *Einführung in die Metaphysik* (Tübingen, 1953); trans. Ralph Mannheim, under the title *An Introduction to Metaphysics* (New Haven, Conn. 1979); hereafter abbreviated *IM.* See also Alexander Schwan, *Politische Philosophie im Denken Heideggers* (Opladen, 1965).

36. Quoted in *Nachlese zu Heidegger. Dokumente zu seinem Leben und Denken,* ed. Guido Schneeberger (Bern, 1962), pp. 149–50. Connections between the "Rektoratsrede" and *Being and Time* are explored in Harries, "Heidegger as a Political Thinker," in *Heidegger and Modern Philosophy: Critical Essays,* ed. Michael Murray (New Haven, Conn., 1978), pp. 304–28.

37. Pöggeler formulates this as a question—though certainly a rhetorical one.

38. Heidegger, *Heraklit,* ed. Manfred S. Frings, vol. 55 of *Gesamtausgabe,* p. 123. For references to similar passages, see *HPT,* p. 279.

39. Heidegger, *Hölderlins Hymne "Der Ister,"* ed. Walter Biemel, vol. 53 of *Gesamtausgabe,* p. 106.

40. Pöggeler, "Heideggers politisches Selbstverständnis," p. 59 n.11.

41. Pöggeler, "Den Führer führen? Heidegger und kein Ende," p. 56.

42. Heidegger, "Überwindung der Metaphysik," *Vorträge und Aufsätze* (1954; Pfullin-

gen, 1978); trans. Joan Stambaugh, under the title "Overcoming Metaphysics," *The End of Philosophy* (New York, 1973), p. 84; hereafter abbreviated "OM."

43. See Habermas, *The Philosophical Discourse of Modernity,* pp. 159–60.

44. On this discussion, which I cannot take up here, see *E,* pp. 152 ff.

45. See "Nur noch ein Gott kann uns retten," interview with Heidegger, *Der Spiegel* 23 (1976): 193–219; trans. William J. Richardson, under the title "Only a God Can Save Us: *Der Spiegel's* Interview with Martin Heidegger,: in *Heidegger: The Man and the Thinker,* ed. Thomas Sheehan (Chicago, 1981), pp. 45–67.

46. "Säuberungsaktion" might also be translated as "purging action"—TRANS.

47. To capture the wordplay in Heidegger's sentence, one could translate it as follows: " 'defense service' I understood neither in a militaristic nor an aggressive sense, but in the sense of self-defense"—TRANS.

48. Habermas, "Zur Veröffentlichung von Vorlesungen aus dem Jahre 1935," Frankfurter Allgemeine Zeitung, 25 July 1953; reprinted in Habermas, *Philosophisch-politische Profile,* pp. 65–72.

49. Christian E. Lewalter, *Die Zeit,* 13 Aug. 1953.

50. Another of Lewalter's sentences deserves to be recorded here: "The extent to which Heidegger's accusers have fallen victim to the passion for persecution is shown by a particularly venomous remark of the present critic. 'A Fascist intelligentsia as such,' says Habermas, 'did not exist only because the mediocrity of the Fascist leadership could not accept the offer of the intellectuals. The forces were indeed there. Only the inferior stature of the political functionaries pressed those intellectual forces into the opposition.' In other words: Heidegger offered himself to Hitler but Hitler, in his 'mediocrity,' rejected the offer and forced Heidegger into opposition. So Habermas presents it." [Ibid.]
Lewalter could have had no idea that Heidegger would eventually confirm my remark, which was rather more clairvoyant than venomous: "National Socialism did, indeed, go in this [correct—J.H.] direction. Those people, however, were far much too poorly equipped for thought to arrive at a really explicit relationship to what is happening today and has been underway for the past 300 years" ("Nur noch ein Gott kann uns retten," p. 214; "Only a God Can Save Us," p. 61).

51. Heidegger, letter to the editor, *Die Zeit,* 24 Sept. 1953.

52. Rainer Marten, "Ein rassistisches Konzept von Humanität," *Badische Zeitung,* 19–20 Dec. 1987. Upon my inquiry, Marten confirmed the matter in a letter of 28 Jan. 1988: "At that time we were reading corrections for Heidegger, for the preparation of the new edition of *Being and Time* (Tübingen, 1953) and the first publication of the lectures from 1935. The passage stood out, to the best of my memory, not because of any explanatory parenthesis, but only through the monstrous nature of its content, which struck all three of us."

53. *Pflasterstrand* (January 1988): 48–49.

54. Ibid., p. 46.

55. See Heinrich Wiegand Petzet, *Auf einen Stern zugehen. Begegnungen und Gespräche mit Martin Heidegger, 1926–76* (Frankfurt am Main, 1983), p. 101.

56. See Heidegger, *Nietzsche*, 2 vols. (Tübingen, 1961).

57. See Hubert L. Dreyfus, "Holism and Hermeneutics," *Review of Metaphysics* 34 (September 1980): 3–23.

58. Ernst Nolte concludes his essay on philosophy and National Socialism with this sentence: "I believe that Heidegger's engagement of 1933 *and* the insight of 1934 into his errors were both more philosophical than the correctness of the consistently distanced and extremely respectable conduct of Nicolai Hartmann" (Philosophie und Nationalsozialismus," in *Heidegger und die praktische Philosophie,* p. 355).

59. On this see Ott, "Wege und Abwege," *Neue Zürcher Zeitung* 27 (November 28–29, 1987): 67. This essay also includes an expert's critical comments on Farias' book.

7

Taking Aim at the Heart of the Present: On Foucault's Lecture on Kant's *What is Enlightenment?*

The current counterpart to neoconservatism is a radical critique of reason stamped by French poststructuralism, which is meeting with a lively response, especially among students and younger intellectuals. In this memorial address for Michel Foucault . . . I tried to bring out the critical impulse in this critique of reason, which occasionally slides off into Germanic obscurity.

Foucault's death came so unexpectedly and so precipitously that one can scarcely resist the thought that the life and teachings of the philosopher were being documented even in the circumstantiality and brutal contingency of his sudden death. Even from a distance, one experiences Foucault's death at fifty-seven as an event whose untimeliness affirms the violence and mercilessness of time—the power of facticity, which, without sense and without triumph, prevails over the painstakingly constructed meaning of each human life. For Foucault, the experience of finiteness became a philosophical stimulus. He observed the power of the contingent, which he ultimately identified with power as such, from the stoic perspective, rather than interpreting it from within the Christian horizon of experience. And yet in him the stoic attitude of keeping an overly precise distance, the attitude of the observer obsessed with objectivity, was peculiarly entwined with the opposite element of passionate, self-consuming participation in the contemporary relevance of the historical moment.

I met Foucault only in 1983, and perhaps I did not understand him well. I can only relate what impressed me: the tension, one that eludes familiar categories, between the almost serene scientific reserve of the scholar striving for objectivity on the one hand, and the political vitality of the vulnerable, subjectively excitable, morally sensitive intellectual on the other. I imagine that Foucault dug through archives with the stubborn energy of a detective in hot pursuit of evidence. When he suggested to me in March 1983 that we meet with some American colleagues in November 1984 for a private conference to discuss Kant's essay *What is Enlightenment?*, which had appeared two hundred years earlier, I knew nothing of a lecture on that very subject that Foucault had just given. I had understood his invitation as a call to a discussion in which we, along with Hubert Dreyfus, Richard Rorty, and Charles Taylor, would debate various interpretations of modernity, using as a basis for discussion a text that in a certain sense initiated the philosophical discourse of modernity. But this was not exactly Foucault's intention in his proposal; I realized that, however, only in May of this year, when an excerpt from Foucault's lecture was published.

In Foucault's lecture we do not meet the Kant familiar from *The Order of Things,* the epistemologist who thrust open the door to the age of anthropological thought and the human sciences with his analysis of finiteness. Instead we encounter a *different* Kant—the precursor of the Young Hegelians, the Kant who was the first to make a serious break with the metaphysical heritage, who turned philosophy away from the Eternal Verities and concentrated on what philosophers had until then considered to be without concept and nonexistent, merely contingent and transitory. In Kant's answer to the question "What is Enlightenment?" Foucault sees the origin of an "ontology of contemporary reality" that leads through Hegel, Nietzsche, and Max Weber to Horkheimer and Adorno. Surprisingly, in the last sentence of his lecture Foucault includes himself in this tradition.

Foucault links the *What is Enlightenment?* text, which appeared in 1784, with Kant's *Dispute of the Faculties,* which appeared fourteen years later and looks back on the events of the French Revolution. The dispute between the Philosophical Faculty and the Faculty of Law concerned the question whether the human race was involved in continual progress toward the better. In his philosophy of law Kant had clarified the end state in terms of which this progress could be measured: A republican constitution would ensure the rule of law internally as well as externally: both the autonomy of citizens under laws they had made for themselves and the elimination of war from international relations. In the *Dispute of the Faculties* Kant is looking for an empirical reference point to demonstrate that a "moral tendency" of the human race, observable in history, actually moves toward these postulates of pure practical reason. He is looking for an "event of our time" that indicates a disposition on the part of the human race toward what is morally better; and he finds this "historical sign" not in the French Revolution itself but in the openly manifested enthusiasm with which a broad public had fearlessly greeted these events as an attempt to realize principles of natural law. Such a phenomenon, Kant believes, cannot be forgotten—"for that event is too great, too closely interwoven with the interest of mankind, not to be remembered by the peoples of the world under the inducement of favorable conditions and awakened for renewed attempts of this kind."

Foucault cites these famous sentences not entirely without a "feeling for collaboration in the good" on his part. In the earlier text on enlightenment Kant had still emphasized that revolution never gives rise to "true reform of a way of thinking," a reform that, as he says later in the *Dispute of the Faculties*, finds expression precisely in enthusiasm for the revolution that has since taken place. Foucault connects the two texts in such a way that a synoptic view emerges. From this angle the question "What is Enlightenment?" fuses with the question "What does the revolution mean for us?" A fusion of philosophy with thought stimulated by contemporary historical actuality is thereby accomplished—the gaze that has been schooled in Eternal Truths immerses itself in the detail of a moment pregnant with decision and bursting under the pressure of anticipated possibilities for the future.

Thus Foucault discovers in Kant the *first* philosopher to take aim like an archer at the heart of a present that is concentrated in the significance of the contemporary moment, and thereby to inaugurate the discourse of modernity. Kant drops the classical dispute over the exemplary status of the ancients and the equal stature of the moderns; transforming thought into a diagnostic instrument, he entangles it in the restless process of self-reassurance that to this day has kept modernity in ceaseless motion within the horizon of a new historical consciousness. For a philosophy claimed by the significance of the contemporary moment, the issue is the relationship of modernity to itself, the "rapport 'sagital' à sa propre actualité." Hölderlin and the young Hegel, Marx and the Young Hegelians, Baudelaire and Nietzsche, Bataille and the Surrealists, Lukács, Merleau-Ponty, the precursors of Western Marxism in general, and not least, Foucault himself—all of them contribute to the sharpening of the modern time consciousness that made its entrance into philosophy with the question "What is Enlightenment?" The philosopher becomes a contemporary; he steps out of the anonymity of an impersonal enterprise and identifies himself as a person of flesh and blood to whom every clinical investigation of a contemporary period confronting him must be directed. Even in retrospect, the period of the Enlightenment fits the description it gave itself: it marks the entrance into a modernity that sees itself condemned to draw on itself for its consciousness of self and its norm.

If this is even a paraphrase of Foucault's own train of thought, the question arises how such an affirmative understanding of modern philosophizing, a philosophizing that is inscribed in our present and always directed to the relevance of our contemporary reality, fits with Foucault's unyielding critique of modernity. How can Foucault's self-understanding as a thinker in the tradition of the Enlightenment be compatible with his unmistakable critique of precisely this form of knowledge, which is that of modernity?

Wouldn't every line of Kant's philosophy of history, his speculations about a constitution of freedom, about world-citizenship and perpetual peace, his interpretation of revolutionary enthusiasm as a sign of historical progress toward the better—wouldn't every line of all this necessarily provoke the scorn of Foucault the theoretician of power? Hasn't history frozen into an *iceberg* under the stoic gaze of Foucault the archaeologist, an iceberg covered with the crystalline forms of arbitrary discourse formations? (This, at least, is how his friend Paul Veyne sees it.) Doesn't this iceberg begin to demonstrate, under the cynical gaze of Foucault the genealogist, a completely different dynamic than the thought of modernity, with its orientation to contemporary reality, would like to acknowledge—merely a senseless back-and-forth movement of anonymous processes of subjugation in which power and nothing but power keeps appearing in ever-changing guises? Didn't Foucault, using Kant as an example, reveal in *The Order of Things* the peculiar dynamic of a will to truth for which every frustration is only a new stimulus to an increased production of knowledge which then fails in its turn? Modernity's form of knowledge is characterized by the aporia that the cognitive subject, having become self-referential, rises from the ruins of metaphysics to pledge itself, in full awareness of its finite powers, to a project that would demand infinite power. As Foucault demonstrates, Kant transforms this aporia into a structural principle of his epistemology by reinterpreting the limitations of our finite faculty of cognition as transcendental conditions of a knowledge that progresses on into infinitude. A subject strained to the limits of its structure becomes entangled in the anthropocentric form of knowledge, and this terrain is then occupied by the human sciences, in which Foucault sees an insidious disciplinary force at work. With their pretentious claims that are never made good, in any case, the human sciences put up the dangerous facade of a universally valid knowledge, behind which is hidden the facticity of a sheer will to self-possession through knowledge. Only in the wake of this bottomless will to knowledge are the subjectivity and the consciousness of self that make up Kant's starting point formed.

If we return to the text of Foucault's lecture with these considerations in mind, we do in fact note certain precautionary measures against all too obvious contradictions. Certainly the Enlightenment, which inaugurates modernity, does not represent merely an arbitrary period in intellectual history for us. But Foucault warns us against the pious attitude of those who are intent only on preserving the remains of the Enlightenment. He explicitly (if only parenthetically) establishes the connection to his earlier analyses. Today it cannot be our task, he says, to maintain enlightenment and revolution as ideal models; rather, the important thing is to inquire into the particular historical forces that since the late eighteenth century have both gained acceptance in universalist thought and hidden within it. Foucault opposes the "thinkers of order" who continue on with Kant's epistemological problematic; still in search of the universal conditions under which propositions as such can be true or false, they are caught in an "analytic of truth." In spite of these precautions it is a surprise to find that Foucault now presents the subversive thinkers who try to grasp the contemporary relevance of their present as the legitimate heirs of the Kantian critique. Under the altered conditions of their own times, they once again pose the fundamental diagnostic question of a modernity engaged in self-reassurance, the question that Kant was the first to pose. Foucault sees himself as carrying on this tradition. For him the challenge of the Kant texts on which his lecture is based consists in deciphering the will that was once revealed in the enthusiasm for the French Revolution. For that is the will to knowledge that the "analytic of truth" cannot acknowledge. Whereas, however, Foucault had previously traced this will to knowledge in modern power formations only to denounce it, he *now* displays it in a completely different light: as the critical impulse that links his own thought with the beginnings of modernity, an impulse worthy of preservation and in need of renewal.

Of the circle of those in my generation engaged in philosophical diagnoses of the times, Foucault has had the most lasting effect on the *Zeitgeist,* not least of all thanks to the earnestness with which he preseveres in productive contradictions. Only complex thought produces instructive contradictions. Kant became entangled in an instructive contradiction of this kind when he explained revolutionary enthusiasm as a historical sign that allowed an intelligible disposition in the human race to appear within the phenomenal world. Equally instructive is the contradiction in which Foucault becomes entangled when he opposes his critique of power, disabled by the relevance of the contemporary moment, to the analytic of the true in such a way that the former is deprived of the normative standards it would have to derive from the latter. Perhaps it is the force of this contradiction that drew Foucault, in this last of his texts, back into a sphere of influence he had tried to blast open, that of the philosophical discourse of modernity.

8

Culture and Politics

Political Culture in Germany Since 1968: An Interview with Dr. Rainer Erd for the *Frankfurter Rundschau*

Erd: Professor Habermas, this spring of 1988, members of my generation, who are now in their forties, are looking back on a date that seemed to make relevant social change possible: May 1968. In the spring of 1968 a movement that wanted more than social movements traditionally demand made its worldwide public debut. The student movement not only advocated institutional changes (like university reform); equally, it advocated individual emancipation in a comprehensive sense. It declared war on classical institutions of bourgeois society like marriage and the nuclear family as much as on the structural division between manual and mental labor.

Not only were the political institutions of parliamentary democracy (and the three fundamental domains of parliament, law, and administration) subjected to a fundamental critique; the international division of labor was subjected to the same critique. The spectrum of demands made by the student movement extended from individual emancipation to new forms of life and living arrangements, to changes in the structure of the economy, society, and the state and the abolition of the division between the First, Second, and Third Worlds.

Obviously, much of what was so emphatically demanded at that time has not become reality. And yet it seems to me that to think that the conservatism of the past years has revoked the changes of the 1970s is to fundamentally misjudge the political situation at the end of the 1980s. How do you see this? What has the student movement left us?

Habermas: Mrs. Süssmuth [Rita Süssmuth, minister of family affairs in the Kohl government]. A liberal minister of family affairs of this type would scarcely have been thinkable in a Christian Democratic government prior to 1968. I am not being altogether ironic; this fact indicates something. If we think of Mr. Dettling [a young colleague of Heiner Geissler, Christian Democratic party general secretary, in the central office of the party], the march through the institutions has reached even the Christian Democratic party—not just social work, the schools, the kindergarten or the media. And furthermore, the fact that Mrs. Süssmuth has extended her province to include women's issues and has given some remarkable twists to traditional family and youth policies, at least in their outward appearance, is symptomatic of a shift in boundaries.

The definition of what is political has changed since 1968. It is now taken for granted that much of what was formerly assumed to be part of the private sphere is a matter of politics—the relations between the sexes, for example ("marital violence"), or the status of housework and childrearing, issues connected with childraising, and so forth. Private needs have been politicized. And then we have to ask what Heiner Geissler, who is so cool and calculating, was responding to when he decided on this kind of woman. He was in fact responding to a subliminal change in attitudes and conceptions of value in segments of the population that even a conservative party needs to stay on the right side of.

It is precisely in these subinstitutional domains that there are now signs of a liberalizing thrust. Karl Mannheim spoke of a fundamental democratization. We haven't got that far yet here. But a process of fundamental liberalization set in motion by the cultural revolution of that period—you can see something of that. Changes in the form of interpersonal relations in families, schools, universities, and sometimes even the courtroom do not affect deeply rooted social inequalities, but still, they are not nothing.

Erd: There is no publicly relevant domain in the Federal Republic where one does not find traces of the 1968 movement. In the legal domain, for instance, in nearly every area of the law and especially, of course, in the socially sensitive areas of labor and constitutional law, there are now judges whose positions cut across prevailing arguments.

Habermas: And in Mutlangen younger lawyers are even engaging in civil disobedience [in protests against the stationing of missiles]. But when we talk about 1968 and what came after it we should also take a step back and look at the incubation period: Adenauer's last years, the Erhard interim, the Grand Coalition up to the election of Heinemann. Bauer, the Hessian state attorney general, had set the first Auschwitz trial in motion. Later the first debate on the statute of limitations [for Nazi crimes] was successful. Discussions about our policy on Eastern Europe and the Soviet Union began. Jaspers became radicalized. The social studies curriculum was reformed. The *edition suhrkamp* and, somewhat later, [Alexander and Margarete Mitscherlich's book] *The Inability to Mourn* were published. In those years between 1960 and 1968 noninstitutionalized public opinion was becoming increasingly important. Then the student movement was the one- to two-year long explosion that no one had foreseen. A neoconservatism that in our country is particularly full of *ressentiment* soon concocted a kind of counterrevolution to this revolt. Marcuse's opposition between "counterrevolution and revolt" fits the German scene in the 1970s quite well—as though the emotions that had been discredited under the shadow of Nazi crimes were only waiting for an occasion to rise to the surface again.

Erd: Professor Habermas, at the end of the 1960s one had the impression that you were one of the student movement's chief opponents. After you spoke of the "Left fascism" of the student movement, the theoreticians of the Left attacked you and reproached you with supporting the conservative cause.

Habermas: To speak to that only briefly: I made this reproach in the form of a hypothetical question in Hannover in 1967, very spontaneously and in a very specific context; I explained it immediately, and in 1977 I retracted it altogether—much to Rudi Dutschke's satisfaction, incidentally. I tried at that time to explain why left-wing intellectuals in the Federal Republic reacted to the first signs of a rhetoric of violence and the use of violence in a way that was touchier, more fastidious, more irritable than their friends in other countries. I had already spoken out in May 1968 (in this paper, by the way) against the dubious distinction between "violence against things" and "violence against persons."

Erd: Be that as it may, your criticism that the student movement overestimated the real possibilities for action has been confirmed by the history of the past twenty years. When we see how such symbolic figures of 1968 as Daniel Cohn-Bendit are now defending the market and parliamentary democracy, we certainly get the impression that at least the portion of the student movement that is currently politically influential implicitly accepted the critique you made then. On the other hand, you have now become someone to be criticized by the other political camp, the conservatives.

Habermas: I see that, my dear Dr. Erd, a little differently. I have always been a red flag for the conservatives. Even in 1953, when I criticized Heidegger, people saw me as a spokesman for Adorno, although at the time, as a naive student in Bonn, I had had no contact with the Frankfurt people. My critique of a specific form of student actionism in 1968–69 had more of an internal character—and that is also how it was received.

Erd: But still, the conservatives' tone has become sharper. Especially in articles in the *Frankfurter Allgemeine Zeitung,* and with Joachim Fest, [one of the editors], and Konrad Adam taking the lead, they are even making you jointly responsible for acts of political terrorism. To be made responsible, first by the Left and now by the conservatives, for things with which you really have nothing to do—is that the price an intellectual who is critical and politically committed has to pay? Or is it specific to the political culture of the Federal Republic that intellectual opponents are called political enemies regardless of the situation?

Habermas: Anybody who enters the political public sphere and criticizes other people cannot be a crybaby himself. There is always something comical in the picture of the innocent prosecutor. And the syndrome of violence is deeply entrenched in all of us. Intellectual controversies are characterized as political battles elsewhere as well. Here, though, we are under the suspicion of being not only political opponents but "domestic enemies"—in that you're right. In a country that has never experienced a revolution, the right-wing intelligentsia—from Carl Schmitt to Ernst Nolte—stirs up the citizens' fear of civil war and constructs theories based upon it. Furthermore, the mandarin consciousness, which Hauke Brunkhorst recently examined in an important book, [*Der Intellektuelle im Land der Mandarine*, Frankfurt, 1987], is specific to the German university tradition. One element in it is hatred of the intellectual, another is a distorted understanding of politics. Mandarins always speak in the exalted name of science and scholarship. Even when they enter the political public sphere, they are completely unwilling to accept the rules of the game and the presuppositions of communication in that sphere—they are above all that.

Clearly this is how the historians Hillgruber and Nolte emerged from the university to disseminate, in a popular paperback or a feuilleton, ideas whose target was our self-understanding as citizens of the Federal Republic. They did not think of themselves as intellectuals who were bringing their technical expertise into the discourse of the public appropriation of tradition. They actually thought—or at least that is what they said—they were engaged in scholarship, nothing but pure scholarship. They were willing to participate in the public discourse of citizens of this country only with the privileges accorded experts and under the cover of scholarship. It is only in terms of this piece of very German ideology that I can explain the reproach leveled against me by these and other historians. When one tried to explain to them that in the politic public sphere comparisons between what happened in the concentration camps and what happened on the Eastern Front, or comparisons between Auschwitz and Dresden, lose their alleged scholarly innocence and necessarily turn into a settling of accounts, they took it as a "ban on thought and inquiry."

Erd: If we compare the current political situation with that of twenty years ago, two things are especially striking. The political spectrum has been extended, on the Left and on the Right. Today left-wing terrorism, which after the Red Army Faction was taken over in part by groups like the Autonomen, is as much a part of everyday politics as radical-right groups. But the spectrum of legal politics has also been extended on the Left and on the Right. Since the beginning of the 1980s, conservatism has been the dominant political grouping in the Federal Republic, relativized to a certain extent, however, by the Greens. And in the realm of journalism the once liberal *Frankfurter Allgemeine Zeitung* has developed into a conservative and sometimes radical-right partisan paper, while the Left has found an organ in the "taz" (*Tageszeitung*, daily paper).

Habermas: For obvious reasons neither a classical Left nor a classical Right has been able to develop in the Federal Republic. We have neither a strong communist party nor a Le Pen [the French neofascist party] nor the Neofascists. But the more things are normalized here, forty years later, the more the integrative power of a strong center proves to be a force of concealment as well. The fluid boundaries between neoconservatism and the radical Right, as at Weikersheim or in "MUT," a radical-right magazine read by our Chancellor, are obscured. The lines are becoming blurred on the Left too, if we think of the neutralist nationalism of some Berlin subcultures.

Erd: My question is, are conservatism and the peace movement as well as left-wing and right-wing radicalism results of the structural problems of the left-liberal era of the 1970s?

Habermas: The agreement on missile deployment that Helmut Schmidt pushed through, a climate in which efforts at reform had failed, and other things drove many people in the Social Democratic Party to the Left, while at the same time, in a climate of *ressentiment,* the unabashed pressure of capital, unemployment, the weakness of the unions, and so forth, advanced the Right. These are normal swings of the pendulum. You ask why the pendulum is swinging again now. Apart from stagnation in international economic problems, structural changes in the economy at home, technical and demographic developments, and especially the social consequences of unemployment—apart from these obvious problems, there has also been a change in the way the public perceives the problems.

We see on the one hand a habituation to crises that are becoming widespread, diffuse, and ongoing, and that appear to be a form in which accelerated change stabilizes itself. But on the other hand the reactions to these crises are also becoming more subjective, more governed by mood, more eccentric. I noticed a certain *fin-de-siècle* mood, a feeling that time is running out. Everyday postmodernism is gaining ground.

This mood is double-edged: it makes some people subdued and causes others to flip out. This may also be connected with our greater distance from 1945. For the first time, the Federal Republic is acquiring historical contours of its own. It is becoming possible to survey its life cycle. We have reached a point from which it is easy to divide postwar history into phases: First there are the years up to the currency reform, the restoration phase, which was important both symbolically and economically—the majority of the population was still dazed by the collapse of the Nazi regime; the voices of an antifascist coalition that would soon disintegrate were still muffled by suspicious Allies. Then, under Adenauer, a long, very long latency period characterized by an aggressive constructive will that was channeled into the private sphere—with a division of labor between "no experiments" and the opposition of the literati. Then the period of incubation, the first stirrings of unrest, the economic crisis of 1967, and the [student] revolt; and finally the two very contrary pulses of thirteen years of a social-liberal coalition that made more changes in the soft flesh of motivations and mentalities under the surface of institutions and structures than in the hard stone of the bureaucracy.

And today we have the ambiguous *juste-milieu*, the "right" environment, of the cheerful Yuppies atop a base of the (as yet) silent unemployed. These phases, I think, are now discernible from the perspective of the ordinary person and not only from that of the historian. And it is only from this distance, with the awareness of a regained normality, that that past, that pluperfect past that will not pass away, acquires tremendous contemporary relevance. Perhaps this is the kind of normality that is possible for us after Auschwitz. And the more extreme swings of the pendulum that you mentioned are part of this.

Erd: It is specific to the contemporary period that the question of who champions an emancipatory concept of society can no longer necessarily be answered in terms of organizations. Whereas earlier one would have had valid grounds for naming the Social Democrats and the unions as the institutions that stood for social change and the dismantling of domination, the situation is now fundamentally different. The political landscape of the Federal Republic can no longer be divided up into "conservative" and "emancipatory" organizations. Instead, one finds both positions throughout the whole spectrum of parties. There are groups in the Christian Democratic party that represent much more emancipatory ideas than the orthodox cadres of the Social Democratic party, although of course the converse is also true. It now seems indisputable that the Left's traditional idea of relativizing positions of economic authority and leveling social inquality through state intervention is no longer applicable. If this is correct . . . .

Habermas: May I interrupt you? When it comes to "right" and "left" I am old-fashioned. Take only the most important social themes, in social policy, for instance—unemployment, the status of gainful employment, which has become problematic, the idea of a minimum income for everyone, which Oscar Lafontaine has now taken up, in other words, a relative decoupling of income and employment. Or in legal policy: the key words there are internal security, the right to asylum, civil disobedience, a communal right to vote for foreign workers, and so forth; or the national theme, the old standby of reunification—on these "issues" opinions diverge very quickly. Of course you are correct in saying that *all* the parties (and the Greens set the pace there) are involved in a reorientation, even the Free Democratic party, which after the ideological shift had initially regressed to a purely economic party of the Weimar type.

Erd: If everyone is looking for alternative orientations, then let me ask what you consider to be the most important political problems of the immediate future.

Habermas: On that I have nothing original to say; I read the paper like everyone else. The problems of armaments and arms exportation, the problem of the ecological reconstruction of industrial society and the Third World, and especially our number one problem: With the labor unions on the defensive, how can we stop the social darwinism of the "two-thirds society" [with two-thirds of the population affluent and one-third permanently marginalized], how can we strengthen the solidarity of those who remain inside with those on the outside, with those who are excluded or marginalized—at least all that is out in the open and is being discussed.

Another theme has become interesting, one which, as you know, I have been concerned with for thirty years: the structural transformation of the public sphere and the prospects for radical democracy. The electoral strategists and the electoral sociologists are most aware of it. We are now feeling the effects of an educational revolution, of the women's movement, which is finally making progress, and of the electronic media. One feels it here in the Frankfurt area: the cultural orientations of broad strata of the population are being transformed. The catch-phrase "postmaterial values" is not completely inaccurate. The new constellation of culture and politics that is emerging interests me. Election results are clearly increasingly dependent on a perception of individual political problems that is theme-dependent, well informed, and thus culturally mediated.

That too is a long-term consequence of 1968. Looser party ties may be symptomatic of the fact that more and more people are suing for the use-value of democracy and the constitutional state. They want democracy in cash, in the ready cash of the active utilization of individual liberties, more political participation, individualized mass consumption. And thus counter-political spheres arise that are close to the base, not only in the metropolitan subcultures, around the Greens, but also in disadvantaged marginal groups that we always said could not be organized and were not capable of action.

The more mass civilization prevails and comes to be taken for granted, the more it loses the aura of a critique of civilization, of the "revolt of the masses," the more the romanticism of mass action, which has dazzled the Left long enough, fades away. The new perspective is that of a culture-society in which autonomous public spheres multiply and can form subversive counter-balances to the highly organized public sphere that was bequeathed to us.

Perhaps at some point even the political parties will be compelled to reorganize, or at least to differentiate clearly between two opposing functions. For they should do more than just select leadership personnel for the next government, be a component of the political system, and extract mass loyalty from the public sphere. They should be a more forceful presence within the public sphere and function more as a catalyst, clarifying and concentrating opinions rather than creating and prompting them.

The utopias of social labor are out of date. Socialism will survive only if it takes seriously the utopian element that lies within democratic procedures themselves. The procedural utopia focuses on the structures and presuppositions for a radical-pluralistic, largely decentralized process of will-formation that produces complexity and is certainly costly, a process of will-formation the content and outcomes of which no one can—or should want to—anticipate.

Erd: We keep hearing it said that to this point the "Historians' Debate" has produced one conspicuous result: It has made the weakness of the conservative argument public and by doing so has hindered conservative groups in the Federal Republic more than it has helped them. In public opinion in the Federal Republic—leaving the *Frankfurter Allgemeine Zeitung* and *Die Welt* aside as important but taking an outside position—there seems quite obviously to be a consensus that Nazism was a

unique historical phenomenon and can certainly not be understood as a reaction to Bolshevism. Looked at this way, the
"Historians' Debate" was the test of the political culture that
arose in the Federal Republic after 1968. And it stood the test
well.

Habermas: The fact that Hans-Ulrich Wehler, one of the German historians most highly regarded here and abroad, has
expressed himself so clearly, unambiguously, and convincingly
in his book on the Historians' Debate may confirm your impression. I don't want to underestimate the political culture's powers of self-purification—think of the Barschel incident. [Uwe
Barchel, Christian Democratic Minister-President of Schleswig
Holstein, resigned his post following allegations of unethical
electioneering tactics against the Social Democrats and was later
found dead in a hotel room]. But without the larger picture,
without détente between the superpowers or the waning of
neoconservatism, the Christian Democratic leadership might
not have hesitated to leap onto the bandwagon that Dregger
and Strauss were piloting to an *"entsorgte Vergangenheit,"* a past
that no longer causes concern.

And further: beneath the debate on the question in what
sense the Nazi mass crimes were unique lies the deeper question of what attitude we want to take toward the continuities
of German history—whether we can affirm our political existence while maintaining a clear awareness of a break with our
more sinister traditions. Can we, and do we want to, give up
the comforts and the dangers of a conventional identity that is
incompatible with a *critical* appropriation of traditions? Nationalism is as virulent as ever. This question, I am afraid, has not
yet come due. Many people regard Dolf Sternberger's phrase
"constitutional patriotism," a phrase I have taken up, as a
provocation—especially when it is intended critically and not
used by "militant democrats" against alleged domestic enemies.

Erd: I believe that now, in contrast to earlier phases in German
history, we can look into the political future of the Federal
Republic with a certain composure. In the past twenty years a

political culture has developed that has enough stability to set limits to fundamental conservative revisions. Can we then, look ahead—with vigilance, of course—but nevertheless without getting worked up?

Habermas: In that I still hear an echo of Max Weber's complaint about the "sterile excitation" of the intellectuals—Gehlen used it to put together his critique of intellectuals. There are things I get upset about—a sentence, for instance, by the New York correspondent to the *Frankfurter Allgemeine Zeitung's* feuilleton section in the February 13 [1988] weekend supplement. The successor to the unforgotten Sabina Leitzmann writes: "Dozens of cosmetic surgeons made their living from the fact that many Jews tried to assimilate their noses to the Anglo-Saxon ideal of beauty. Only after Barbara Streisand created a furor with her characteristic nose did the 'nose-job' lose its attraction." Completely apart from its context, a complaint that had been stirred up about the Jews having too much influence in Washington, a formulation like that is offensive in *any* context when one reads it not in "MUT" but in one of Germany's leading dailies. It simply displays a lack of sensitivity.

On the other hand, I agree with you: I too breathe a little more easily when I see how the government of the ideological shift has to take the more liberal portion of its clientele into consideration, that it has to direct itself toward what I have somewhat optimistically called fundamental liberalization. Today there are majorities in Germany that we don't have to be afraid of. At any rate our *juste-milieu* doesn't arouse the kind of anxiety one hears in every line of Max Horkheimer's journals from the 1950s and 1960s.

But I don't feel cozy and settled. A *juste-milieu* can have clay feet too. What would a nonoppressive normality be like? It would be a normality that managed not to be apathetic toward the unbearable. Sensitivity to what society has produced in the form of suffering and injustice that *could be avoided* would be normal. In my contact with my children, and with younger people in general, I notice how my own responses have become dulled. Perhaps, and I say this as a university teacher, contact with younger generations is the most reassuring thing there is in our country. If distrust of one generation for the other, and distrust within the same generation, ever becomes unnecessary, we will also be able to look into the future without getting worked up.

The New Intimacy between
Politics and Culture: Theses
on Enlightenment in Germany

Political competition for the scarce resource "meaning" has narrowed the distance between politics and culture. The new political attentiveness to the cultural forms in which the *Zeitgeist* expresses itself can be explained by, among other things, a change in the way politics itself is perceived: politics seems to be suffering a loss of maneuverability and competence. At least three convictions go to make up this more sober image of politics. First, interventions into the economic system that are in conformity with the system have not had the desired effects. Still less is expected of interventions designed to change the system; their effects would be counterproductive. Second, not only is the economic system proving resistant; the administrative measures that politics must make use of in its interventions also constitute a medium with characteristics of its own. Bureaucracy and law have lost their innocence in the eyes of their clients. Third, crises have become widespread and persistent. They are becoming the dominant form in which an accelerated social change stabilizes itself.

Politicians who share this image of politics are tempted to displace their unsolved problems onto a third medium. They slip over into the arena of mass culture. In celebrating its seven-hundred and fiftieth year, the state did not put on a show by holding military parades and religious services for a week. Instead, it basked in a year-long cultural bubble bath of interviews, discussions, and exhibitions concocted of pop, punk, and Prussia. One level higher, an intellectual President of the Republic is making successful use of niches in cultural activity.

The new intimacy between politics and culture has double-edged consequences for the politician. On the one hand, there is broader scope for a symbolic politics that compensates for disappointments that have arisen in other areas in a way that almost balances out the costs. On the other hand, cultural meaning is a substance with a mind of its own. It cannot be increased at will, nor can it be given arbitrary forms. The pejorative term *"Stimmungsdemokratie,"* a "democracy of moods," obscures the fact that the legitimation process is subject to this new kind of limitation. More instructive is the interest of electoral sociologists in the so-called "service-sector centers," where a perception of politics that is theme-dependent, informed, and in all cases culturally mediated is most pronounced. The directness with which [Christian Democratic party secretary] Heiner Geissler, who is a cool, calculating man, propagandistically places his bets on postmaterial values (and sends Norbert Blüm to Chile [to confer with representatives of persons illegally interned by the Chilean government, thus as a symbolic move in support of Chilean democracy] is extremely revealing.

In short, culture, which is disseminated through the mass media but also emerges in discussions, displays the Janus face of all rhetoric. Once a person becomes involved in culture, he can be persuasive only within the dangerous medium of convictions. To be sure, culture that is propagated through the mass media often enough pays for its dissemination with a dedifferentiation of its intellectual content; but dissemination through the media also means that possibilities for counterargument become decentralized. Being able to say no is the reverse side of being convinced—and even the person who has been persuaded must at least feel convinced. To this extent, the utilization of culture by politics could even promote enlightenment tendencies. This does not have to be the case, as experience tells us.

Enlightenment in Germany—Two Opinions

One recent example of the political relevance of culture is the dispute over Frankfurt's Börneplatz [where real estate developers turned up part of the old Jewish ghetto; the question then was whether to preserve the ruins or to go ahead with construction]. On this occasion the mayor of the city turned the city council meeting, to its credit, into a lecture on history. His talk, which was probably prepared by experts, is relevant to our topic in another respect as well. Not only did the mayor engage in a historical-critical discussion, thus in a discourse dedicated to the spirit of the Enlightenment; he made enlightenment the theme of his talk.

At issue was the connection in intellectual history between the rise of racist anti-Semitism in Germany and the loss of authority, due to the Enlightenment, on the part of the Christian religion and the church: "It was not Christian anti-Judaism but the path the German people has followed since the Enlightenment that led to the German catastrophe" (*Frankfurter Rundschau,* September 26, 1987). It is clear from the context that the phrase "since the Enlightenment" is not meant merely in the sense of something *post hoc.* The diminishing "influence of the churches on national and private life" is documented in such consequences as the French Revolution, the nation state and nationalism, Marx and Nietzsche. This fundamentalist Christian interpretation of history, however, is to hold only for Germans, not for Jews, who under the aegis of the Enlightenment entered into a more or less harmonious symbiosis with German culture: "I understand the dismay a Jew would feel, something that would lead to disagreement with my evaluation. That goes without saying. He makes his evaluation on the basis of the fate of his people, his religion, and I make mine on the basis of the fate of our people, and thus may arrive at different conclusions." Whatever the mayor may have meant, the idea that only those who share the same fate or are "of the same kind" can understand one another is a maxim so obviously incompatible with the universalism of the Enlightenment that its stock has risen in the world since 1933, even in academic circles.

My colleague in philosophy, Günther Rohrmoser, who sees opposition to the Enlightenment, then as now, as what is specifically German, proceeds in a more consistent fashion: "We Germans, with Fichte and since Fichte, have raised the claim to be in possession of our own answer to ... modern society and the problems of human alienation connected with it. Until now it has been possible to say with some truth that the answers emerging from the tradition of the Enlightenment have been better than the German answers. It was possible to say that mankind was still inspired by a belief in the successful completion of the historical process through science, technology, and the unchecked exploitation of nature. But now this belief, and with it the project of modernity, finds itself in a deep crisis . . . . Is it really the case that the answers of an ideologically exhausted liberalism and a socialism that has failed in all its variants are better than those we can derive from the memory of the greatest philosophical and cultural achievements of the Germans? If we look for the cause of the neuroticization of our national self-understanding, which is currently leading us into a progressive decline, we will find it in the determination, announced in 1945, to see nothing but an error in the difference between the Germans and all the ahistorical-abstract traditions of the West founded on natural law, and to set this difference aside in a radical way, that is, through a cultural revolution" (quoted from Hans-Uwe Otto/Heinz Sünker, eds., *Soziale Arbeit und Faschismus*, Bielefeld: Bollert, 1986). That was in Weikersheim in 1983 [at a congress on "German Identity Today" headed by Hans Filbinger, a former CDU Minister-President of Baden-Württemberg who had been asked to resign when his past as a Nazi naval judge was exposed].

Reaction Formations

Today we know that the advice Bernhard Willms [a professor of political science and prominent Neonationalist] gave the government on that occasion was not followed only by Filbinger's friends: "The Germans must neutralize the 'mastering of the past' and make it a matter of science and scholarship. Anyone who preaches guilt or keeps the wound of Hitler open is fighting not for but against identity." How is it that precisely in this country a "grand coalition" of critics of enlightenment has formed, a coalition in which the brown, black, and green fringes meet?

Rohrmoser is not so wrong. In Germany it is only since 1945 and in the Federal Republic that the tradition of the Enlightenment in its full breadth has become a possession to be taken more or less for granted. By the end of the crippling latency period, at the beginning of the 1960s, intellectuals had brought about a degree of Westernization of German culture. They now understood Herder and Kant not as thinkers who overcame the Enlightenment but as its exponents; they no longer excluded Börne, Heine, and Tucholsky—to name only a few; they took Freud and psychoanalysis, Western Marxism, the positivism of Vienna and Berlin seriously as major intellectual movements. This was more than a rehabilitation. For those elements in the German, and especially the German-Jewish intelligentsia that had been suppressed, cut off, and made the object of contempt were now making their home with us *for the first time*—which is not, of course, to claim nationality for ideas that by their very nature circulate. This process was also mediated in our universities by the emigrants who had returned from exile. In the eyes of the students of that period it was primarily in exile that it had been possible to maintain continuities undamaged and to preserve a heritage from corruption.

Traces of a reaction formation may be discernible in a mentality that sprang from a reaction to fascism in this way. In any case, given the background of this kind of mentality it is understandable that in Germany the international youth revolt of the 1960s became involved with the specific themes of the effort to work through our national past. And this genealogy may also explain why after all that was over the protest movement *again* elicited compulsive reactions here. For stereotypes of a very German struggle against the ideas of the French Revolution, stereotypes we thought had been long overcome, had been flushed up to the surface from the collective unconscious.

Enlightenment about the Enlightenment

The revolt evoked reactions from two sides—which, simplifying somewhat, I shall call the camp of the older generation and the camp of the younger generation. Both sides claim to represent enlightenment about the Enlightenment. The neoconservative disciples of Gehlen and Forsthoff, Schelsky and Joachim Ritter consider the rationality of the state and the economy to be jeopardized by those who take modernism in art and universalism in science, scholarship, and morality seriously and who go so far as to expose religion and morals to the pressure of reflection and innovative experiment. From this perspective, the need for affirmation that characterizes a disenchanted modernity has to be satisfied by a process of re-enchantment, by narrative without argument, inspirational literature, the creation of meaning, and empathic historicism. The Young-Conservative heirs of the revolt, on the other hand, are not at all satisfied with this culture that represents a settling of damages, with a notion of compensation that simply divides the legacy of the Enlightenment in half. They are existential and want the whole thing. Following the trail of Heidegger or Nietzsche, they hope to find something completely different in something thoroughly old; from their perspective, what culminates in the Enlightenment is only the doom of a logocentric destiny that has been building for a long time.

Both versions, the more moderate as much as the radical, however, make the same mistake. They ignore the fact that it is precisely in Germany that the self-critique of the Enlightenment is as old as the Enlightenment itself. Anyone who did not know the limits of the intellect [*Verstand*] was always considered irrational. If the intellect is inflated to the totality and usurps the place of reason [*Vernunft*], the mind loses its capacity to reflect on the limits of intellectual activity. Thus it is of the very nature of the Enlightenment to enlighten itself about itself, and about the harm that it does. Only when this fact is repressed can the counter-Enlightenment present itself as enlightenment about the Enlightenment.

Religion, Enlightenment, and New Mythology

In a discussion with Eugon Kogon in 1957, Adorno made the following statement*: "The current religious renaissances seem

*In what follows, Habermas quotes from Adorno's "Vernunft und Offenbarung," in

to me to be philosophy of religion rather than religion. In any case they are in agreement with eighteenth and early nineteenth century apologetics in attempting to use rational reflection to conjure up its opposite; now, however, they attempt to do so through rational reflection on reason itself, with a smouldering readiness to attack reason, a propensity for obscurantism that is more vicious than all the narrow-minded orthodoxy of the earlier period because it does not quite believe what it is saying" (22). This is true for a theory of compensation that justifies the powers of tradition in functionalist terms. And in opposition to a negativistic critique of reason that negates itself as critique, Adorno insists that the dialectic of enlightenment should not be broken off too quickly: "Certainly self-examination is required of a reason that does not wantonly absolutize itself as an unyielding means of domination, and the current need for religion expresses something of this. But this self-examination cannot stop at the mere negation of thought by thought itself, at a kind of mythic sacrifice; it cannot be accomplished by a 'leap'—that would bear too close a resemblance to the politics of catastrophe" (23). At the time, this statement was directed against a leap into a revelation disguised as philosophy and not against the praise that is now widely accorded a secular polytheism, or against the new mythologies that announce the end of the autonomy of the subject and can no longer claim any resemblance to the mythology of reason once invoked by the youthful friends Hegel, Hölderlin, and Schelling. Faced with the new mythologies as they are currently being propagated, Adorno would have emphasized what *links* radical enlightenment with monotheism: the moment of self-transcendence by which the ego, trapped in its world, is granted a detachment from the world as a whole and from itself, and thereby a perspective without which autonomy—on the basis of mutual acknowledgement—and individuality cannot be achieved. At the same time, however, this commonality of monotheism and enlightenment does not affect Adorno's conviction that "no theological content will remain untrans-

Stichworte (Frankfurt, 1969). Page numbers in parentheses refer to that text (translator's note).

formed; every aspect of it will have to undergo the trial of immigrating into the dimension of the secular, the profane" (20). But to draw theological contents into the universe of justificatory discourse and the solidarity of communal life, thus to render them profane, is the opposite of a neopagan regression to a point behind the self-understanding of autonomy and individuality that entered the world with the teachings of the prophets.

Discouragement

The normative content of the Enlightenment was expressed in the ideas of self-consciousness, self-determination, and self-realization. This "self," to be sure, was understood in the sense of cold bourgeois subjectivity and self-assertion, in the sense of an individualism that organizes things and has them at its disposal. Thus the ideas themselves have entered a twilight zone. Doubt in them is ubiquitous these days; it is nourished by experiences with an overly complex, exploitative, and inexplicably risky society. The origins of the contingencies that are overwhelming us today lie in social contexts and no longer directly in nature. Functionalist Marxism, structuralism, and the systems theory that is the heir of both reflect the experience of impotence even in their theoretical structures. As Luhmann put it, everything is possible and nothing works any more. The paradigm shift that has occurred in the realm of theory speaks for itself: An anonymous society without a subject is taking the place of an association of free and equal individuals who regulate their communal life themselves through democratic will-formation. One's will to give form to social life vanishes with one's confidence in the possibilities for doing so.

Certainly the twentieth century has given us cause to shudder at the spectacle of mobilized masses. The farther mass civilization progresses, the more the romance of mass action fades. Belief in large-scale subjects and in the possibility of controlling social systems has disintegrated. Even social movements have now become a mechanism for multiplication and individualization. But praise of multiplicity, apology for the contingent and the private, celebration of rupture, difference, and the moment, the revolt of the marginal areas against the centers, the mustering of the extraordinary against triviality—all this should not become an escape from problems that can be solved, if at all, only by daylight, only cooperatively, only with the last drops of a solidarity that is almost completely drained of its life blood. But what do the new mythologies put in the place of self-determination and solidarity?

Even when they teach a background affirmation of life, the most advanced works of literature and film seem to be surrounded by an aura of awakening discouragement. In the film *Wings of Desire,* a film rich in allusions, Peter Handke's texts and to an even greater degree the views of [director] Wim Wenders produce a structure that elevates the incursion of the extraordinary into daily life, a science-fiction theme, to the mythical. Several levels mesh in the dramaturgy of the action. The gaze of the angels lingers as though behind glass on the triviality of small worries, on the normality and despair of everyday life. In the soulful eyes of childlike visitors to the circus and in the historical reminiscences of the narrator, truth has not yet been completely destroyed. But only the angels who descend freely into human life and mingle inconspicuously with mortals experience the authenticity of earthly existence and become the spokespersons of the great affirmation. Conversely, both the unearthly angels who shy away from painful embodiment, who do not know pain and pleasure, and those immersed in daily life, who with their dull drives are merely subjected to pleasure and pain, experience a deficit in fulfilled life, the one deficit the mirror image of the other. Only the angels who *have descended,* who, not without narcissism, are wholly absorbed in pleasure and pain, experience the exaltation of happiness, loneliness, union—and pay for it with *amor fati,* a song to a life that is removed from life.

I wonder whether these demigods remain the select few, as in myth, or whether they are meant to indicate in exemplary fashion a path that could be taken by everyone? Having no special cineastic preparation, I do not know whether I have understood the film correctly. Does it not transfigure the extraordinary at the expense of the more trivial experiences from which we learn? Does it not blur the distinction between Benjamin and Heidegger—between profane illumination and an awakening directed against the profane?

The Cultural Obsolescence of Political Premises

The future of enlightenment—what might it consist of? We would need to be able to explain how responsibilities for longer and longer and ever less comprehensible chains of action are increasing even as the scope for action narrows. And we would have to be able to show this in the hesitant awareness of the danger that even the successes of goal-oriented collaboration pose, as Benjamin well knew, for the possibility of happiness.

Today a skeptical but nondefeatist enlightenment can feel encouraged by the fact that the cultural orientations of the broad population are currently being re-formed in discussions within the political public sphere and under the prompting of social movements. Such an enlightenment can feel encouraged, because with these subcutaneous revolutions in attitude a change in mentality is taking place that abandons the political commonplaces of yesterday as though they were ruins. Even social structure seems open to cultural mobilization. Culture can wash away a politics that has become caked and hard. Do Reagan and Gorbachev realize that they have just provided an example of this kind of cultural obsolescence of premises that even yesterday seemed solid as a rock?

9

A Kind of Settling of Damages

Wolfgang Mommsen's talk at the Römerberg Colloquium in Frankfurt provided the occasion for a first response to the article by Ernst Nolte that had appeared the day before, "*Vergangenheit, die nicht vergehen will*" ["The Past That Will Not Pass Away"] (*Frankfurter Allgemeine Zeitung*, June 6, 1986). "Apologetic Tendencies," my article in *Die Zeit* a month later, took up in a larger context the theme of a revisionism that makes the past innocuous. (In *Die Zeit*, Section I and the notes at the end of the article, included here, were omitted at the request of the editor.) A further article, "On the Public Use of History," brought the debate, which was set off by the *Frankfurter Allgemeine Zeitung*'s vehement reactions and continued in *Die Zeit*, to a temporary close. My "Closing Remarks" of February 23, 1987, respond to a polemic by Andreas Hillgruber.

Remarks from the Römerberg Colloquium

I'd like to return to Wolfgang Mommsen's talk. Professor Mommsen, I am interested in the question whether and, if so, to what extent historical scholarship can carry out the tasks of ideology planning today. You have laid out an impressive counterproposal to that of some of your colleagues, that is, to those among them who for some years have been trying to make use of historical scholarship in a wholly functionalist manner (not only in founding museums but also through the background interpretations produced in connection with such efforts) to strengthen historical consciousness, or what they call historical consciousness—to strengthen the forces of social integration in order to counteract suspected instabilities.

Of course historical scholarship has always assumed ideological functions in addition to others—you pointed this out, and Hans-Ulrich Wehler has also discussed it in the most recent issue of *Parlament*; it did so from an offensive position after 1849 and under Bismarck, and then from a defensive position in the Weimar Republic. But still, in the exceptional phase, as you call it, that followed, two things occurred that have a direct bearing on my question.

One is the extensive instrumentalization of historical scholarship for manipulative purposes under the conditions of political dictatorship. Those of us who were students after the war had only to go into the philosophy department libraries to see how a "German philosophy" had been written by our teachers, how Greek philosophy had been traced to the second or third wave of Aryan immigration, and so forth. The other event is the moral catastrophe (Auschwitz, in other words) that made it definitively impossible to carry on with continuities in a naive fashion.

I wonder what functions for the formation of ideologies, as it were, one can continue to expect historical scholarship to fulfill after the end of fascism. It would seem instead that this moral catastrophe brought with it completely different opportunities. First of all, having been torn out of continuities, we are subject to the constraint of being able to relate to the past only with a reflexive attitude; but then every reading of the past results in an ambivalent picture of what has come down to us. Second, we can now appropriate traditions only in terms of precisely those universalist value orientations that were violated in such an unprecedented way at that time. And third, we have to live with a dynamic, conflicting pluralism of readings of our own history, not under the premise "anything goes," but under the premise that the historical consciousness of a whole population can now take only a decentered form. These, at least, were the constraints and the opportunities that fell to us in greater measure than to other nations.

Yet for about ten years now we have seen an attempt on the part of a journalistically active group of historians who at the moment exercise influence through government office to put historiography to work for functionalistically defined purposes again—for the creation of, let us say, positive pasts, pasts that "one can approve of."

Under the slogan "freedom or totalitarianism," the "Bolshevist danger" often forms the actual point of reference in these attempts, which has the advantage that it can be linked to a widespread repressive anticommunism that already exists and does not need to be created. One has only to look at the *Frankfurter Allgemeine Zeitung* and its prompt contribution to our discussion.

A functionalist view of history of this kind, however, will run up against two stumbling blocks in the Federal Republic today. The first obstacle is what you yourself called the "exceptional" character of the Nazi period, and what forms the moral background of the unique events that we in Germany have become accustomed to referring to in a detached way with foreign words like "Holocaust" or "*Shoah*," despite the fact that we have had the plain word "Auschwitz" for them from the beginning. Auschwitz is an obstacle not because it creates a kind of "guilt-tripping" but because it puts a whole population, as it were, under a compulsion to reflect that makes naive external self-definition and the marginalization of potential domestic enemies at least more difficult. The second obstacle, I believe, consists in the fact that given the current political and military situation, a polarization of the superpowers, or shall we say the actualization of anticommunist stereotypes of the enemy, does not exactly fit our interest position. These obstacles make special efforts necessary. One has to begin by constructing an external enemy, for a so-called "historical" consciousness in the conventional prereflexive sense cannot exist without one. This is also how I understand Ernst Nolte's article in the *Frankfurter Allgemeine Zeitung,* which I read yesterday and which I consider astonishing. At least that was my first reaction. What is involved here is an attempt to make Auschwitz unexceptional by remarking, among other things, that with the sole exception of the technical procedure of gassing, what the Nazis did had already been described in an extensive literature dating from the early 1920s. With the lovely, almost Heideggerian words, "Was not the Gulag Archipelago more original than Auschwitz?" Nolte presents German fascism, even in its "aberrations," as merely a response and reaction to the Bolschevist threat of annihilation. One can then see the revival of anticommunism as the reverse side of the same argument.

I am not a historian, and I am known for making emphatic judgments and perhaps also for having emphatic prejudices; but even if I take that into account to my detriment, as a daily reader of the *Frankfurt Allgemeine Zeitung,* after reading this article I have to note a "qualitative leap" in dealing with our historical consciousness. This is what is behind my question: If historians proceed in such a transparent manner, so functionalistically, how can they hope to be successful, given the conditions in which we live today?

Apologetic Tendencies

A conspicuous shortcoming of the literature of National Socialism is that it doesn't know, or doesn't want to admit, to what extent everything that was later done by the Nazis, with the sole exception of the technical procedure of gassing, had already been described in an extensive literature dating from the early 1920s. . . . Could it be that the Nazis, that Hitler carried out an 'Asiatic' deed only because they regarded themselves and those like them as potential or actual victims of an 'Asiatic' deed?

—*Ernst Nolte,* in the *Frankfurter Allgemeine Zeitung,* June 6, 1986

I

"To the victims of war and tyranny"—This inscription on the memorial in Bonn's North Cemetery demands a prodigious act of abstraction on the part of the viewer. On Judgment Day, as we learned growing up as Christians, each of us, individually and with no one to take our place, will face a God of Judgment on whose mercy we are dependent precisely because we do not doubt the justice of His verdict. In view of the uniqueness of the life history for which each person must account, all, each in turn, may expect equal treatment. The conceptual connection between individuality and equality, a connection on which the universalist principles of our constitution are based even though they are tailored to the fallibility of the human capacity for judgment, also emerged from the abstraction involved in this conception of Judgment Day. It was thus to deeply anchored moral intuitions that Alfred Dregger [parliamentary party chairman of the Christian Democrats] appealed when, in the Bundestag discussion of April 25, 1986, concerning the erection of a new memorial in Bonn, he emphatically opposed the view that one must after all differentiate between the perpetrators and the victims of the Nazi regime. The debate about the question whether a public memorial that did not differentiate between perpetrators and victims should be erected, about whether perpetrators and victims could be honored in the same context, at the same time and in the same place, is a debate about whether an abstraction can be required. In other contexts, this abstraction has a valid place. If it were really an issue of remembering the *individual* dead, who would presume to classify the unspeakable suffering of children, women, and men, a suffering that is impenetrable to mortal eyes, in terms of the characteristics of perpetrators and victims?

After the spectacle [at Bitburg] on May 8, 1985, no one can be blamed for being suspicious of the demand for a central national memorial. The remoteness of the existing "provisional" memorial in the North Cemetery in Bonn is felt as a shortcoming only by those who do not place the remembrance of the victims of war and tyranny under the individualizing abstraction of Judgment Day but instead want to commemorate collective fates. This was the view of the memorial culture of the nineteenth century—ritualized commemoration of a triumph struggled for in common and a defeat suffered in common was to help stabilize the cohesiveness and identity of the polity. There are still valid grounds for this view. Death on the front or as a prisoner of war, death by the side of the road or in a bomb shelter was both an individual and a shared fate; being wounded, being exiled, being raped; the hunger, want, and desperate loneliness of individuals are representative of what many had to endure under similar circumstances— soldiers, war widows, those who were bombed out, refugees. Suffering is always concrete suffering; it cannot be detached from its context. And from this context of a shared experience of suffering, traditions are formed. Mourning and remembrance, practiced communally, secure these traditions.

A memorial that gives expression to this legitimate need presupposes a life context in which both the good and the bad are shared. Of course, everything depends on what kind of form of life it is. The less internal communality such a collective life context has preserved, the more it has survived externally, through the usurpation and destruction of life that is alien to it, the greater is the ambivalence toward the burden of reconciliation imposed upon the griefwork of succeeding generations. In such a case would not the compulsory posthumous integration of those who in their lifetimes were oppressed or ostracized into an undifferentiated remembrance be only a continuation of the usurpation—an extorted reconciliation? Dregger and his friends cannot have both: a tradition-building remembrance that in any case maintains its power of social integration only as long as it is directed to the collective fate— and the abstraction from this very fate in which, regardless of individual differences, many were involved as perpetrators and accomplices and some were involved as resisters and victims. Mr. Dregger's strange calculations that show "that almost ten million of our people have been forcibly dispatched from life to death since 1914"[1]— which probably means, double the number of Jews, gypsies, Russians, and Poles murdered by the Nazis—are no help here.

One cannot simultaneously undertake a moral abstraction and insist on historical concreteness. Someone who nevertheless persists in mourning collective fates without distinguishing between perpetrators and victims must be up to something else. Someone who "does" Bergen-Belsen in the morning and holds a veterans meeting in Bitburg in the afternoon has something else in mind—something that not only formed the background for May 8, 1985, but also inspires current planning for new memorials and new museums: a Federal Republic of Germany that is solidly anchored in the Atlantic community of values is to regain its national self-confidence through identification with an acceptable past, without going astray to become a neutral nation state. Of course, such a seizure of national history for purposes of promoting identification[2] requires the support of two screening operations. First of all, the memory of the negatively charged portions of recent history, which would inhibit identification, has to be leveled; then, under the banner of freedom or totalitarianism, the ever virulent fear of

Bolshevism has to be kept alive through an appropriate stereotype of the enemy. The scenario of Bitburg contains precisely these three elements. The aura of the military cemetery served to mobilize historical consciousness through national sentiment. The juxtaposition of Bitburg and Bergen-Belsen, of SS graves and the mass graves of concentration camp victims, relieved the Nazi crimes of their uniqueness; the veteran generals' handshake in the presence of the American president finally confirmed that we had always been on the right side in the struggle against the Bolshevist enemy. In the weeks prior to Bitburg, Dregger and the *Frankfurter Allgemeine Zeitung* went out of their way to explain these elements to us.[3]

But there are narrow limits to the bureaucratic creation of meaning; that is why the services of historians are needed. Historians acquire a secure position in the planning of ideology. They are to treat historical consciousness as a substance to be used in maneuvers to provide the political system's need for legitimation with appropriate positive pasts. How are established contemporary historians responding to this demand?

II

The Erlangen historian Michael Stürmer favors a functionalist interpretation of historical consciousness: "In a land without history, the future belongs to those who fill memory, coin concepts, and interpret the past."[4] In line with Joachim Ritter's neoconservative worldview, which was made topical in the 1970s by his students, Stürmer envisions modernization processes as a kind of settling of damages. The individual has to be provided with identity-creating meaning in compensation for the unavoidable alienation that he experiences as a "social molecule" in the environment of an objectified industrial society. To be sure, Stürmer is less concerned with the identity of the individual than with the integration of the polity. "When it no longer finds a common ground," pluralism of values and interests leads "sooner or later to social civil war."[5] What is needed is "the foundation of higher meaning, something which, after religion, only nation and patriotism have previously been capable of accomplishing."[6] A historical scholarship that is aware of its political responsibilities will not refuse the call to produce and disseminate a view of history that will promote national consciousness. Academic history is in any case "propelled by collective, largely unconscious needs for the establishment of secular meaning, but [it] must"—and Stürmer definitely experiences this as a dilemma—"work them out in accordance with scientific methodology." This is why it walks "the line between creating meaning and demythologizing."[7]

Let us now watch the Cologne historian Andreas Hillgruber as he walks this line. Having no technical expertise in his field, I venture to approach the most recent work of this renowned contemporary historian only because, in a bibliophile edition put out by [the conservative publisher] Wolf Jobst Siedler under the title *Two Sorts of Destruction* [*Zweierlei Untergang*], his study is obviously addressed to the layman. One can watch in it the self-observations of a patient submitting to a revisionist operation on his historical consciousness.[8]

In the first part of his study Hillgruber describes the collapse of the German Eastern Front during the last year of the war, 1944–45. He begins by discussing the "problem of identification," that is, the question with which of the parties involved at the time the author should identify in his presentation. Hillgruber has already rejected, on the grounds that it is based on an "ethics of conviction," the interpretation of the situation given by those involved in the July 20th assassination attempt, a position he contrasts with that of the commanders-in-chief, district officials, and mayors on the scene, whose attitude he sees as based on an ethics of responsibility. Thus there are three positions left. Hillgruber rejects Hitler's attitude of holding out to the end as social-darwinistic. And he rules out identification with the victors. The perspective of liberation is appropriate only for the victims of the concentration camps, not for the German nation as a whole. The historian has only one option: "He has to identify with the concrete fate of the German population in the East and with the desperate and self-sacrificing efforts of the German army in the East and the German naval forces in the Baltic Sea area, who were trying to save the population of the German East from the Red Army's orgies of revenge, from mass rapes, arbitrary murder, and indiscriminate deportations, and . . . to keep the escape route to the West open" (p. 24f.).

Bewildered, one asks why the historian of 1986 should not attempt a retrospective view from the distance of forty years, that is, assume his own perspective, from which he cannot detach himself in any case. That would also offer the hermeneutic advantage of allowing him to establish relationships between the selective perceptions of the parties directly involved, to weigh them against one another and supplement them with the knowledge of subsequent generations. Hillgruber does not want, however, to write his account from this, one would almost like to say "normal" point of view, for then questions of the "morality of wars of extermination" would inevitably arise. But those questions are to be set aside. In this context, Hillgruber refers to Norbert Blüm's statement that as long as the German "Eastern Front" held, the extermination operations in the camps could continue. This fact would necessarily cast a long shadow over the "picture of the horrors of women and children who had been raped and murdered" that was presented to the German soldiers after the recapture of Nemmersdorf, for example. Hillgruber is concerned with representing what happened from the point of view of brave soldiers, a desperate civilian population, and the "tried and true" higher officials of the Nazi party; he wants to project himself into the experiences of the combatants of the time, experiences not yet framed and devalued by our retrospective knowledge. This intention accounts for the principle of dividing the study into two parts, the "collapse in the East" and the "extermination of the Jews," two events that Hillgruber wishes precisely *not* to show, as the dust jacket announces, "in their sinister entanglement."

III

Following this operation, the credit for which should probably go to the dilemma of meaning-creating history that Stürmer remarks on, however, Hillgruber does not hesitate after all to call on the knowledge of the historian of a later generation to support the thesis he introduces in his preface, namely that the expulsion of the Germans from the East is in no way to be understood as a "response" to the crimes committed in the concentration camps. Referring to the Allied war aims, he shows that "in the case of a German defeat there was at no point in the war any prospect of saving the Prusso-German Eastern provinces" (p. 61); he explains the Western powers' lack of interest in terms of their "clichéd image of Prussia." It does not occur to Hillgruber that the power structure of the German Reich could have anything to do with its social structure, which was especially well preserved in Prussia. He makes no use of information from the social sciences—otherwise he could scarcely have traced the fact that outrages occurred during the Red Army's invasion not only of Germany but also, and earlier, of Poland, Rumania, and Hungary, to the Stalinist era's barbaric "conceptions of war." Be that as it may, the Western powers, according to Hillgruber, were blinded by their illusory military objective, the destruction of Prussia. They learned too late that with the advance of the Russians "all Europe became the loser in the catastrophe of 1945."

Having set this scene, Hillgruber can now put the struggle of the German army in the East in its proper light—a "desperate defensive battle to preserve the independence of the great-power position of the Third Reich that it was the Allies' will to destroy. The Germany army in the East offered protection to an area that had been settled by Germans for hundreds of years, to the homeland of millions living in a core area of the German Reich" (p. 63f.). The dramatic presentation then closes with a wishful interpretation of May 8, 1945: Forty years later the question of a "reconstruction of the destroyed Central Europe ... was as open as it was when contemporaries witnessed, as active participants or as victims, the catastrophe of the German East" (p. 74). The moral of the story is obvious: at least today the alliance is the right one.

In the second part of his book Hillgruber treats, in twenty-two pages, the aspect of the event that he has until then kept out of his "tragic" heroic epic. The subtitle of the book already indicates a different perspective. To the "smashing of the German Reich" (which apparently took place only on the "Eastern Front"), evoked in the rhetoric of cheap war paperbacks, is opposed the soberly recorded "End of European Jewry."

"Smashing" requires an aggressive opponent; an "end" takes place on its own, as it were. Whereas in the first case Hillgruber speaks of "the annihilation of whole armies side by side with the courageous sacrifices of individuals," here he speaks of the "stationary successor organizations of the *Einsatzkommandos*." Whereas there "many anonymous individuals rose above themselves in the catastrophe that was overwhelming them," here the gas chambers are paraphrased as "more effective means" of liquidation. There we find the musty unrevised clichés of a jargon carried around since boyhood, here the frozen language of the bureaucrat. The historian has changed more than the perspective of the presentation. Now he is concerned with proving that the "murder of the Jews" was "solely a consequence of the radical race doctrine" (p. 9).

Stürmer was interested in the question "to what extent it was Hitler's war and to what extent it was the Germans' war."[9] Hillgruber poses the analogous question with regard to the extermination of the Jews. He sets up hypothetical reflections about what the life of the Jews would have been like if the German nationalists and the Stahlhelm had come to power in 1933 instead of the Nazis. The Nuremberg Laws would have been enacted anyway, as would all the other measures up until 1938 that "imposed a special consciousness of the Jews," for they were "in harmony with the sentiments of a large part of the society" (p. 87). Hillgruber doubts, however, that between 1938 and 1941 *all* the functionaries would have considered a policy of forced emigration the best solution to the Jewish question. Nonetheless, by then two thirds of the German Jews would have "reached other countries." Finally, as far as the final solution after 1941 is concerned, it was Hitler alone who had it in mind from the very beginning. Hitler wanted the physical destruction of all Jews "because only through a 'racial revolution' of this kind could the position of world power for which his *Reich* was striving be made lasting" (p. 89). Since the word "could" in this sentence is not put in the subjunctive in German, we do not know whether or not the historian has assumed the perspective of the participant this time as well.

At any rate Hillgruber draws a sharp line between the euthanasia measures, to which 100,00 mentally ill persons had already fallen victim, and the extermination of the Jews. Against the background of a social-darwinist humanitarian genetics, the killing of "life that was unworthy to live" found widespread endorsement among the population. In contrast, Hitler was isolated with the idea of the "final solution," even among the innermost leadership clique, "including Göring, Himmler, and Heydrich." After Hitler has been identified as the person solely responsible for originating the idea and the decision, it remains only to carry the explanation out to its conclusion—but there also remains the frightening fact that the bulk of the population, as Hillgruber certainly assumes, kept quiet while it all went on.

The objective of this laborious revision would of course be jeopardized if this phenomenon ultimately had to be submitted for moral judgment after all. At this point, therefore, the historian, who has been proceeding narratively and who attaches no value to social-scientific attempts at explanation, shifts into the realm of the anthropological and universal. In his opinion, "the acceptance by the bulk of the population of this gruesome event, of which they had at least a vague suspicion . . . points beyond the historical uniqueness of the event" (p. 98). Standing firmly within the tradition of the German mandarins, moreover, Hillgruber is most deeply alarmed by the large number of academics involved—as if there were not quite plausible explanations for that as well. In short, the fact that a civilized population allowed the monstrous to occur is a phenomenon that Hillgruber dismissed from the technical jurisdiction of the overtaxed historian—and expels without justification into the dimension of the human condition.

IV

Writing in the *Historische Zeitschrift* (vol. 242, 1986, p. 465f.) Klaus Hildebrand, Hillgruber's colleague at the University of Bonn, commends a work by Ernst Nolte as "pioneering" because it has the merit of removing the "apparent uniqueness" from the history of the "Third Reich" and integrating the "annihilatory capacity of the worldview and the regime" historically into the overall development of totalitarianism. Nolte, who had already been widely acknowledged for his book *Three Faces of Fascism* (1963), is in fact cut from different cloth than Hillgruber.

In his article "Between Myth and Revisionism?"[10] Nolte now establishes the necessity for a revison with the statement that the history of the "Third Reich" has been written largely by the victors and has thus been made into a "negative myth." To illustrate his point, Nolte invites the reader to the tasteful thought experiment of imagining the picture of Israel presented by a victorious PLO *after* the total destruction of Israel: "For decades and possibly centuries, nobody would dare to trace the moving origins of Zionism to the spirit of resistance against European anti-Semitism" (p. 21). Even the theory of totalitarianism of the 1950s did not provide a different perspective but only led to incorporating the Soviet Union into the negative image as well. Nolte is not satisfied with a concept that owes its existence in this way to the opposition between it and the democratic constitutional state; he is concerned with the dialectic of reciprocal threats of annihilation. Long before Auschwitz, Nolte thinks, Hitler had valid grounds for his conviction that his opponents wanted to annihilate him too—"annihilate" is the word used in the original English. Proof of this he considers the "declaration of war" that Chaim Weizmann delivered for the Jewish World Congress in September 1939, thus *justifying* Hitler in treating German Jews as prisoners of war—and in deporting them (p. 27f). Recently one read in *Die Zeit* (albeit reported anonymously) that Nolte served this fantastic argument to a Jewish guest, his colleague Saul Friedländer from Tel Aviv, for dessert—and now I am reading it firsthand.

Nolte is not the concerned conservative narrator struggling with the "problem of identification." He resolves Stürmer's dilemma of scholarship *vs.* the creation of meaning with a bold decision and chooses as the point of reference for his account the terror of the Pol Pot regime in Combodia. From there he reconstructs a prehistory that extends from the "gulag," the expulsion of the kulaks by Stalin and the Bolshevist revolution, back to Babeuf, the early socialists, and the English agrarian reformers of the early nineteenth century—a line of revolt against cultural and social modernization fueled by an illusory nostalgia for the return of a comprehensible, self-sufficient world. In this context of horror the destruction of the Jews appears as only the regrettable result of a nevertheless understandable reaction to what Hitler must have experienced as a threat of annihilation: "The so-called annihilation of the Jews during the Third Reich was a reaction or a distorted copy and not a first act or an original" (p. 36).

In another essay Nolte attempts to clarify the philosophical background of his "trilogy on the history of modern ideologies."[11] I will not discuss that work here. Only the "philosophical" in what Nolte, a former student of Heidegger, calls his "philosophical historiography" interests me.

In the early 1950s there was a debate in philosophical anthropology about the interlocking of "openness to the world" [*Weltoffenheit*] and "enmeshedness in the world" [*Umweltverhaftung*]—a discussion in which Arnold Gehlen, Helmut Plessner, Konrad Lorenz, and Erich Rothacker participated. Nolte's peculiar use of the Heideggerian concept of "transcendence" reminds me of that debate. Since 1963 he has used this expression to shift the great turning point, the historical event of the breakup of a traditional lifeworld in the transition to modernity, into the realm of the anthropological-original. In this dimension of profundity in which all cats are gray he then campaigns for an understanding of the antimodernist impulses that are directed against modernity's "unconditional affirmation of practical transcendance." By this Nolte means the allegedly ontologically grounded "unity of world economy, technology, science, and emancipation." This is all marvelously suited to current prevailing moods—and to the parade of California worldviews that spring from them. More annoying is the dedifferentiation that makes "Marx and Maurras, Engels and Hitler, for all the emphasis on the oppositions between them, nevertheless related figures." Only when Marxism and fascism have been understood as attempts to provide a response to "the frightening realities of modernity" can the true intention of Nazism be distinguished clearly from its fatal praxis: "The 'monstrous crime' consisted not in the ultimate intention but in the ascription of guilt, which was directed against a group of people who were themselves so greatly bewildered by the emancipation process of liberal society that important representatives of the group declared them mortally endangered" (p. 281).

There would be no need for further discussion of the scurrilous background philosophy of a significant-eccentric mind if neoconservative contemporary historians had not felt it necessary to make use of precisely this variety of revisionism.

As a contribution to this year's Römerberg colloquium, which, in the papers of [the contemporary historians] Hans and Wolfgang Mommsen, also dealt with the theme of the "past that will not pass away," the feuilleton section of the June 6, 1986, *Frankfurter Allgemeine Zeitung* bestowed upon us a militant article by Ernst Nolte—under a hypocritical pretext, I might add (and I say this in the knowledge of the correspondence between Nolte, who was allegedly disinvited, and the organizers of the colloquium). On this occasion Stürmer was also in solidarity with the newspaper article, in which Nolte reduced the uniqueness of the extermination of the Jews to the "technical procedure of gassing," and supported his thesis that the Gulag Archipelago was more "original" than Auschwitz with a rather abstruse example from the Russian Civil War. The only thing Nolte had learned from Claude Lanzmann's film *Shoah* was that "the SS personnel in the death camps might be victims in their own right, and conversely there was virulent anti-Semitism among the Polish victims of Nazism." These unappetizing tidbits show that Nolte far eclipses a Fassbinder. If the *Frankfurter Allgemeine Zeitung* rightly took up arms against the planned Frankfurt performance of [Fassbinder's] play [*Trash, the City, and Death*], then why this?

I can account for it only by the fact that Nolte not only gets around the dilemma of scholarship *vs.* the creation of meaning more elegantly than others but also has a ready solution to a further dilemma. Stürmer describes that second dilemma: "Germans must find their identity in the reality of a divided Germany, an identity that can no longer be grounded in a nation state but can also not be grounded without a nation."[12] The planners of ideology want to create consensus through a revival of national consciousness, but at the same time they have to keep the enemy stereotypes of the nation state out of the sphere of NATO. Nolte's theory has a great advantage for purposes of this manipulation. He kills two birds with one stone: The Nazi crimes lose their uniqueness by being made at least understandable as a response to (now permanent) Bolshevist threats of annihilation. Auschwitz is reduced to the format of a technical innovation and explained through the "Asiatic" threat of an enemy who is still at our doors.

V

If one looks at the composition of the commissions that worked out the ideas for the museums planned by the West German government—the German Historical Museum in Berlin and the House of the History of the Federal Republic in Bonn— one cannot help getting the impression that ideas from the New Revisionism are also to be converted into the form of exhibitions, objects for display that will have a broad pedagogical influence. The documents submitted do have a pluralistic look. But it can hardly be otherwise with new museums than with new Max Planck Institutes: the programmatic concept papers that regularly precede the founding of a new institution do not have much to do with what the appointed directors later make of the institutions. Jürgen Kocka, the token liberal on the Experts' Commission in Berlin, suspects as much: "Ultimately, what matters is who takes charge of the thing. . . . Here, too, the devil is in the details."[13]

Who would want to oppose sincere efforts to strengthen the historical consciousness of the West German people? And there are good reasons for distancing oneself historically from a past that doesn't want to pass away. Martin Broszat has presented them convincingly. The complex connections between criminality and the ambiguous normality of daily life in Nazi Germany, between destruction and vigorous productivity, between a devastating systemic perspective and an inconspicuous-ambivalent nearsightedness on the local level could certainly do with wholesome objectifying attention. The practice of breathlessly collecting an illogically moralized past from fathers and grandfathers for pedagogical purposes could then yield to detached understanding. Careful differentiation between understanding and condemnation of a shocking past could also help to dissolve the hypnotic paralysis. But unlike the revisionism of Hillgruber or Nolte recommended by Hildebrand and Stürmer, this kind of historicizing would not be guided by the impulse to *shake off* the debts of a successfully de-moralized past. I do not want to impute bad intentions to anyone. There is a simple criterion that separates the one view from the other: Some proceed on the assumption that the work of detached understanding liberates the power of reflective remembrance and thus extends the possibilities for dealing autonomously with an ambivalent tradition; others would like to put a revisionist history to work furnishing a conventional identity with a national history.

Perhaps this formulation is still not sufficiently unambiguous. Anyone whose aim is to revive an identity anchored in quasi-natural fashion in a national consciousness, anyone who is guided by the functional imperatives of predictability, of securing consensus, of social integration through the creation of meaning, must of necessity shy away from historiography's power to enlighten and reject a pluralism of interpretations of history that would influence a broad public. It is hardly an injustice to Michael Stürmer to read his lead article [in the *Frankfurter Allgemeine Zeitung* of April 25, 1986] in this sense: "Looking at the Germans in relation to their history, our neighbors ask themselves where all this is leading. The Federal Republic . . . is a central piece in the European defense arc of the Atlantic system. But it now appears that each of the generations living in Germany today has a different, even opposing image of the past and the future. . . . The search for a lost history is not an abstract educational endeavor: it is morally legitimate and politically necessary. What is at stake is the inner continuity of the German republic and the predictability of its foreign policy."[14] Stürmer advocates a uniform picture of history that can secure identity and social integration, replacing forms of religious belief that have drifted off into the private sphere.

Historical consciousness as a substitute for religion—isn't historiography somewhat overextended with this old dream of historicism? Certainly, German historians can look back to a genuine tradition in their guild of supporting the state. Hans-Ulrich Wehler has recently reminded us of the contribution of ideology to the stabilization of the *kleindeutsche* or Lesser German Reich and its internal marginalization of "enemies of the *Reich.*" This mentality, which developed after the failure of the revolution of 1848–49 and the defeat of a liberal historiography of Gervinus's type, was dominant up into the late 1950s: "For almost a hundred years one could find liberal, enlightened historians only in isolation or in small marginal groups. The majority of the guild thought and argued nationalistically (in terms of the Reich), with an eye to the state, and in terms of power politics."[15] The fact, however, that after 1945—at least with the generation of younger historians educated after 1945—not only another spirit but a pluralism of readings and methodological approaches has become dominant, is by no means simply a mishap to be repaired. On the contrary, the old mentality was only the specific disciplinary expression of a mandarin consciousness that for good reasons did not survive the Nazi period: through its demonstrated impotence in the face of, or even complicity with the Nazi regime, it was publicly convicted of a lack of substance. This historically compelled advance in reflection not only affected the ideological premises of German historiography; it also intensified methodological awareness of the context-dependency of all historiography.

It is, however, a misunderstanding of this hermeneutic insight to proceed, as the revisionists are currently doing, on the assumption that one can turn the spotlights of arbitrarily reconstructed past histories on the present and from the options illuminated select a particularly appropriate picture of history. Rather, the intensified methodological awareness signals the end of all images of history that are closed or ordained by government historians. The inevitable pluralism of readings, which is by no means unmonitored but on the contrary rendered transparent, only reflects the structure of open societies. It provides an opportunity to clarify one's own identity-forming traditions in their ambivalences. This is precisely what is needed for the critical appropriation of ambiguous traditions, that is, for the development of a historical consciousness that is equally incompatible with closed images of history that have a secondary quasi-natural character and with all forms of conventional, that is, uniformly and prereflexively *shared* identity.

What is currently lamented as a "loss of history" involves more than hiding something away and repressing it, more than a fixation on a past that is burdened and has therefore come to a standstill. If national symbols have lost their influence with the young, if naive identification with one's heritage has yielded to a more tentative relationship to history, if discontinuities are felt more strongly and continuities not celebrated at any price, if national pride and collective self-esteem are filtered through universalist value orientations—to the extent to which all this is really the case, indications of the development of a postconventional identity are increasing. In [the] Allensbach [Institute for Public Opinion Research] these indications are pondered in Cassandran tones; if they are not misleading, they reveal only one thing: that we have not completely wasted the opportunity that the moral catastrophe could also represent.

That the Federal Republic opened itself without reservation to the political culture of the West is the great intellectual accomplishment of the postwar period, an accomplishment of which precisely my generation could be proud. It will not be given stability by a NATO philosophy with German-nationalist overtones. That opening was accomplished by overcoming the very ideology of the middle that our revisionists are reviving with their geopolitical chatter about "the old European middle position of the Germans" (Stürmer) and "the reconstruction of a destroyed Central Europe" (Hillgruber). The only patriotism that does not alienate us from the West is a constitutional patriotism. Unfortunately, in the cultural nation of the Germans, a connection to universalist constitutional principles that was anchored in convictions could be formed only after—and through—Auschwitz. Anyone who wants to dispel our shame about this fact with an empty phrase like "obsession with guilt" (Stürmer and Oppenheimer), anyone who wants to recall the Germans to a conventional form of their national identity, is destroying the only reliable basis for our tie to the West.

Notes

1. Alfred Dregger, "Nicht in Opfer und Täter einteilen," in *Das Parlament*, May 17–24, 1986, p. 21.

2. K. E. Jeismann, "Identität statt Emanzipation. Zum Geschichtsbewusstsein in der Bundesrepublik," in *Beilage zu Das Parlament* B 20–21, 1986, p. 3ff.

3. Jürgen Habermas, "Entsorgung der Vergangenheit," in his *Die Neue Unübersichlichkeit* (Frankfurt, 1985), p. 261ff.

4. Michael Stürmer, "Suche nach der verlorenen Erinnerung," in *Das Parlament*, May 17–24, 1986, p. 1.

5. Michael Stürmer, "Kein Eigentum der Deutschen: die deutsche Frage," in W. Weidenfels, ed., *Die Identität der Deutschen* (Bonn, 1983), p. 84.

6. Stürmer, "Kein Eigentum," p. 86.

7. Michael Stïrmer, *Dissonanzen des Fortschritts* (Munich, 1986), p. 12.

8. Andreas Hillgruber, *Zweierlei Untergang* (Corso bei Siedler, 1986). Page numbers in the text refer to this edition.

9. Stürmer, *Dissonanzen*, p. 190.

10. Ernst Nolte, "Between Myth and Revisionism? The Third Reich in the Perspective of the 1980s," in H. W. Koch, *Aspects of the Third Reich* (London, 1985), p. 16ff. Page numbers in the text refer to this edition.

11. Ernst Nolte, "Philosophische Geschichtsschreibung heute?" in *Historische Zeitschrift* 242 (1986), p. 265ff.

12. Stürmer, "Kein Eigentum," p. 98; see also Stürmer, *Dissonanzen*, p. 328ff.

13. Jürgen Kocka, "Ein Jahrhundertunternehmen," in *Das Parlament*, May 17–24, 1986, p. 18.

14. *Frankfurter Allgemeine Zeitung*, April 25, 1986.

15. Hans-Ulrich Wehler, "Den rationalen Argumenten standhalten," in *Das Parlament*, May 17–24, 1986, p. 2; see also his "Historiography in Germany today," in *Observations on the "Spiritual Situation of the Age*," ed. Jürgen Habermas (Cambridge, MA, 1984), pp. 221–259.

On the Public Use of History

Anyone who reads Ernst Nolte's circumspect article in the last issue of *Die Zeit* and has not followed the emotional discussion in the *Frankfurter Allgemeine Zeitung* must get the impression that this is a debate about historical details. In reality, what is involved is the translation into politics of the revisionism appearing in contemporary historiography, a translation that is impatiently urged on by the [conservative] government of the "ideological shift." This is why Hans Mommsen sets the controversy in the context of a "regrouping of historical-political thought"; his essay in the September-October issue of *Merkur* provides us with the fullest and most substantial account to date. At the center of the debate stands the question *how* the Nazi period is being dealt with historically in the public consciousness. Our increasing distance from it makes a "historicization" necessary, one way or another.

Today the grandchildren of those who at the close of World War II were too young to be able to experience personal guilt are already growing up. Memory, however, has not become correspondingly distantiated. Contemporary history remains fixated on the period between 1933 and 1945. It does not move beyond the horizon of its own life-history; it remains tied up in sensitivities and reactions that, while spread over a broad spectrum depending on age and political stance, still always have the same point of departure: the images of that unloading ramp at Auschwitz. This traumatic refusal to pass away of a moral imperfect past tense that has been burned into our national history entered the consciousness of the general population only in the 1980s, with the fiftieth anniversary of January 30, 1933 [the Nazi seizure of power], and the fortieth anniversaries of July 20, 1944 [the German officers' attempt to assassinate Hitler], and May 8, 1945 [when Germany surrendered]. And yet barriers that held up even yesterday are now breaking down.

Remembrance of the Victims and the Perpetrators

Recently the memoirs of those who for decades were unable to speak about what they had undergone are increasing in number: I think of Cordelia Edvardson, daughter of the Langässers, or of Lisa Fitko. We were able to follow the almost physical process of the work of remembering in scenes [in his film *Shoah*] where the relentness Claude Lanzmann loosened the tongues of the victims of Auschwitz and Maidanek. In the barber he interviewed, horror that had grown rigid and mute was put into words for the first time—leaving one unsure whether to continue to believe in the liberating power of words. And on the other side too, words flowed again from mouths that had long been kept shut—words that for good reasons had not been used since 1945, at least not in public. Collective memory spontaneously produces other phenomena in the perpetrators than in the victims. Saul Friedländer has noted how a gap has opened up in the last few years between the wish on the part of the Germans to normalize the past and an increasingly intense involvement with the Holocaust on the part of the Jews. As far as the Germans are concerned, a look at the recent press can only confirm this diagnosis.

In the Frankfurt trial of two physicians directly involved in "*Aktion Gnadentod*," the "euthanasia program," the counsel for the defense argued that a Göttingen psychiatrist was biased, on the grounds that the expert witness had a Jewish grandfather and might be emotionally encumbered. In the same week Alfred Dregger expressed a similar concern in the Bundestag: "Lack of a history and lack of regard for our own nation are cause for concern. Without an elementary patriotism, which other peoples take for granted, our people will not be able to survive. Anyone who misuses the so-called 'mastering of the past,' which was necessary, to be sure, to make our people incapable of having a future will meet with opposition from us." The attorney introduces a racist argument into a criminal trial; the party chairman demands an outspoken relativization of the encumbered Nazi past. Is the accidental coincidence of the two statements so accidental? Or is an intellectual climate in which such things simply go together gradually spreading in this republic? Then there is the sensational demand by the well known patron of the arts that the art of the Nazi period no longer be kept under "censorship." And then the Chancellor, with his historical sensitivity, draws parallels between Gorbachev and Goebbels.

Three moments had already come into play in the Bitburg scenario: The aura of the military cemetery was to awaken national sentiment and thereby "historical consciousness"; the juxtaposition of the mass graves in the concentration camp and the SS graves in the cemetery for those buried with honors, Bergen-Belsen in the morning and Bitburg in the afternoon, implicitly contested the uniqueness of the Nazi criminals; and the handshake of the veteran generals in the presence of the American president finally confirmed that we had always been on the right side in the fight against Bolshevism. Since then we have experienced agonizing discussions, discussions that smoulder rather than clarify, discussions on planned historical museums, on the production of a Fassbinder play, on a national monument that is as superfluous as a goiter. And yet Ernst Nolte complains that Bitburg did not open the gates wide enough, did not sufficiently remove the obstacles to a process of "settling accounts." "Fear of being accused of 'balancing claims,' and of comparisons in general forbade the asking of the simple question what it would have meant if in 1953 the then Chancellor had refused to visit the military cemetery in Arlington on the grounds that men who had participated in the terrorist attacks on the German civilian population were buried there" (*Frankfurter Allgemeine Zeitung*, June 6, 1986). Anyone who thinks out the presuppositions of this strangely constructed example will wonder at the naiveté with which an internationally renowned German historian balances Auschwitz against Dresden.

This mixing of what can still be said with the unspeakable is probably a reaction to a need that has become greater with increasing historical distance. One need, in any case, is unmistakable, and those who wrote the series on the Germans in World War II under the auspices of Bavarian Television assumed it in their older viewers: the wish to remove the subjective experience of the war period from a framework that of necessity provides everything with a different meaning in retrospect. This wish for unframed memories from the veteran's perspective can also be satisfied by reading Andreas Hillgruber's account of the events on the Eastern Front in 1944–45. The author poses the "problem of identification," an unusual problem for a historian, for himself only because he wants to take the experiential perspective of the combat troops and the civilian population affected. It may be true that Hillgruber's work as a whole conveys a different impression. But the little book published by Siegler (*Two Sorts of Destruction*) is not meant for readers with specialized knowledge that would permit them to put the contrasting accounts of "The Smashing of the German Reich" and "The End of European Jewry" in the proper context.

These examples show that despite everything history does not stand still. Mortality intervenes even in a life that has been damaged. Compared with the situation forty years ago, when Karl Jaspers wrote his famous treatise *The Question of Guilt*, our situation has changed fundamentally. At that time the issue was the distinction between the personal guilt of the perpetrators and the collective liability of those who—however understandable the reasons for it may have been—failed to do anything. This distinction no longer fits the problem of later generations, who cannot be blamed for their parents' and grandparents' failure to act. Is there still a problem of joint liability for them?

Jaspers's Questions Today

As before, there is the simple fact that subsequent generations also grew up within a form of life in which *that* was possible.

Our own life is linked to the life context in which Auschwitz was possible not by contingent circumstances but intrinsically. Our form of life is connected with that of our parents and grandparents through a web of familial, local, political, and intellectual traditions that is difficult to disentangle—that is, through a historical milieu that made us what and who we are today. None of us can escape this milieu, because our identities, both as individuals and as Germans, are indissolubly interwoven with it. This holds true from mimicry and physical gestures to language and into the capillary ramifications of one's intellectual stance. As though when teaching at universities outside Germany I could ever disclaim a mentality in which the traces of a very German intellectual dynamic from Kant to Marx and Max Weber are inscribed. We have to stand by our traditions, then, if we do not want to disavow ourselves. I agree even with Mr. Dregger that there are no grounds for such evasive maneuvers. But what follows from this existential connection between traditions and forms of life that have been poisoned by unspeakable crimes? At one time a whole civilized population, proud of its constitutional state and its humanistic culture, could be made liable for these crimes—in Jaspers's sense of a collective joint liability. Does something of this liability carry over to the next generation and the one after that as well? There are two reasons, I believe, why we should answer this question affirmatively.

First, there is the obligation incumbent upon us in Germany—even if no one else were to feel it any longer—to keep alive, without distortion and not only in an intellectual form, the memory of the sufferings of those who were murdered by German hands. It is especially these dead who have a claim to the weak anamnestic power of a solidarity that later generations can continue to practice only in the medium of a remembrance that is repeatedly renewed, often desperate, and continually on one's mind. If we were to brush aside this Benjaminian legacy, our fellow Jewish citizens and the sons, daughters, and grandchildren of all those who were murdered would feel themselves unable to breathe in our country. This has political implications as well. In any case I do not see how the relationship of the Federal Republic to Israel, for instance, could be "normalized" in the foreseeable future. For many, of course, the "indebted memory" is only in the title, while the text itself denounces public manifestations of a corresponding feeling as rituals of false subordination and gestures of feigned humility. It amazes me that these gentlemen cannot even distinguish—if we are to use Christian terminology—between humility and atonement.

The current debate, however, concerns not an indebted memory but the more narcissistic question of the attitude we are to take—for our own sakes—toward our own traditions. If we do not resolve this question without illusions, remembrance of the victims will also become a farce. Until now, the Federal Republic's officially proclaimed self-understanding has had a clear and simple answer. The answer was the same with Weiszäcker as with Heinemann and Heuss. After Auschwitz our national self-consciousness can be derived only from the better traditions in our history, a history that is not unexamined but instead appropriated critically. The context of our national life, which once permitted incomparable injury to the substance of human solidarity, can be continued and further developed only in the light of the traditions that stand up to the scrutiny of a gaze educated by the moral catastrophe, a gaze that is, in a word, suspicious. Otherwise we cannot respect ourselves and cannot expect from others.

Until now the official self-understanding of the Federal Republic has been based on this premise. This consensus has now been terminated by the Right. For there is concern about the result: An appropriation of tradition that takes a critical view does not in fact promote naive trust in the morality of conditions to which one is merely habituated; it does not facilitate identification with unexamined models. Martin Broszat identifies this correctly as the point on which opinions divide. The more we can regard the National Socialist period calmly as the filter through which cultural substance that is adopted voluntarily and with awareness must pass, the less that period will block our path like a locked door.

Dregger and those who share his convictions are now opposing this continuity in the self-understanding of the Federal

Republic. In my understanding, their discomfort stems from three sources.

Three Sources of Discomfort

First, neoconservative-derived interpretations of the situation play a role. According to those interpretations, a moralistic defense against the recent past is blocking the view of a thousand-year history prior to 1933. Without the memory of this national history, which has come under a "thought ban," a positive self-image cannot be created. Without a collective identity, the forces of social integration decline. The lamented "loss of history" is even said to contribute to the weakness of the political system's legitimation and to threaten this country's domestic peace and international predictability. This is used to justify the compensatory "creation of meaning" through which historiography is to provide for those uprooted by the process of modernization. But an appropriation of national history for purposes of facilitating identification requires that the status of the negatively cathected Nazi period be relativized; for these purposes it is no longer sufficient to shunt this period aside; its significance must be leveled off.

Second, there is a deeper motivation for a revisionism that wants to make the past harmless, a motivation that is completely independent of functionalist considerations à la Michael Stürmer. Since I am not a social psychologist, I can only make some conjectures about it. Edith Jacobson once gave a very penetrating exposition of the psychoanalytic insight that the developing child has to gradually learn to connect his experiences with a loving and permissive mother with experiences derived from contact with a withholding and withdrawing mother. Obviously the process in which we learn to synthesize the initially competing images of the good and bad parents into complex images of *the same* person is a long and painful one. The weak ego acquires its strength only through nonselective interaction with an ambivalent environment. In adults the need to defuse the corresponding cognitive dissonances is still alive. It is all the more understandable the more the extremes diverge: as, for example, in the contrast between the positive experiential impressions of one's own father or brother and problematizing information provided us by abstract reports on the actions and entanglements of persons close to us. Thus it is by no means the morally insensitive who feel compelled to free the collective fate in which those closest to them were involved from the stigma of unusual moral obligations.

The third motivation lies at still another level—the struggle to reclaim encumbered traditions. As long as the appropriating gaze is directed toward ambivalences that are disclosed to later generations by virtue of their knowledge of the later course of history rather than through their own efforts, even what was exemplary cannot escape the retroactive force of a corrupted effective history. After 1945 we read Carl Schmitt and Heidegger and Hans Freyer, and even Ernst Jünger differently than before 1933. This is often hard to bear, especially for my generation, who—after the war, in the long latency period up to the end of the 1950s—were under the intellectual sway of prominent figures of this sort. This may, incidentally, explain the persistent efforts at rehabilitation so earnestly expended— and not only in the *Frankfurter Allgemeine Zeitung*—on the legacy of the Young Conservatives.

Forty years later, then, the debate that Jaspers in his time managed, albeit with difficulty, to settle has broken out again in another form. Can one become the legal successor to the German Reich and continue the traditions of German culture without taking on historical liability for the form of life in which Auschwitz was possible? Is there any way to bear the liability for the context in which such crimes originated, a context with which one's own existence is historically interwoven, other than through remembrance, practiced in solidarity, of what cannot be made good, other than through a reflexive, scrutinizing attitude toward one's own identity-forming traditions? Can we not say in general that the less internal communality a collective context of life has preserved, the more it has maintained itself externally, through the usurpation and destruction of life that is alien to it, the greater is the burden of reconciliation imposed on the griefwork and the critical self-examination of subsequent generations? And does not this very thesis forbid us to use leveling comparisons to play down the fact that no one can take our place in the liability required of us? This is the question of the uniqueness of the Nazi crimes. What can be going on in the mind of a historian who would claim that I had "invented" this question?

The debate about the correct answer to this question is conducted from the first-person point of view. This arena, in which none of us can be nonparticipants, should not be confused with discussion among scientists and scholars who have to take the observational perspective of a third person in their work. The political culture of the Federal Republic is, of course, affected by the comparative work of historical scholars and others engaged in the *Geisteswissenschaften*, but the results of scholarly work reach the public flow of the appropriation of tradition, with the corresponding return to the perspective of the participant, only by way of mediators and the mass media. It is only here, in the public sphere, that comparisons can be used to settle damages. Prissy indignation about an ostensible conflation of politics and scholarship puts the issue on a false basis. Nipperdey and Hildebrand's criticisms are misdirected. Apparently they live in an ideologically closed milieu to which reality no longer has access. It is not a question of Popper versus Adorno, not a question of scholarly theoretical debates or of value freedom—it is a question of the public use of history.

From Comparisons Comes an Offsetting of Claims

In the academic discipline of history if I assess it correctly as an outsider, three primary positions on the Nazi period have been developed: one describes it from the perspective of the theory of totalitarianism, one focuses on the person and worldview of Hitler, and one is directed toward structures of power and authority or the social system. To be sure, one position will be more suitable than another for externally derived purposes of relativizing and leveling. But even the view that focuses on Hitler's person and his delusions about race works as a revisionism that renders the past harmless and relieves the conservative elites in particular of their burden only when it is presented in the corresponding perspective and in a certain tone of voice. The same is true of the comparison between Nazi crimes and Bolshevist extermination operations, even of the abstruse thesis that the Gulag Archipelago was more of "an original" than Auschwitz. Only when a daily newspaper publishes a corresponding article can the question of the uniqueness of the Nazi crimes assume the significance for us, who appropriate traditions from the perspective of participants, that makes it so explosive in this context. In the public sphere, in connection with political education, museums, and the teaching of history, the question of the apologetic production of images of history is a directly political one. Are we to undertake macabre reckonings of damages with the help of historical comparisons in order to evade our liability for the collective risks of the Germans? Joachim Fest, an editor of the *Frankfurter Allgemeine Zeitung*, complains (in the issue of August 29, 1986) about the lack of sensitivity "with which professors at their desks set about deciding who the victims were." This sentence, the worst in a bad article, can only reflect back on Fest himself. Why does he give an official air, in public, to the kind of reckoning of damages that until now has been current only in radical right-wing circles?

That certainly has nothing to do with forbidding scholars to discuss certain questions. If the dispute that began with the rejoinders of Eberhard Jackel, Jürgen Kocka (in the *Frankfurter Rundschau* of September 23, 1986), and Hans Mommsen (in the *Blätter für deutsche und internationale Politik*, October 1986) had taken place in an academic journal, I could not have been offended by it—I would not even have seen it. Of course the mere publication of Nolte's article by the *Frankfurter Allgemeine Zeitung* is not a sin, as [the historian] Thomas Nipperdey says mockingly, but it does mark a watershed in the political culture and self-understanding of the Federal Republic. The article was seen as indicating this by other countries as well.

Fest does not defuse this turning point by making Auschwitz's moral significance for us dependent on one's partiality to more pessimistic or more optimistic interpretations of history. The practical conclusions suggested by pessimistic interpretations of history differ depending on whether one holds the wickedness of human nature accountable for the constants of disaster or conceives them as socially produced—Gehlen versus Adorno. Nor are so-called optimistic interpretations of history always focused on the "new man"; we all know that American culture is incomprehensible without its meliorism. Finally, there are intuitions less one-sided than these. If historical progress consists of diminishing, eliminating, or preventing the suffering of a vulnerable creature, and if historical experience teaches us that progress finally achieved is followed only by new disasters, then we may certainly suppose that a balance of tolerability can be maintained only if we do our utmost for the sake of whatever progress is possible.

In the beginning my opponents tried to evade a debate on substance by attempting to discredit me as a scholar. I do not need to return to those opportunistic accusations here. To acquaint readers of *Die Zeit* with a diversionary technique one would expect more of brawling politicians than of scholars and publicists at their desks, I will give only one example. Joachim Fest asserts that on the main issue I imputed a completely false thesis to Nolte; Nolte, he says, "does not [deny] the uniqueness of the Nazi extermination operations." Nolte had in fact written that the mass crimes of the Nazis were far more irrational than their Soviet-Russian prototypes: "All of this," Nolte writes, summarizing his reasons, "constitutes their uniqueness," and then he continues, "But that does not alter the fact that the so-called annihilation of the Jews during the Third Reich was a reaction or a distorted copy and not a first act or an original." Then in the *Historische Zeitschrift* his well-meaning colleague Klaus Hildebrand also praised this very essay as pioneering because Nolte "tried to explain . . . the apparent uniqueness in the history of the 'Third Reich.'" I was able to adopt this reading, which sees all assurances to the contrary as escape clauses, all the more readily in that in the meantime Nolte had written the sentence in the *Frankfurter Allgemeine Zeitung* that first got the controversy rolling: Nolte had reduced the uniqueness of the Nazi crimes to the "technical procedure of gassing." Fest does not even let it rest at that distinction—referring expressly to the gas chambers, he asks, "Can it really be said that the mass liquidations by shooting in the back of the neck that were customary for years during the Red Terror were something qualitatively different? For all the differences, isn't the similarity stronger?"

I accept the remark that "extermination" rather than "expulsion" of the kulaks is the proper description of that barbaric process; for enlightenment is a mutual enterprise. But the balancing of accounts that Nolte and Fest are conducting in full public view is not in the service of enlightenment. It affects the political morality of a polity which—after a liberation by Allied troops to which it did not contribute—was founded in the spirit of the occidental understanding of freedom, responsibility, and self-determination.

Closing Remarks

1. The first reactions to my article ["Apologetic Tendencies"] (in *Die Zeit*, July 11, 1986) made it clear that Hildebrand, Stürmer, Hillgruber, and Fest wanted to be done with the theme of a revisionism that makes the past harmless: they denied the facts and their political context; they challenged the assertion that the activities of the historians I had mentioned had anything to do with each other; and they implied that I had fabricated the evidence myself. I would have let even the shabbiest element in this defensive strategy, the reproach of scholarly dishonesty, drop if it had not been taken up again by Andreas Hillgruber in the journal *Geschichte in Wissenschaft und Unterricht*, edited by K. D. Erdmann (12, 1986, p. 625ff.), in a manner unusual in both substance and tenor.*

2. With the dispute about quotations, Hillgruber chose a level of discussion on which he could evade argumentation about the issue itself. This forces me to return to my critique. After the fact, to be sure, Hillgruber did express himself cautiously on the extreme assertions of Nolte and Fest (in *Geschichte in Wissenschaft und Unterricht*), but of course his own book is not apologetic in the sense that he weighs the Nazi mass crimes against those of the Soviets in such a way as to relieve moral burdens. His account is apologetic in a different sense: the title *Two Sorts of Destruction* represents a relativizing of Auschwitz

---

*In the German text a section, here omitted, follows in which Habermas discusses accusations that he has falsified citations and been guilty of various misinterpretations. (translator's note)

in relation to "The Smashing of the German Reich." Auschwitz is no longer to be the signature of the era. Hillgruber is concerned with a normalization of our view of the Nazi period that will allows the events on the "Eastern Front" to regain, even in retrospect, a meaning of their own—unaffected by an unjust regime and its mass crimes.

Recently, in a noteworthy article on "The Blocked Past," the social historian Karl Schlögel formulated the task that Hillgruber's topic poses for the writer: "It was the tanks and the death factories of the Germans that depopulated Central Europe and altered it beyond recognition. The extermination of the Central-European Jews, the enslavement of the people of this area, the murder of the Polish and Czechoslovakian intelligentsia, the view of all Slavs as beasts of burden, and the systematic extermination of Soviet prisoners of war—all that is still on the public agenda in the Germans' mastering of the past. The German crime has a fairly specific locus: eastern Central Europe was the Nazi regime's death zone. Precisely because this needs to be brought to awareness, the opportunity also arises to speak of the crimes that were committed against the German civilian population in eastern Central Europe, of the mass expulsion of the Germans" (*Frankfurter Allgemeine Zeitung*, February 21, 1987). This terrible story, says Schlögel, cannot be told in the language of a dogmatic point of view: "only someone who can at least take the part of all those involved in the process can do justice to a story."

Hillgruber begins with a dogmatic point of view that would like to shift the moral emphasis: Following Alfred Heuss, whom he cites several times, he sets himself the goal of developing the German's people currently weak awareness of what was "probably the most serious consequence of the war"—by which he means the expulsion of the Germans from the former eastern territories and the ceding of those territories to Poland (*Geschichte in Wissenschaft und Unterricht*, p. 730). On this question of what the "gravest" consequence of the war was, moreover, Hillgruber was not to be moved by the skeptical inquiries of his colleague Jürgen Kocka [of Bielefeld University] (in a broadcast on Austrian television the first weekend in February 1987). Hillgruber takes as his theme not "the history of the peoples involved in Central Europe, which is both a shared history and a history of opposition to one another" (Schlögel), not their dreadful entanglements, but the disentangling of events on the "Eastern Front" from the crimes of the Germans that both preceded and coincided with them. This explains why Hillgruber takes as his point of departure Norbert Blüm's statement (*Two Sorts of Destruction,* p. 18) that the crimes in the concentration camps continued only as long as the German military fronts held up. Hillgruber wants to understand this indisputable causal connection as a tragic linkage of events but not a relationship that needs to be accounted for. Otherwise one could draw the conclusion that "it would have been desirable to let the fronts, and that means the German Eastern Front as well . . . collapse as quickly as possible in order to put a stop to the horrors in the concentration camps" (p. 18). To counter this, Hillgruber holds up "Nemmersdorf," the reconquered village where a picture of horror presented itself to the German soldiers: "'Nemmersdorf' became the word for what the German population could expect when the dam broke" (p. 19).

Hillgruber sketches the panorama of the "desperate defensive battle to maintain the independence of the great-power position of the German Reich that it was the Allies' will to destroy" (p. 64), in order to return normality and meaning to this portion of German history. Many Germans did not experience the spring of 1945 as a liberation. Does that mean that even forty years later the historian has to depict the defeat from the perspective of the destruction of the German Reich? If we were to present it retrospectively as a liberation from the Nazi regime, of course, the objective senselessness of the war that Hitler unleashed would become clear to us. With his version Hillgruber resists this insight, an insight that colleagues like Hans and Wolfgang Mommsen rightly insist on: "We cannot get away from the bitter truth that the defeat of Nazi Germany was in the interest not only of the peoples to whom Hitler had carried the war and the population groups singled out by his henchmen for annihilation or oppression or exploitation, but of the Germans themselves" (Wolfgang Mommsen in the *Frankfurter Rundschau,* December 1, 1986).

The Nazi period represents an object particularly ill-suited for the project of meaning-creating normalization. This is why Hillgruber finds himself compelled to engage in four operations.

(a) First there is the author's decision to identify with the perspective of the German population and the troops in combat—and only with these—in his account of the events on the "Eastern Front" (p. 24f.). Hillgruber met the disapproving comments of his colleague Christian Meier [of the University of Munich] (*Frankfurter Allgemeine Zeitung*, November 20, 1986), not with an explanation but with an avowal of German nationalism to the effect that a German historian has to identify with the German fate (*Frankfurter Allgemeine Zeitung*, November 29, 1986). He responded to my critique of this veteran's perspective, which is somewhat remarkable in a historian forty years later, with the grotesque question: "Are regulations to be issued here—in contradiction to our liberal constitution—on what historians may and may not do?" (*Geschichte in Wissenschaft und Unterricht*, p. 731.) Saul Friedländer, a colleague from Tel Aviv who has expressed himself on the Historians' Debate at length in a leading Israeli daily, also finds Hillgruber's methodological one-sidedness "amazing" [Habermas quotes from an original manuscript, written in English; the quotes are here retranslated into English from Habermas's German translation, as the manuscript was not available]: "Was identification with the Red Army solely the perspective of the inmates of the camps? Was it not the hope of hundreds of millions of people in all of Europe and beyond that the German Eastern front and the Western front would both collapse? At that time—and Hillgruber will be able to identify with the context of that time—even those outside the borders of Germany who were afraid of the Red Army waited fervently for the end of Nazi Germany. Perhaps it is understandable that this was not the case inside Germany, but it may be, as Heinrich Böll once remarked, that this is precisely where the real problem of the Germans' relationship to their past lies."

(b) Next, Hillgruber brings a perspective to bear from which World War II appears as a completely normal example of national self-assertion. To do this he has to start somewhat earlier: "In fact the 1920s and the 1930s offered a remarkable chance not only to restore and consolidate Germany's position as a great power, which had been shaken in World War I but not destroyed; there was still the possibility of a leading role for the Reich in Central Europe" (p. 70). Hitler may well have lost this opportunity through his claims to power based on race ideology, but the war would have been lost anyway through the usual logic of power politics. This is why Hillgruber puts so much emphasis on proving that the Allied war aims can by no means be understood as a response to the crimes of the Nazi tyranny. These aims resulted from the usual calculations of interests (obscured, to be sure, by prejudices against Prussian militarism). On this point one needs to read the Harvard historian Charles Maier: "It does not seem relevant to Hillgruber's way of thinking that German aggression might indeed have led the Allies to contemplate partition; in any case the notion was rejected in theory, and partition came about only as a result of circumstances when the war ended. Hillgruber's historical contribution to 'winning the future' thus amounts to the old Prusso-German lament . . . that the Machiavellian British were always conspiring to encircle the Reich. Predictably enough, the essay closes with a lament that after 1945, Prussia and Germany would no longer be able to fulfill their mediating role between East and West. But precisely what sort of a 'mediating role' had brought all those German soldiers to Stalingrad in the first place? Unfortunately, this is vulgar *Historismus* at best" ("Immoral Equivalence," in *The New Republic*, December 1, 1986, p. 38).

(c) The normal image of valiant self-assertion, however, can be created only if obvious distinctions between patriotic defense of one's country and maintenance of the Nazi regime are avoided. Thus Hillgruber tries to devalue political resistance against the tyranny at home as unrealistic and based on an ethics of conviction (p. 20f.). Joachim Perls, the Hannover political scientist, observes of this "that the . . . position of the opponents of Nazism is cast into doubt as a framework for the analysis of the 'Third Reich'" (*Frankfurter Rundschau*, Dec. 29, 1986). Hillgruber's presentation is directed to such an extent by his focus on the external enemy that only the "fate of the

German nation as a whole" still counts (p. 24). In this higher totality, the Nazi regime fuses with the country that was worth fighting for.

(d) These three operations—the identification of the historian with the Germans in combat, the normalizing view of the opposition between Allied war aims and German interests, and the trivializing of the German Resistance—make the decisive step possible: a redistribution of the moral weight between what the German nation suffered in the course of and as a consequence of the war it had contrived, and the suffering that German troops and German terror had caused others. It is only these three operations that make it possible to decouple the extermination of the European Jews from the battle on the "Eastern Front"—and to ascribe it to Hitler as the exclusive consequence of his race doctrine (as Hillgruber had said in his preface). Of course Hillgruber abhors the mass crimes of the Nazis. But Micha Brumlik has correctly interpreted the message his narrative conveys to the reader: Given the evils that continued resistance to the Red Army was to avoid, from the German perspective the other evil—continued murder and suffering in the concentration camps—could be "put up with." Similarly, Hans Mommsen sees a "relativization of the Holocaust" in Hillgruber's "placing the organized murder of millions of European Jews on the same level as the sacrifices of the final phase of World War II in the East" (Hans Mommsen, "Die Wende im Geschichtsbild," in *Vorwärts*, December 20, 1986, p. 40).

3. What most irritates me in the course of the debate up to now is the fact that an important segment of German historians is ready to deny or ignore the apologetic content of Hillgruber's book. I would be relieved to think this was occurring only out of opportunism—Hillgruber is an influential man.

Hillgruber himself sets his text, which is intended for a broad public, in the context of the political discussion about May 8th (p. 161f.). From this May 8, 1985, that is, from the performance at Bitburg, there is a direct line to the standard election speech with which [the Christian Socialist leader] Franz Joseph Strauss toured the country. In that speech he says: "It is now high time for us to step out of the shadow of the Third Reich and the aura of Hitler and become a normal nation again . . . . Without a national identity in which Germans can find their relationship to themselves and their past, but also to their future, the German people cannot fulfill their mission in the world . . . . And therefore, ladies and gentlemen, we need—and I do not say this presumptuously—to hold our heads higher here" (*Frankfurter Rundschau*, January 14, 1987). At a conference sponsored by the Konrad Adenauer Foundation, Hans-Peter Schwarz, the historian and biographer of Adenauer, "formulated the Historian's Debate clearly in terms of power politics," as the reporter Rolf Zundel noted, by saying that "precisely in the last decade West Germans have been visibly longing to reassure themselves of their roots in an unabridged German history that can be experienced in living terms, but they are constantly reminded only of the twelve years on which patriotic feelings of self-esteem cannot be based. When national consciousness is replaced by consciousness of guilt, patriotism is programmed to degenerate into defeatist pacifism" (*Die Zeit*, February 6, 1987). As one can see, politicians and contemporary historians are currently vying to see who will define what we can expect, politically, from contemporary historiography. In a situation like this Hillgruber and his associates can no longer feign ignorance. Instead of insinuating that I intended some kind of prohibition of thought or questioning, one might well recommend to one historian or another greater sensitivity to his own scholarly independence of the political context.

Where the political self-understanding of the Federal Republic is concerned, the debate so far has at least resulted in the clarification of an alternative: One group has a functionalist understanding of the public use of history; they dispense the slogan, which is formulated in terms of power politics but self-contradictory, of promoting loyalty to NATO and internal cohesion through "national consciousness instead of guilt consciousness." In opposition to this kind of "politics of history," to manipulated historical consciousness in general, the other group advocates enlightenment. They do not confuse a constitutional-patriotic tie to the principles of the constitutional state, identification with Western forms of life, and a solid political tie to the West with an uncritical willingness to follow any and all policies of the United States, even one so extravagant as the "Star Wars" program. They trust above all a national self-consciousness that draws its strength solely from the critical appropriation, educated by Auschwitz, of our traditions, which, fortunately, are not lacking in unambiguous models.

Historical Consciousness and Post-Traditional Identity: The Federal Republic's Orientation to the West

I

In referring to European culture, the dedication of the Sonning Prize calls to mind the milieu that joins us today. By that I mean "we Western Europeans," who are not only nourished by the heritage of European intellectual history but also share democratic forms of government and occidental forms of life. This "West" was given its definition by the first generation of states in modern Europe; it was taken for granted that Englishmen and Frenchmen as well as Danes and Swedes belonged to it. Only in the decades since the end of World War II has it become a matter of course for Germans this side of the Elbe and the Werra to consider themselves a part of Western Europe.

Midway through World War I, Friedrich Naumann, a liberal, published a book with the title *Central Europe*. And a year before the Nazi seizure of power Giselher Wirsing, a member of the circle around *Die Tat*, was writing about "Central Europe and the German Future." Those titles reflect the dream of a hegemony of the Central European powers and an ideology of "the middle" that had deep roots in the "anti-civilizing, anti-Western undercurrent in the German tradition" from the Romantics to Heidegger.[1] This self-consciousness fixated on its intermediate geographical situation was given a social darwinist

The first four sections of this essay are based on Habermas's Sonning Prize acceptance speech in Copenhagen on May 14, 1987.

turn during the Nazi period. And this mentality is among the factors that explain how it was possible for an entire civilized population to close its eyes to mass crimes. The consciousness of having taken a *Sonderweg,* a special path that set Germany apart and gave it special privilege in relation to the West was discredited only by Auschwitz. After Auschwitz, at any rate, it lost its power to generate myths. That through which we Germans dissociated ourselves from Western civilization, and indeed from any and every civilization, set off a shock-wave; and though many citizens of the Federal Republic fended off this shock at first, they remained under its influence as they gradually abandoned their reservations about the political culture and social forms of the West. A mentality changed.

This, at least, is how it seemed to me, and it still seems that way. Doubts about this diagnosis arise, however, when one considers, with the obligatory attitude of suspicion, the debate that has been going on among historians for the past year, a debate that in reality concerns the Federal Republic's self-understanding. To be sure, both sides in the debate emphatically defend the Federal Republic's orientation to the West. But the one side conceives these ties to the West primarily in terms of power politics and thinks primarily of the military alliance and foreign policy, whereas the other side stresses the ties to the West's Enlightenment culture. What is in dispute is not whether the Federal Republic is part of Western Europe but the question raised by the neoconservatives, the question whether the choice in favor of the West does not have to be broadly anchored in a renewed national self-consciousness. According to the one side, the identity of the Germans, which is allegedly in jeopardy, has to be strengthened through a historical presentation of "pasts that one can approve of." This side is concerned with a neohistoricist illumination of the continuities in German national history that extend into and through the 1930s and the 1940s. On this view, one would expect the generations of today to be able to relate more freely and with greater detachment to a Nazi period that had regained a measure of normalcy.

The critics on the other side argue that historical truth could get lost in this kind of historiographic politics. They have another reason as well to fear a historical leveling of what was exceptional in the events and circumstances that made Auschwitz possible. To redistribute the moral emphasis and make the extraordinary banal in this way could defuse consciousness of the discontinuities in our recent history. For it is only in the untroubled consciousness of a break with our disastrous traditions that the Federal Republic's unreserved openness to the political culture of the West will mean more than an opportunity that is economically attractive and inevitable in terms of power politics. What I am concerned with is this "more," the possibility of a greater meaning in the new intellectual orientation.

I would hardly trouble a Danish audience with what is almost an intimate German problem if I did not believe that we could find more general issues in it as well. Of course, I do not want to make any hasty generalizations. In Denmark "only" one percent of the Jewish population fell into the hands of the SS.[2] This is not grounds for celebration—for every single one who was deported leaves behind traces of a history of suffering for which amends can never be made. Nevertheless, you can be proud of what many of your compatriots did at a time when the great mass of our population at least allowed something monstrous to happen of which they at least had some suspicion. Some of us are the heirs of the victims and of those who helped the intended victims or offered resistance. Others are the heirs of the perpetrators or of those who kept quiet. For those born later, this *divided* legacy establishes neither personal merit nor personal guilt. Beyond guilt that can be ascribed to individuals, however, different contexts can mean different historical burdens. With the life forms into which we were born and which have stamped our identity we take on very different sorts of historical liability (in Jaspers' sense).[3] For the way we continue the traditions in which we find ourselves is up to us.

No hasty generalizations, then. And yet on another level Auschwitz has become the signature of an entire epoch—and it concerns all of us. Something happened there that no one could previously have thought even possible. It touched a deep layer of solidarity among all who have a human face. Until then—in spite of all the quasi-natural brutalities of world history—we had simply taken the integrity of this deep layer for granted. At that point a bond of naiveté was torn to shreds—a naiveté from which unquestioned traditions drew their authority, a naiveté that as such had nourished historical continuities. Auschwitz altered the conditions for the continuation of historical life contexts—and not only in Germany.

You may be familiar with that strangely archaic feeling of shame in the face of a catastrophe that one has survived not through one's own efforts but by chance. I first observed this reaction in others—in those who had escaped the concentration camps, who had gone into hiding or emigrated—and who could show solidarity with those who did not survive the extermination operations only in an inexplicably self-tormenting way. By the criteria of personal guilt, this feeling is unfounded. But those who have come under the influence of this kind of melancholy act as though they could still somehow render the pastness of an irreparable calamity less definitive through a remembrance that shared in the suffering. I do not want to deny the specificity of this phenomenon. But since that moral catastrophe doesn't the survival of all of us stand under the curse, in attentuated form, of having merely escaped? And doesn't the fortuitousness of unmerited escape establish an intersubjective liability—a liability for distorted life circumstances that grant happiness, or even mere existence, to some only at the cost of destroying the happiness of others, denying them life and causing them suffering?

II

In his "Theses on the Philosophy of History," Walter Benjamin anticipated this intuition and gave it conceptual formulation: "There is no document of culture which is not at the same time a document of barbarism. And just as such a document is not free of barbarism, barbarism taints also the manner in which it was transmitted from one owner to another."[4]

This sentence appears in the context of Benjamin's critique of a way of viewing history that neohistoricism now wants to revive—even with regard to, and in fact precisely with regard to the Nazi period. At that time historiography was carried on under the banner of a historicism that empathized with the victors without thinking of the victims—except in its celebratory transfiguration of the sacrifice of its own heroes. Benjamin was thinking of the public use made of history by national movements and nation states in the nineteenth century—the kind of historical writing with a broad influence that could serve as the medium for the self-reassurance of a nation, a people becoming conscious of its own identity. I would like to begin by recalling some of the connections between historicism and nationalism in order then to explain why recourse to this kind of national-historical identity formation is denied us today, at least in Western societies.

Nationalism as it has developed in Europe since the end of the eighteenth century is a specifically modern form of the manifestation of a collective identity. After the break with the *ancien régime* and the dissolution of the traditional social order of early bourgeois society, individuals were emancipated within a framework of abstract civil liberties. The mass of these emancipated individuals became mobile—not only politically mobile as citizens but economically mobile as labor power, militarily mobile as liable for military service, and culturally mobile as subject to compulsory education, as people who learned to read and write and thus became subject to the influence of mass communication and mass culture. In that situation it was nationalism that satisfied the need for new forms of identification. It differed from previous forms of identity formation in several respects.[5] First, the ideas on which identity was founded were drawn from a heritage that was independent of church and religion, a profane heritage that was processed and supplied by the *Geisteswissenschaften* that emerged at that time. This explains something of the character of the new ideas, which were both penetrating and conscious; they took hold of all strata of the population in similar ways and were dependent upon a self-directed reflexive mode of appropriating tradition. Second, nationalism made the shared cultural heritage of language, literature, and history congruent with the organizational form of the state. The democratic nation state that emerged from the French Revolution remained the model to which all nationalist movements were oriented. Third, there was a tension in national consciousness between two elements that had been more or less in balance in the classical nation states—that is, in nations that became conscious of themselves only within the framework of preexisting forms of state organization. I am referring to the tension between the universalist value orientations of democracy and the constitutional state on the one hand, and the particularism of a nation distinguishing itself from what is outside it on the other hand.

In the context of nationalism, freedom and political self-determination have double meanings: they mean both the popular soveriegnty of citizens with equal rights and the self-assertion through power politics of a nation that has become sovereign. The first element is reflected in international solidarity with the oppressed, from enthusiasm for Greek and Polish causes in the early nineteenth century to the hero cults and tourist trade in revolutions of our times (China, Vietnam, Cuba, Portugal, Nicaragua). The second element is manifested in the stereotypical images of the enemy that have lined the paths of all national movements. For the Germans between 1806 and 1914 it was images of the French, the Danes, and the English. The symptoms of this unresolved tension, however, are revealed not only in such opposing responses but also in the very state and the very historical consciousness in which nationalism took form.

The form of national identity makes it necessary for every nation to organize itself as a state in order to be independent. In historical reality, however, the state with a homogeneous national population was always a fiction. It was the nation state itself that generated movements for autonomy in which oppressed national minorities fought for their rights. And by subjecting minorities to its central administration, the nation state contradicts the very premises of self-determination on which it rests. A similar contradiction runs through the historical consciousness in the medium of which a nation's self-consciousness is formed. In order to form and maintain a collective identity, the linguistic-cultural life context has to be given representation in the present in such a way as to produce meaning. But the medium in which affirmative pasts are given present representation, the *Geisteswissenschaften*, works against this.

Their claim to truth commits the *Geisteswissenschaften* to critique; it stands opposed to the function of social integration, in the service of which the nation state put historical scholarship to public use. Normally the compromise took the form of a historiography that elevated empathy with what existed to a methodological ideal and refrained from "brushing history against the grain" (Benjamin). The gaze that turns away from the victor's backside can conceal its selectiveness from itself all the more readily in that its own selectiveness disappears in that of the narrative form.

The classical nation states and those that emerged from the *Risorgimento* movements managed to live more or less unobtrusively with such contradictions. It was the original nationalism embodied in such figures as Hitler and Mussolini that destroyed that precarious balance and released national egoism altogether from its ties to the universalist origins of the democratic constitutional state. In Nazi Germany the particularist element that until then had been repeatedly pacified finally became inflated into the idea of the racial supremacy of one's own people. This strengthened a mentality without which the organized large-scale extermination of pseudoscientifically defined categories of internal and external enemies would not have been possible. In the shock that followed the exaltation, narratively established continuities of national history were shattered in Germany, even if at first only in that the negatively cathected period was warded off and shunted aside. Over a longer period, this shock also brought about an incursion of reflection into public historical consciousness and shook things that had been taken for granted in a collective identity shaped by nationalism.

The question is whether we ought to see in this only the continuation of a national pathology with the signs reversed, a sort of negative nationalism (Nolte), or whether under the particular conditions of the Federal Republic we are only seeing more clearly, and in a more compulsive and unbalanced form, a change of form that is also taking place in the classical nation states. What I have in mind is a transformation in the form of national identity such that there is a shift in the relative weights of the two elements mentioned above. If my conjecture is correct, the constellation of the two elements is changing in such a way that the imperatives of the self-assertion of national forms of life through power politics no longer simply dominate the mode of action of the constitutional state but also find their limits in postulates of the universalization of democracy and human rights.

III

In the year 1949, six new nations were founded. Vietnam, Laos, Cambodia, and Indonesia belong to the third generation of nation states that emerged from the dissolution of colonial empires in Asia and Africa and that followed, *mutatis mutandis,* the model of their predecessors. The Federal Republic of Germany and the German Democratic Republic, which came into being at the same time, do not form part of this series. According to one version, the two successor states to the German Reich are transitory creations whose unity as a nation state is being temporarily withheld. The hypothesis of a general transformation in the form of national identity calls for a different reading. In this version, an unfortunate episode, not even seventy-five years long, of in any case incomplete unification as a nation state came to an end in 1945. After that the cultural identity of the Germans became detached from the organizational form of the unified state—something that happened even earlier in the case of Austria.

The historian Rudolf von Thadden has remarked, without resentment, that Kant remains a part of German intellectual history even though Königsberg is now called Kaliningrad— that is to say, lies in neither West German nor East German territory.[6] With this decoupling of shared cultural identity from the formation of society and the form of the state, a nationality that has certainly become more diffuse becomes detached from nationality in the sense of citizenship in a nation and leaves room for political identification with what the population considers worthy of preserving in the postwar development of its own state at any given time. In the Federal Republic, Dolf Sternberger has observed a certain constitutional patriotism, that is, a readiness to identify with the political order and the principles of the Basic Law.

This more sober political identity has detached itself from the background of a past centered on national history. The universalist content of a form of patriotism crystallized around the democratic constitutional state is no longer pledged to continuities filled with victories; this form of patriotism is incompatible with the secondary quasi-natural character of a consciousness that has no insight into the deep ambivalance of every tradition, into the concatenation of things for which amends cannot be made, into the barbaric dark side of all cultural achievements to the present day.

To be sure, the current debate shows that this reading is a disputed one. In the same phenomena others see only indications of the pathology of a national identity that has been damaged. In either case, certainly, the beginnings of a post-national identity linked to the constitutional state could develop and stabilize only within the framework of more general tendencies extending beyond the Federal Republic.

Do such more general tendencies exist? I will not go into the familiar functional aspects in terms of which the significance of the nation state's level of integration has currently declined everywhere; nor into what the nation state's loss of sovereignty (it is increasingly dependent on the capitalistic world economy and on superpowers with nuclear arms) may mean in the perception of its citizens. I will limit myself to some trivial observations that attest to a weakening here of the particularist element in the nationalist form of consciousness.[7]

1. In section 324 of his *Philosophy of Right,* Hegel—who as we know kept his distance from the national movements of his time—provides, quite ingenuously, arguments for the "ethical moment of war" and the individual's duty to expose himself to "the sacrifice of his property and his life" in war. Under the name of a sovereignty conceived in modern terms, the nation state inherited the classical duty to die for one's fatherland, thereby confirming the primacy of the nation over all other earthly goods. This core content of nationalism, which stamped its mentality, has not withstood the development of weapons technology. Today, anyone who actually uses the weapons with

which he threatens another country knows that he is destroying his own country in the same moment. Thus in the meantime refusal of military service has become easier to justify in moral terms than military service itself, which has become paradoxical.

2. Hannah Arendt saw in the camps the symbol of the most essential characteristic of our century. She was referring not only to the extermination camps but to detention and refugee camps in general, to reception and transit camps for political emigrants, for those expelled from their native lands and those seeking economic asylum, for foreign workers, and so on. The massive population shifts imposed by war, political oppression, economic distress, and the international labor market have left scarcely a one of the developed societies unchanged in its ethnic composition. Contact with people deprived of their rights, the direct confrontation of indigenous populations with foreign forms of life, religions, and races has, to be sure, given rise to defensive reactions; but these experiences also provide a stimulus to learning processes, to the recognition of one's own privileged situation. They constrain one to relativize one's own form of life, and they represent a challenge to take the universalist bases of one's own tradition seriously.

3. The effects of mass communication and mass tourism are less drastic, more subcutaneous. Both have the effect of altering a nearsighted vision focused on contemplation and a group morality tailored to what is close to home. They accustom the gaze to the heterogeneity of life forms and to the reality of the differential between conditions of life here and elsewhere. This habituation is, of course, ambivalent: it opens our eyes but also dulls them. We could not live if we had to look at those pictures of [famine in] the sub-Sahara region every day. But even the fact that we cannot survive without repression reveals the unsettling presence of a society that has expanded to include the world as a whole. In this society the stereotypes and the images of the enemy that shield what is one's own from what is foreign and other become less and less reliable. The more insistently an asynchronous variety of different, competing, and mutually exploitative forms of life assert their rights to coexistence and equal treatment, the more it becomes clear that there is no

alternative to the extension of moral consciousness in the direction of universalism.

4. Finally, the scholarly disciplines that served as the medium in which the cultural heritage of a nation could be given present representation have changed. During the nineteenth century the *Geisteswissenschaften* were still directly connected, within their national boundaries, to flows of communication among the educated public and its public appropriation of tradition. With the disintegration of the educated bourgeois strata this tie became looser. Then the international integration of the system of science and scholarship extended to the *Geisteswissenschaften* as well and rendered national traditions of scholarship more accessible to one another. Finally, the rapprochement of the social sciences and the *Geisteswissenschaften* gave rise to a push for theorizing in the latter and promoted greater differentiation between research and presentation, expert scholarship and exoteric historiography. In general, the distance between the historical disciplines and the public process of cultural transmission has become greater. The fallibility of knowledge and the conflict of interpretations promote the problematization of historical consciousness rather than identity formation and the creation of meaning.

If we accept for the moment that these and other like tendencies do in fact indicate a change in the form of national identity, at least within the domain of Western industrial societies, how are we to understand the relationship between a historical consciousness that has become problematic and a postnational state identity? Every identity that establishes membership in a collectivity and that defines the set of situations in which those belonging to the collectivity can say "we" in the emphatic sense seems to be part of an unquestioned background that necessarily remains untouched by reflection.

IV

Søren Kierkegaard, the religious writer and thinker who to this day has inspired our thinking far beyond the bounds of existential philosophy, was a contemporary of the national movements. But he did not speak of collective identities at all;

he spoke only of the identity of the individual person. In *Either/ Or* he focuses on the decision, taken in solitude, through which the moral individual assumes responsibility for his life history and "makes himself the man he is."[8] This practical act of transformation has a cognitive side as well; with it the individual is converted to an "ethical view of life": he "discovers now that the self he chooses contains an endless multiplicity, inasmuch as it has a history, a history in which he acknowledges identity with himself" (181). Anyone who remembers the *Confessions* of Saint Augustine will recognize in this authentic life-project an old Christian motif, the experience of conversion. The "absolute choice" transforms the individual in the same way that conversion transforms the Christian: "He becomes himself, quite the same self he was before, and yet he becomes another, for the choice permeates everything and transforms it" (172). Every individual first encounters himself as the historical product of contingent life circumstances, but in "choosing" himself as this product he constitutes a self to which the rich concreteness of the life history in which he merely found himself is attributed as something for which he will account retrospectively. From this perspective, a life that is accepted with responsibility is revealed as being at the same time an irreversible series of lapses. The Danish Protestant insists on the interlocking of existential authenticity and the consciousness of sin: "But one can choose oneself ethically only by repenting of oneself; and only by repenting does one become concrete" (207).

This concept of an ego-identity produced through the reconstruction of one's own life history in the light of an absolute responsibility for oneself can also be read in a somewhat more secular way. Then one sees that in the middle of the nineteenth century Kierkegaard had to think under the presuppositions of Kantian ethics and wanted to offer an alternative to Hegel's attempt at a dubious "concretization" of Kant's universalist morality. For Hegel had wanted to provide support for subjective freedom and moral conscience in the institutions of a rational state. Kierkegaard, who distrusted this objective spirit as much as Marx did, anchored both instead in a radicalized inwardness. In this way he arrived at a concept of personal identity that is clearly more suited to our posttraditional, but not yet in itself rational world.

Yet Kierkegaard was completely aware of the fact that the personal self is at the same time a social self and a self that is a citizen—for him Robinson Crusoe remained an adventurer. He envisaged personal life being "translated" into the life of the citizen and returning from that sphere into the sphere of inwardness (220). Then, of course, we may ask how intersubjectively shared life contexts must be structured in order not only to leave room for the development of exacting personal identities but also to support such processes of self-discovery. What would group identities have to be like to be capable of complementing and stabilizing the improbable and endangered type of ego identity that Kierkegaard outlines?

It would be a mistake to think of group identities as ego identities on a large scale—the relationship between the two is not one of analogy but one of complementarity. It is easy to see that nationalism could not serve as such a complement to Kierkegaard's ethical view of life. Nationalism does, to be sure, represent a first step toward reflexive appropriation of traditions to which one identifies oneself as belonging; national identity is already posttraditional. But this form of consciousness develops a strong prejudicial force: that can be seen in the limiting case in which it actualizes itself in purest form— in the moment of mobilization for patriotic war. This situation of voluntarily falling into line is the sheer opposite of the existential "either/or" with which Kierkegaard confronted the individual. Apparently, in the identifications that the nation state expected of its citizens more was predecided than Kierkegaard, with the interest of the individual in mind, could allow.

The situation is different with a constitutional patriotism that does not arise until after culture and national politics have become more emphatically differentiated from one another than they were in the nation states of the old type. Here identifications with one's own forms of life and traditions are overlaid with a patriotism that has become more abstract, that now relates not to the concrete totality of a nation but rather to abstract procedures and principles. These focus on the conditions for communal life and for communication among different, equally entitled coexisting forms of life—both within the nation and outside it. Of course constitutional patriotism's ties to these principles have to be nourished by a heritage of cultural traditions that is consonant with them. National traditions continue to confer privileged status on one form of life, even if it is only one in a hierarchy of life forms of varying scope. To these forms of life correspond, in turn, collective identities that overlap one another but no longer need a *central point* around which they can be grouped and integrated into a national identity. Instead, the abstract idea of the universalization of democracy and human rights forms the hard substance through which the rays of national tradition—the language, literature, and history of one's own nation—are refracted.

The analogies between this process of appropriation and Kierkegaard's model of the responsible assumption of one's individual life history should not be taken too far. The decisionism of "either/or" represents an extreme stylization, even with regard to an individual life. The weight of the "decision" here is meant primarily to stress the autonomous and conscious character of the act of taking hold of oneself. The only thing that can correspond to this on the level of the appropriation of intersubjectively shared traditions, which are not subject to the will of any one individual, is the autonomous and conscious character of a publicly conducted debate. We Germans, for instance, are debating how we want to understand ourselves as citizens of the Federal Republic—the public process of cultural transmission takes place in the mode of this debate about conflicting interpretations. And the historical disciplines—and other expert cultures as well—are involved in that debate only in terms of their public use, not as scholarly disciplines.

There is another, equally important difference. Kierkegaard places the art of choosing oneself wholly under the viewpoint of moral justification. But it is only what we can attribute to an individual person that is subject to moral evaluation; we cannot feel responsible for historical processes in the same sense. For those born later, only a kind of intersubjective liability arises from the historical complex of forms of life that have been passed on from generation to generation. It is here, however, that the moment of repentance that follows on the heels of self-reassurance finds its counterpart—a melancholy in view of the victims whose sufferings cannot be made good, a melancholy that places us under an obligation. Whether or not we view this historical liability as broadly as Benjamin did, today we bear a greater responsibility than ever for the proportion of continuity and discontinuity in the forms of life we pass on.

In an illuminating passage, Kierkegaard uses the image of the editor: the individual who lives ethically is the editor of his own life history, but he has to be "fully conscious that he is responsible" (218). Once the individual has made the existential decision who he wants to be, he assumes responsibility for deciding what will henceforth be considered essential in the life history he has taken on morally—and what will not: "He who lives ethically abolishes to a certain degree the distinction between the accidental and the essential, for he accepts himself, every inch of him, as equally essential. But the distinction returns, for when he has done this, he distinguishes again, yet in such a way that for the accidental which he excludes he accepts an essential responsibility for excluding it" (175). Today we can see that there is a counterpart to this in the life of a people. In the public process of transmitting a culture we decide which of our traditions we want to continue and which we do not. The debate on this rages all the more intensely the less we can rely on a triumphal national history, on the unbroken normality of what has come to prevail, and the more clearly we become conscious of the ambivalence in every tradition.

V

In the personal sphere, then, Kierkegaard speaks of a "distinction" we make when we recall ourselves from distraction and collect ourselves in the focus of responsibly being ourselves. Then one knows who one wants to be and who one doesn't want to be, what is to be an essential part of oneself and what isn't. Existential philosophy's conceptualizations of authenticity and inauthenticity cannot be transferred directly from the personal sphere to the mentality of a population. But in that sphere, too, historical decisions of political-cultural significance have left their distinguishing marks—as in the case of the Federal Republic's orientation to the West. One can certainly ask how such a decision is reflected in the political-cultural self-understanding of the population: does it establish a distinction, a desire to be different? Does integration into the West also mean for us today a break with the context of the German consciousness of having taken a special path, or do we think of it only as an opportunistic decision, the decision which, given the way things stand, is most likely to permit the maximum continuity in the domestic life of the nation?

The Federal Republic's integration into the West took place in several steps: economically, with the currency reform and the European Economic Community; politically, with the division of the nation and the consolidation of the Federal Republic into a state in its own right; militarily, with rearmament and admission to NATO; and culturally, through a long process of internationalization of science and scholarship, literature and art that was not completed until the end of the 1950s. These processes took place in a constellation of power politics determined initially by Yalta and Postdam and later by the relationship of the superpowers to one another. But from the beginning they met in the population of West Germany "a widespread basic pro-Western sentiment that was nourished by the radical failure of Nazi policies and the repugnant image of Soviet communism."[9] Well into the 1960s, the mentality that formed the background of our political culture was defined by a twofold antitotalitarian consensus. With the breakup of this compromise we are now faced explicitly for the first time with the question of what that orientation to the West actually means for us: mere adaptation to a constellation, or a new, principled intellectual orientation rooted in convictions.

Of course the best guarantee that processes for which the ground was being cleared anyway would find acceptance was the mute persuasiveness of economic success and increasingly of the achievements of the welfare state as well. This was supplemented by the rejection of the Soviet Union—the anticommunism of refugees who had had personal experience with it, the anticommunism of the Social Democratic Party, which had been unable to prevent the formation of the Socialist Unity Party in the other half of Germany, and the anticommunism of those who had always been anticommunist, especially the anticommunism under the aegis of which the governing parties put through rearmament. Under Adenauer the latter were not squeamish in their propaganda and linked domestic opponents and external enemies in their stereotypes.

Whereas the early economic decisions had essentially restored relationships that had been temporarily damaged, and the new political-institutional order could still be understood as a reform of the Weimar state, there were new beginnings externally, in the politics of alliances, and internally, in political culture. It was themes from these two areas that set off the great controversies that had a decisive influence on the mentality of the country. The government and the Opposition were in conflict on the politics of rearmament and later on policies toward the Soviet bloc, sometimes against the background of extraparliamentary movements. The debates on political culture were set off by what the intellectuals, now established for the first time as a social stratum, and later the rebelling students and the new social movements perceived as authoritarian tendencies—and as lack of sensitivity toward the moral bases, which they took at their word, of a democratic and social-welfare constitutional state, and in general of a polity established in the spirit of antifascism. Of course it is not possible to characterize the history of the mentality of the Federal Republic in a few sentences. What I want to emphasize is this: If one disregards marginal groups, both of these ongoing controversies were conducted on the basis of a choice in favor of the West that was not seriously questioned.[10]

The second thematic area, however, did affect the antitotalitarian consensus, whose composition had changed in character shortly after the war: anticommunism, in the sense of a rejection of Soviet communism, was taken for granted, up through the antiauthoritarian students of 1968, but antifascism—even the word seemed suspicious—was quicky specified to mean not much more than the general rejection of a period that was distanced as a whole and written off as "the age of the tyrants." To the extent to which it united the whole population, the antitotalitarian consensus rested on an implicit asymmetry; it remained a consensus only on the condition that antifascism not become an antifascism of principle. But then liberal and leftist-minorities repeatedly made those very conditions problematic:

• when they publicly thematized details of the Nazi period, which though negatively cathected was shunted aside as a whole (reparations, "working through the past," the Auschwitz trials, debates on the statute of limitations, and so forth);

• when they played off the principles of the constitutional state and a society of social justice against actions taken within the Federal Republic (the Spiegel affair, the Springer campaign, professional proscription, debates on asylum and sanctuary, and so forth);

• or when they criticized the policies of America, the protecting power, and thus criticized the contrast with totalitarianism, in terms of standards shared by both countries (Vietnam, Libya, opposition to a policy of détente, and so forth).

The Historians' Debate also forms part of this context. There is no need to inquire into the motives behind the undisguised political aims connected with the attempt to historicize the Nazi period for the public in such a way that it is normalized and distanced. As it becomes more and more difficult to fulfill the condition for the antitotalitarian consensus of the 1950s, that is, reticence with regard to our own past, we are left with these alternatives: either to explicitly problematize a past that we no longer shunt aside, or to affirm, still a little defiantly, continuities that extend on through the Nazi period.

Thus only now has the question of how we want to understand our orientation to the West come up for debate—whether we want to understand it pragmatically, as a matter of alliances, or intellectually as well, as a new beginning in political culture.[11] To be content with a rhetorical "both" is to evade the issue and turn an existential question into one of semantics: Kierkegaard's *Either/Or* is concerned with the way responsibility for a piece of history is assumed *consciously.* Nor should our postwar history be abandoned to hollow lip service in its decisive point, the renunciation of our own disastrous traditions.

Notes

1. Theodor W. Adorno, "Was bedeutet: Aufarbeitung der Vergangenheit," in *Eingriffe* (Frankfurt, 1963), p. 137.

2. H. U. Thamer, *Verführung und Gewalt* (Berlin, 1986), p. 707.

3. Karl Jaspers, *Die Schuldfrage* (Heidelberg, 1946).

4. Walter Benjamin, "Theses on the Philosophy of History," in *Illuminations* (New York, 1969), p. 256.

5. On this topic, see P. Alter, *Nationalismus* (Frankfurt, 1985).

6. Rudolf von Thadden, "Das verschobene Vaterland," in *Süddeutsche Zeitung*, April 11/12, 1987.

7. Jürgen Habermas, "Können komplexe Gesellschaften eine vernünftige Identität ausbilden?" in the *Zur Rekonstruktion des Historischen Materialismus* (Frankfurt, 1976), p. 144f. Abridged translation "On Social Identity," *Telos* 19, Spring 1974, pp. 91–103.

8. Søren Kierkegaard, *Either/Or*, Vol. II, tr. Walter Lowrie (Princeton, NJ, 1944), p. 180. Page numbers in the text for further citations refer to this edition.

9. D. Thränhardt, *Geschichte der Bundesrepublik Deutschland* (Frankfurt, 1986). p. 34.

10. This is directed against the common prejudice that the choice in favor of the West is identical with a choice for Adenauer's policies or for the NATO doctrine dominant at any given time.

11. Ralf Dahrendorff emphasizes this aspect of the Historians' Debate: "In the well-meaning protection of the broad shadow cast by the Chancellor, a search for an identity has begun which is characterized above all by the wish for an unbroken continuity. Confusing to many, it is conducted primarily by those who favor Reagan in current politics in the United States, whereas, conversely, leftist critics of American politics swear by the Western Enlightenment. Thus combinations arise that *appear* to be contradictory: Those who are for the Strategic Defense Initiative and missile deployment are also prepared to compare Auschwitz with Asiatic prototypes and to weigh the horrors of history against one another. And vice-versa." In "Zur politischen Kultur der Bundesrepublik," in *Merkur*, January 1987, p. 71.

Name Index

Adorno, Theodor, vii, x, xi, xxiv–xxv, 13–14, 52, 77, 80, 148, 201–203
Arendt, Hannah, 258

Ball, Hugo, 137
Bataille, Georges, 137
Becher, Johannes R., 78
Bell, Daniel, 23, 27–31, 43–44
Benevolo, Leonardo, 3–4
Benjamin, Walter, 43, 137, 252–253, 255
Benn, Gottfried, 84–85
Berger, Peter, 23
Bering, Dietz, 37, 75–76
Bloch, Ernst, 50, 78
Blüm, Norbert, 243
Böll, Heinrich, 93
Bröcker, Walter, 156
Broszat, Martin, 224
Brumlik, Micha, 246

Curtius, Ernst Robert, 78

Dregger, Alfred, xiv, 212–213, 214, 215, 230, 234–235

Ellwein, Thomas, 115
Epstein, Carl, 78
Erd, Dr. Rainer, 183–194

Farias, Victor, 140, 141, 161
Fest, Joachim, 238–240, 241
Fichte, Johann G., 111
Fischer, Wend, 6
Forsthoff, Ernst, 32, 33–34, 35–36, 201
Foucault, Michel, 52, 173–179
Fourier, 50
France, Anatole, 73
Frank, Manfred, 145

Franzen, Winfried, 140–141, 148, 153, 162–163, 167

Gehlen, Arnold, 32, 34–35, 35–36, 37, 40, 94–95, 137, 194, 201
Glazer, Nathan, 23
Glotz, Peter, 24
Gorz, Andre, 53
Grass, Günter, x
Gropius, 15, 16

Hegel, 11–12, 81, 82, 111, 201, 257, 260
Heidegger, Martin, 140–172
Heidorn, Joachim, 27
Heigert, Hans, 31–32
Heine, Heinrich, 72–99
Heinemann, Gustav, 43
Herzog, Wilhelm, 89–90
Hesse, Hermann, 78, 87
Heuss, Alfred, 242
Heuss, Theodor, 71–72, 78, 79
Hildebrand, Klaus, 220, 241
Hiller, Kurt, 71, 78
Hillgruber, Andreas, xiv–xvi, xviii, xx, 187–188, 207, 216–220, 232, 241–248
Hobbes, 129–131
Hohendahl, Peter Uwe, 75
Hölderlin, Friedrich, 148, 160, 202
Horkheimer, Max, viii–ix, 44, 52, 194
Humboldt, Wilhelm von, 101, 102, 108–109, 113, 115–116, 124

Inglehart, Ronald, 30

Jaspers, Karl, 78, 100–103, 115, 117–118, 141–142, 232–233, 236
Jencks, Charles, 5, 19

Studies in Contemporary German Social Thought
Thomas McCarthy, General Editor

Theodor W. Adorno, *Against Epistemology: A Metacritique*

Theodor W. Adorno, *Prisms*

Karl-Otto Apel, *Understanding and Explanation: A Transcendental-Pragmatic Perspective*

Richard J. Bernstein, editor, *Habermas and Modernity*

Ernst Bloch, *Natural Law and Human Dignity*

Ernst Bloch, *The Principle of Hope*

Ernst Bloch, *The Utopian Function of Art and Literature: Selected Essays*

Hans Blumenberg, *The Genesis of the Copernican World*

Hans Blumenberg, *The Legitimacy of the Modern Age*

Hans Blumenberg, *Work on Myth*

Susan Buck-Morss, *The Dialectics of Seeing: Walter Benjamin and the* Arcades Project

Helmut Dubiel, *Theory and Politics: Studies in the Development of Critical Theory*

John Forester, editor, *Critical Theory and Public Life*

David Frisby, *Fragments of Modernity: Theories of Modernity in the Work of Simmel, Kracauer and Benjamin*

Hans-Georg Gadamer, *Philosophical Apprenticeships*

Hans-Georg Gadamer, *Reason in the Age of Science*

Jürgen Habermas, *On the Logic of the Social Sciences*

Jürgen Habermas, *The New Conservatism: Cultural Criticism and the Historians' Debate*

Jürgen Habermas, *The Philosophical Discourse of Modernity: Twelve Lectures*

Jürgen Habermas, *Philosophical-Political Profiles*

Jürgen Habermas, editor, *Observations on "The Spiritual Situation of the Age"*

Jürgen Habermas, *The Structural Transformation of the Public Sphere: An Inquiry into a Category of Bourgeois Society*

Hans Joas, *G. H. Mead: A Contemporary Re-examination of His Thought*

Reinhart Koselleck, *Critique and Crisis: Enlightenment and the Pathogenesis of Modern Society*

Reinhart Koselleck, *Futures Past: On the Semantics of Historical Time*

Harry Liebersohn, *Fate and Utopia in German Sociology, 1887–1923*

Herbert Marcuse, *Hegel's Ontology and the Theory of Historicity*

Guy Oakes, *Weber and Rickert: Concept Formation in the Cultural Sciences*

Claus Offe, *Contradictions of the Welfare State*

Claus Offe, *Disorganized Capitalism: Contemporary Transformations of Work and Politics*

Helmut Peukert, *Science, Action, and Fundamental Theology: Toward a Theology of Communicative Action*

Joachim Ritter, *Hegel and the French Revolution: Essays on the* Philosophy of Right

Alfred Schmidt, *History and Structure: An Essay on Hegelian-Marxist and Structuralist Theories of History*

Dennis Schmidt, *The Ubiquity of the Finite: Hegel, Heidegger, and the Entitlements of Philosophy*

Carl Schmitt, *The Crisis of Parliamentary Democracy*

Carl Schmitt, *Political Romanticism*

Carl Schmitt, *Political Theology: Four Chapters on the Concept of Sovereignty*

Gary Smith, editor, *On Walter Benjamin: Critical Essays and Recollections*

Michael Theunissen, *The Other: Studies in the Social Ontology of Husserl, Heidegger, Sartre, and Buber*

Ernst Tugendhat, *Self-Consciousness and Self-Determination*

Mark Warren, *Nietzsche and Political Thought*